THE WORD PARENTS HANDBOOK

THE WORD PARENTS HANDBOOK

Lawrence O. Richards

WORD BOOKS
PUBLISHER
WACO, TEXAS

A DIVISION OF
WORD, INCORPORATED

Library of Congress Cataloging in Publication Data
Richards, Lawrence O., 1931–

   Includes index.
   1. Parenting. 2. Parenting—Religious aspects—
Christianity. 3. Children—Religious life. 4. Bible
stories, English. I. Title.
HQ755.8.R52 1983   649′.1   83–3550
ISBN 0–8499–0328–9

Printed in the United States of America

ACKNOWLEDGMENTS

I want to express special appreciation to my daughter-in-law, Beth
Hutchins Richards, who provided invaluable aid as my research
assistant, and to my grandson, Matthew Nathaniel, who has reminded me of the joy of having young children in the home.

CONTENTS

Friends values of, peer pressures, unsuitable friends. *Play* playing alone, with others, "make believe." *Sleep* getting enough, bedtime, bed-wetting, nightmares. *Security* fears and worries, the shy child. *Self-control* temper tantrums, lies, stealing, fighting, running away. *Health* good diet, eating habits, illness, going to the hospital. *Achievement* encouraging creativity, hobbies, place of praise, building self-esteem.

Communication the basic skill, listening, sharing feelings, making time. *Discipline* discipline vs. punishment, need for obedience, learning right from wrong, role of approval. *Brothers and Sisters* the new baby, arguing, competition, sharing a room, being a family. *Adoption* when to tell. *Family Responsibilities* chores, allowances, pets, babysitting. *Times of Stress* moving, divorce and remarriage, deaths, handicaps. *Holidays and Vacations*

Choosing a School private or public? what to look for. *Relationships with Teachers* getting involved, when your child has a poor teacher. *Setting Goals* how well do you expect your child to do? *Reading* the basic skill, helping your child learn to read. *Sports* importance, dangers. *Television* how much is too much? setting limits. *Going to Church* choosing a church, what to expect, children's ideas and questions about God.

67270

SUBJECTS DISCUSSED IN THIS HANDBOOK

THE BIBLE STORIES IN THIS HANDBOOK

CHRISTIAN NURTURE

It's no great secret. And it's not hard. All it takes is love and understanding. As you grow with your boys and girls the love comes naturally. And God, who is himself a Parent, enhances your natural love for the growing children entrusted to you. All you and I need to add is the understanding.

What we need to understand

The understanding doesn't come automatically. We have to learn. Sometimes you and I feel frustrated. We notice a pattern in our child's behavior, and just don't know what to do. Where can we gain the understanding we need to turn such problems into teachable moments, and our frustrations into opportunities? There are three sources of the understanding you and I need to provide a truly Christian nurture for our children. Each source is drawn on in this *Word Parents Handbook*.

Understanding children's development. Boys and girls are not just miniature adults. They are children who think, feel, act, and understand as children. So we need insight into how children think and feel and act and understand. When we have some grasp of children's characteristics we're able to match our guidance to their ways and their needs.

Years ago the great Hebrew scholar Franz Delitzsch explained Proverbs 22:6 ("Train a child in the way he should go, and when he is old he will not turn from it") this way: "the education of youth ought to be conformed to the nature of youth; the matter of instruction, the manner of instruction, ought to regulate itself according to the degree of development which the mental and bodily life of the youth has arrived at" (*Commentary,* Vol 11, p. 86, 87). When we fit our guidance to the characteristics of the child we'll be successful in our Christian nurture.

Understanding God's parenting principles. God, who parents us, shares many principles which govern parent/child relationships. When we understand these principles, we can apply them in our own home. God's principles focus on basic attitudes and the quality of our relationship with our children. Bible principles, for instance, seldom tell us when to spank, and when not. But they do provide a frame of reference. They help us see that we are not to punish in anger, but for our children's good (cf. Heb. 12:5,10).

Understanding Scripture's unique contribution. The Bible *is* an adult book, and there is much children will simply not be able to understand. But great truths of Scripture are expressed in stories which children can grasp, and respond to. The people whose experiences are told in Bible stories had many of the same feelings and fears as our children have today. Boys and girls can identify with them, and through their experiences sense God's involvement in daily life today. Understanding how to help children discover the practical meaning of familiar Bible stories provides another wonderful resource for truly Christian nurture.

What *The Word Parents Handbook* provides

This *Handbook* is designed to enrich your understanding. It is intended to help you discover the opportunity disguised in every parenting problem, and help you grow as an effective, nurturing Christian parent.

The first three chapters of the *Handbook* explore your child's needs between the ages of 6 and 11, look at your family life style, and provide an overview of your child at school and church. Each chapter looks at many everyday problems of boys and girls, and suggests ways that each problem can be an occasion for personal growth. Numbered paragraphs provide illustrations, suggest options for problem solving, and review biblical parenting principles.

The last chapter of this *Handbook* retells Old and New Testament Bible stories in a fresh, nurturing way. Each story is designed with *talkables*—thoughts and questions for you and your child to talk over together as you read the Bible story. These *talkables* will help your boys and girls to relate their own experiences, feelings, and choices to the experiences of Bible characters, and to discover how God can meet their own needs. Your *talkable* Bible stories, geared to age levels and specific needs, bring a special guiding, supportive word from God himself to your children.

Most importantly, each *talkable* Bible story is keyed to one or more of the problems/opportunities discussed in the first part of the *Handbook*. If you notice your boy or girl is afraid of the dark, you can find suggestions on how to understand and deal with the fear in Chapter 1. And there you'll be referred to several *talkable*

Bible stories which link overcoming fear with trust in our loving, caring Heavenly Father.

Christian nurture really isn't difficult. All it takes is love and understanding. You already have that love for your boy or girl, and much understanding. As you enrich your understanding with more knowledge of children's development and needs, more insight into God's parenting principles, and more grasp of Scripture's great contribution, God the Holy Spirit will surely guide you to nurture your children wisely and well.

Note: You will notice that each new division within the chapters of this book begins with a numbered paragraph (1, 2, 3 and so on). For easy cross-referencing, these marked sections are referred to as paragraph 1, 2, 3 and so on, throughout the body of the book, and these numbered paragraphs begin with a statement or a question in italic type (see, for example, the first page of chapter 1).

THE WORD PARENTS HANDBOOK

Your love, not the advice of experts, is the key to effective Christian nurture.

1. Your Child's Needs

1. *Children need parents most of all.* Boys and girls between six and eleven are growing, stretching, exploring. It's an exciting time of life: a time of growth and change. But it's a time during which six- through eleven-year-olds are still children—still dependent on mom and dad. Children are dependent on you for more than their food, clothing, and shelter. They are dependent on you emotionally. Mom and dad are the pillars on which a child's world rests. Knowing you are there, and that you love them, provides the warmth and security so necessary for healthy growth.

Your children are dependent on you in another important way. They are beginning to make their own choices now, but they need you to give them guidance and to set limits. You continue to make the most significant choices, those which shape the pattern of their lives.

Children with loving, stable parents already have their one greatest need met. In the climate provided by your love and your own growing maturity, most boys and girls will grow up to become healthy, loving persons themselves.

2. *Parents don't need the experts.* The "experts" are those with theories that tell you how to raise your child. The experts may tell you to be more permissive, or more strict, or teach you a particular communication skill (such as reflective listening) which is supposed to be "the key" to effective parenting. But hundreds of generations of healthy, happy children grew up in strong families before the experts were ever born. You and I really don't need the experts. Instead we need to be suspicious of their systems.

This is because parenting is, at heart, an expression of your relationship with your children. If that relationship is healthy, most of the things you do spontaneously—your feeling about the right way to handle a particular situation—are likely to be right. This is particularly true if you were brought up in a happy home and look back on your own growing-up years with warmth and appreciation. The chances are you'll treat your children the way your

Growth comes in natural, gradual stages. We prepare our children for adulthood by tending to today's growth today.

parents treated you, and they will grow up just as happily as you did.

There are times, of course, when you and I make mistakes. Usually parenting mistakes are self-correcting. We yell at Johnny, and find that instead of helping, our anger makes him dissolve into tears, or become angry in return. We feel a little ashamed of our anger. So usually we talk it over with our spouse, or a friend, or look up the particular situation in a handbook like this one, and next time try a different approach. When we love and respect our children, we're unlikely to repeat the actions that cause hurt.

It is true, however, that parents whose childhoods were painful are at a disadvantage. The parenting they saw modeled by their mothers and fathers is likely to be repeated now. Even when a mom or dad wants to do what's best, the bad example of his or her own upbringing is almost sure to spill over into parenting behavior. Since we tend to carry on the pattern of parenting established by our parents, such moms and dads simply do not know how to parent well.

But even parents like these don't need the experts. What do they need? *The most helpful thing such parents can do is join a discussion group of other moms and dads. Some churches have elective Sunday morning classes that focus on parenting. When these classes provide for free discussion and sharing by group members, they can be especially helpful. It's not the word of experts, but the sympathetic insights and suggestions of other parents living through similar experiences which are most likely to help. *The second most helpful thing such parents can do is plan ahead how they will respond in everyday situations. This *Handbook* suggests many alternative ways to deal lovingly and constructively with problems in daily life. When an incident occurs about which you do not feel comfortable, look it up in the *Handbook* index, and consciously select a different response to make when the situation recurs. Ask God to fill your heart with love for your child, and to bring the planned response to mind so you can act lovingly.

Someone has suggested that only when our children are grown up do we really know how to be good parents—and then it's too late. He was wrong. We learn to be good parents as we go along, living through each change with our boys and girls. As we keep on loving them, we can count on God to help us parent well. The Lord graciously forgives us, heals the hurts, and cleanses our mistakes. He uses you and me in a wonderful, creative way in the lives of our boys and girls.

3. *Your moral sensibility.* One of the most important contributions that parents make to children is moral. We communicate our own sense of orderliness and values. We share our own standards of right and wrong—of what is appropriate and good. Parents provide the moral framework for children's understanding of the world.

You and I will probably stress different values in the way we bring up our children. Some parents will insist on politeness, others will encourage free expression of feelings. One will stress responsibility in doing chores, and another will show concern over thoughtfulness and consideration. Many different good qualities are expressed in Scripture. All are appropriate for God's people to exhibit. Those values we reinforce and encourage are the values that will probably be adopted by our children and become part of their mature character.

There are so many good qualities that different parents should feel free to stress different ones. But there are also basic Christian values, which all believing moms and dads will want to communicate. Some of these are: love and appreciation for others, acceptance and caring, forgiving and accepting forgiveness. These are basic because all believers are called by God to build such relationships with others. To communicate these basic values we need to treat our children with the love, the appreciation, the acceptance, the caring, and the readiness to forgive that we want God to instill within them.

Children need parents with moral sensibilities. Children need to sense that we know right from wrong by the way we relate to other persons. Parents who treat children in this loving, Christian way will generally be successful in communicating their values and standards. Children will welcome such parents' values as their own, and grow freely within the moral framework mom and dad provide.

It is only when parents are harsh and overbearing, or constantly disapproving, that boys and girls are likely to grow up either cowed and sullen, or rebellious. How much better to love warmly, and lead our boys and girls into the joyful freedom that is theirs as the children of God.

4. *What are our goals?* Wise parents don't look too far ahead. We can't tell what our children will do when they grow up. We can't know, now, their adult abilities and interests. We can't be sure of the direction God may lead them. And surely, we'll not want to live their lives for them. So the best we can hope for is that our children will grow up to become loving, responsible persons, responsive to God, and caring about others. We can hope that each of our children will be mature enough to find his way along God's path to abundant life.

To achieve this long-range goal, you and I need to focus on the present, on our children's daily experiences. You see, like other living, growing things, children grow through natural stages. A baby learns to crawl, then to toddle, then to walk, and then to run. An older child learns to play alone, then beside other children, then with them, and then to follow the rules of organized games. Each stage builds naturally on the one before. As each level is successfully attained, the child is prepared for a new stage of growth.

In our ministry to our children we guide and guard this growth process. We want the process to take place in a natural, healthy sequence. We have the greatest impact on the kind of adults our children become by living through each stage with them, providing the guidance they need to succeed at each stage. The loving support and guidance we provide our children today is the greatest contribution we make to the fine, vital adults God wants them to become.

5. *Recognizing individual differences.* While all children pass in sequence through the stages of normal growth, there will be individual differences. One child in a family will be placid, happy to curl up quietly with a book. Another child in the same family will be bursting with energy, unwilling to sit for one unnecessary moment. One child in a family will respond quickly to correction. Another child in the same family will launch into angry argument.

Such individual differences have an impact on how children work through the growth stages. We'll need to take individual differences into account as we guide our boys and girls. Because children do differ, there is no one "best way" that works with every child; no one "best way" to solve a child-rearing problem, or to meet a child's need.

The apostle Paul makes this clear in 1 Thessalonians. There he writes of new believers, telling how he came to know "each one of you." "As a father deals with his own children," Paul went on, he found himself "encouraging, comforting, and urging you to live lives worthy of God" (2:11, 12). The apostle adjusted his ministry to individual differences. For each he had the common goal of a worthy life. But to reach that goal he needed to give some encouragement, others comfort, and still others urging.

This is another reason why none of the experts can give you "the system" that you can safely follow. Individuals differ. The system may fit some children. But it may not fit yours.

This makes it particularly important for us to take time to listen to our children. Like Paul with his spiritual children, you and I need to understand our boys and girls as individuals. Yes, we'll want to know what to expect in general of children passing through normal growth stages. But most of all we'll want to understand how our child feels and thinks and responds as he meets each fresh challenge.

Come to know each child as an individual, continue to love him or her unstintingly, and God will surely show you the best way to help him or her grow in a normal, healthy way.

6. *Your child's other needs.* Loving parents, who provide the supportive relationships so vital to a healthy childhood, are your

children's most basic need. But many other needs emerge as a child grows into and through early and middle childhood. In this first chapter we'll explore a number of need areas, and examine ways we can guide children's growth. We'll look at children's needs for friendship, and discuss the problems and opportunities that chums provide. We'll look at play, at sleep, and at children's need for security. We'll also look at every child's need for self-control, and how we can help our children develop it. We'll think about their physical health, and the mental well-being which comes with a sense of personal achievement.

These, and other aspects of your children's lives, are exciting for us. Each one, with its challenges, gives us many opportunities to provide a distinctively Christian nurture. As we add biblical principles of parenting, we'll find many ways that we can be God's ministers to our boys and girls, enriching their lives, and gently guiding them into healthy personal and spiritual growth.

Friends

7. *Why children need friends.* Friendships are important to children. They provide companionship, someone to walk to school with, someone to go places with, and have fun with. More important, friendships provide children with an opportunity to develop social skills.

Adult/child relationships are different from child/child relationships in a basic way. Adults always retain what one researcher calls the "right of unilateral imposition." Children realize that the adult has the inherent right to control. But when children play with each other, no one has that right of automatic control. No one has the unquestioned authority to determine what the individual or group will do next. In this kind of social setting, children learn the give and take of interpersonal relationships. They learn to both lead and follow. They learn to receive, and to share. They learn that friendliness and a smile will attract others, while hitting and anger drive them away. Children need the opportunity to learn these vital social lessons as they grow up—lessons that can only be truly learned through experience.

Sometimes a mom or dad becomes concerned when he or she sees a child quarreling with friends. But unless one of the children is being physically abused, it's usually best not to intrude. Quarreling is a natural part of that social learning process. In quarreling, boys and girls learn to express their feelings and to adjust to the feelings of others. In fact, quarreling is more common among good friends than among children who are indifferent to each other. If we adults avoid taking sides, our children are likely to learn important lessons through their bickering as well as through their times of happy play together. See *talkables* on pp. 153–155.

8. *Where will our children find friends?* Children's friends are nearly always determined by availability. Children come to know and play with other boys and girls who are about their age, who go to the same school or who live in the same neighborhood. In the lower grades, children's friendships are superficial and short-lived. Children who name each other as "best friends" one month will almost invariably name others next month. They will consider friends those who play with them, who are nice to them, who like to do the same things, who smile and are friendly, or who look nice.

Older boys and girls are more selective. Still, they will choose friends from within the pool of available school or neighborhood acquaintances. Older children tend to select friends who are like them, with similar values and interests. Between the ages of six and twelve, children tend to select friends of the same sex. While older children will often cluster in groups, or form clubs, it's more important for a child to have one or two close friends at a time than to have many superficial relationships.

Sometimes a neighborhood or school may provide few available children the same age as our children. Then church and Sunday school may provide options. But parents cannot expect friendship to develop between children who see each other only on Sunday morning, or only in a program directed by an adult. What we need to do is to try to build a relationship between our family and another family with same-aged children. Visiting each other's homes Sunday afternoons, sharing picnics or even camping trips, can give children a chance to become acquainted. When there are few friends available in the neighborhood, it's worth the effort to invite our children's church friends over for an evening or weekend. And older girls and boys will enjoy talking with such friends on the phone.

Another alternative for parents who have a back yard is to set up play equipment—swings and slides, or a club house—to attract other children. Having children in your home or yard does call for some supervision (and a check on your homeowner's accident policy!). But it does not demand constant adult supervision, especially as your goal is to give your children a chance to learn to relate to other boys and girls on their own.

9. *What are younger children's friendships like?* Children between six and eight, in first through third grades, have a limited notion of "friendship." Entering this age group children are poor group members, but will play well with one or two companions. There is no sense of group loyalty, and a child will tend to run to an adult to tattle when another child displeases him or does something wrong. As a child grows through this period a sense of group loyalty begins to develop, and the child engages in loosely organized play. It becomes fun to have secrets with friends, and children begin to draw away from those of the opposite sex. By the end of this period children often join larger groups for play of more organized games.

Children's general traits will be expressed in their relationships with friends. The child entering this age will tend to be preoccupied with himself or herself, and yet like to help. As they grow you'll note a number of typical childhood behaviors expressed in their relationships with other children. They will be competitive, blaming, sulk at times, seem loud and argumentative, and yet be sensitive to criticism. A child this age is becoming able to think about his or her friendship needs and to evaluate his and others' behavior. *Talkable Bible stories* on pages 215, 237, 269 will help you and your child talk about the meaning of his friendships.

10. *What are older children's friendships like?* Children between nine and eleven, in fourth through sixth grades, have more significant and deeper friendships. They easily join groups for spontaneous play—but in groups of the same sex. Now friends may be found outside the immediate neighborhood. Now, too, children express contempt for the opposite sex. They enjoy clubs, with secret codes and limited membership. As children grow through this period friendships become more intense, and boys and girls become more selective in their friends. They like rules and teamwork, and tend to reject others who won't keep the rules or work together with the group. At the end of the period, by the sixth grade, children are interested in competitive games, and clubs are important. Physical skills are admired by boys, and girls are beginning to become interested in boys.

General traits of children that are reflected in friendships of older children include strong peer orientation, competitiveness, independence, a strong sense of fairness, and quickness to judge others who fall short. Children can be critical of adults, and feel a much greater need to conform to their peer group. *Talkable Bible stories* on pages 196–198, 329–331 will help children this age begin to think of qualities and attitudes which can affect their friendship patterns, and their relationship with God.

11. *How do boys' and girls' friendships differ?* Despite the popular unisex notions, research shows that there are sex-based differences in the youngest of children. These sex differences are expressed in many ways. While recently there has been an observed tendency toward greater involvement by girls in sports and competitive games, boys still choose boy-type activities to do with friends, and girls choose more feminine activities. Boys' friendships are linked with their sports and games and activities. It is the *things they do* together that are important. Girls' friendships are more social. It is the fact that they *do the things together* that is significant. For girls, telling each other how you feel, or talking it over when you've done something wrong, is more important than a particular activity.

For both boys and girls, having a "best friend" is important. What are some of the things that mark off best-friend relationships? They take turns being the leader in games. They walk to school together, and help each other with classwork if one gets behind. They share toys or sports equipment, and stick up for each other if an outsider threatens. They do fun things together, phone each other about school assignments, and sleep over at each other's home. They talk about things that are important to them, and about the opposite sex, and try to be on the same team for sports or in the same group for a school project. Children who have a best friend would usually rather spend time with him or her than with a group of friends.

12. *What if my child is rejected by others?* Seven-year-old Ron stands by the window and watches the other children play. "They hate me," he mutters, as self-pity and anger struggle for control. When the other children are invited into the house for cookies they come readily enough. But when Ronny goes out, they ignore him or run away.

Jenny's eleven-year-old tears aren't hidden. Her best friend at school told Jenny she couldn't play with her any more. The other girls don't like her, Jenny was told, and no one is supposed to play with her. What are parents to do?

These are very typical childhood problems, but parents cannot—and should not—try to isolate boys and girls from all hurts. Life itself is unfair. All of us need to learn to cope and to go on. When we understand the fleeting and changeable nature of children's friendships, we can expect these situations to correct themselves soon. So we listen and empathize, without expressing pity or anger at the children who are excluding our precious one.

It's possible, of course, that these are not isolated incidents, but consistent patterns. In this case we probably do need to consider taking some active step to intervene. There are three approaches we might consider. The first is to honestly look at the way our child relates to others and see if he needs help in learning social skills (see paragraph 13). The second is to look at the ages and characteristics of the friends available in the neighborhood (see paragraph 14). The third is to consider ways of building play with friends into the pattern of our own home and/or yard (see paragraph 8). See *talkables* on pages 167–171, 269–273.

13. *How does my child relate to others? What skills can I teach him?* Not all children mature at the same pace or rate, and so

Rejection by friends is painful, but usually temporary. If the rejection is part of a pattern, there are ways parents can help.

we can expect many individual differences. It's possible that the rejection experienced by Ron and Jenny (paragraph 12) reflects the lack of social skills they have not yet developed. It's also possible that you can actually teach them the needed skills!

Children like Ron (in grades 1–3) are socially immature if they will not take turns, want to be "it" all the time, are demanding and jealous, refuse to share, push and shove, or do not cooperate in group activities. Children like Jenny (in grades 4–6) are socially immature if they do not work well with others in a group, drop out of games or groups when decisions are made against them, insist on their own way, pick fights, report to adults every unimportant infraction of rules, interrupt, fail to say "please" and "thank you," and refuse to follow the rules of the group.

If you notice behaviors like these when your child is playing with others, you've got a good indication that his or her rejection is caused by his own actions.

Since there are great individual differences in the rate of children's development, it may be that your child simply isn't ready to relate to children in his or her own age group. However, if other development is typical, it may be that your child simply needs help to relate well to other boys and girls. Research has shown that children can be trained in social skills, and that such training can make quick and lasting changes in their acceptance by others.

How can you and I train our children? And what kind of training do they need? The list (above) of socially immature behavior gives us many clues. For instance, let's suppose that Ron wants to be "it" all the time. To help Ron, we cut out the figures of several children from a catalog, and back them with cardboard. Now we sit at a table and ask Ron to show us what happens when he plays tag with the others. Or we act out a setting in which a "Ron" figure insists, "I wanna be it." We let him tell how the others react. Then we act out the same situation again, but this time have the Ron figure generously say to another, "It's your turn now." We can talk about how the others may respond, and how the different actions by Ron may make the other children feel. Ron can act out the new behavior a number of times as practice for the new response he'll make when the children play tag again.

A number of needed social skills can be illustrated and practiced with such simple, available tools. As children grow older, direct role-play can be substituted. Mom or an older sibling can pretend to be the rejecting friend, or the group planning an activity. Jenny can practice what to say and do in this pretend, but lifelike, situation.

Taking time to teach children what they can say and do to win friends is an important contribution that we can make to their growth and development. Along with the training, the *talkable Bible stories* on pages 167–171, 193–196, 264–267, 275–278, 329–331, 335–337 can provide insights.

14. *What are the ages and characteristics of friends in the neighborhood?* Often friendship problems come because of age or developmental differences between children. For instance, if all the boys in the neighborhood are a year or two older than Ron, or are more developed physically, we can see why the seven-year-old might have trouble fitting in. Boys' games are active, and great stress is placed on ability to compete. If a boy is younger, or smaller, and can't run as fast and hit the ball as well, he's likely to be chosen last or told he can't play.

It's not fair. But life is never completely fair for any of us. And it is a fact that some children develop more slowly than others in their age group, just as some develop more rapidly than the average. So some boys will be of lower strength and agility. Some boys and girls will not have developed the cognitive abilities necessary for certain kinds of friendship behavior. For instance, few preschool children have the ability to adopt social roles—cultivating the ability to see things from the other child's point of view, and take his or her feelings into account. Some third graders will not have developed this ability to a significant degree, and thus find it hard to function on the social level of other third graders.

One thing we can do if our child is a slow developer is to permit or encourage him to play with younger children who are at his stage of social development. Unless our child is physically overpowering among his juniors, play with younger children may provide the friends he needs, and the social experiences so important for his development.

It's helpful for you and me to remember that a different rate of development is no reflection on our boy or girl. It doesn't necessarily mean he is "slow," or inferior in any way. In fact, the chances are our child will grow into effective adulthood, and may well later surpass those who have a head start now. If we're sensitive to our child's own pace of development, and do not push him too fast, we can remain confident that he will catch up as he continues to grow. See *talkables* on pages 269–273.

15. *What do we do about bullies?* Almost every child will have some experience with another boy or girl who is rough, physical,

and apparently cruel. Typically, children's play groups will deal with the individual bully. You won't need to tell your child not to play with the bully; the neighborhood children simply won't want to. And they'll be very open about why. "Go away; you're too mean." Or, "We won't play with you because you're too rough." Often a lonely bully will change his ways to gain acceptance. "Can I play?" may even be accompanied by a promise, "I won't be mean if you'll let me."

Generally it's best if moms and dads don't jump in if they see the bully in action when there are a number of children playing, and there's no threat of serious physical harm. The bully too must learn how to get along with others. Learning early, from neighborhood children, may head off adolescent delinquency.

What if the bully is playing only with your own child? One mother invited the neighborhood bully into her home and yard to play, and made sure the children had fun things to do. But she also set clear limits. "You can play here at our house as long as you don't hit or shove." When the bully did act aggressively, he was told he had to leave for an hour. After the hour was up, he could come back again, but would be able to stay only as long as he followed the rules and stayed within the limits mom set.

When parents care enough to help their own children establish limits and learn to stay within them, they can have a significant ministry. It will cost you in terms of time and active supervision. And you may need to explain to your own child how playing with the neighborhood bully may help him learn to be good. But the rewards are great if your involvement helps change the direction of a child's life.

Sometimes, though, several bullies form a gang, and pick on younger children or those who are afraid. When this happens it's often wise for adults to intervene. Teachers should be alerted to reports of bullies on the school yard, and sometimes a parent may want to walk a child to and from school. Surely fear of groups of bullies is one of the security problems you'll want to help your child work through (see paragraphs 28–34).

16. *How can I help my child defend himself?* It's not unusual for children to quarrel. Friends will come to blows at times. And every playground has its bully, who looks for fights. Most children don't like to fight. But sometimes a child is in a situation where he almost has to hit back. If he doesn't he'll be judged by others— and perhaps by himself—as a sissy. It's doubly hard if mom or

dad have told the child he isn't allowed to fight. Then, whether he fights or doesn't, he's sure to be in trouble.

It's understandable, of course, that Christian parents should teach children not to strike out to hurt others. Jesus' words to his disciples about turning the other cheek are often quoted, and many understand them as an absolute prohibition against fighting. But it's never enough for us parents to simply tell our children, "Don't fight." We have to help them by giving positive guidance on how to handle situations in which childhood fights may occur.

What our children need most is a set of options that will give them several possible responses to make when the challenge comes to fight. A child might say, "You're my friend. I don't want to fight you. Why do you want to fight me?" This response is an invitation to begin talking about the problem instead of fighting over it.

Should Christian parents ever permit their children to fight?

Or a child might say, "Fighting isn't right," and simply walk away. Most boys and girls between six and eleven would agree that fighting isn't right. The appeal to what is right, and then acting on it, takes a courage that other children can appreciate.

While we want to help children live out the spirit of Jesus' admonition to "turn the other cheek," we need to realize that this is not an absolute prohibition against necessary self-defense or the defense of the helpless. God wants us to "strive for peace with all men" (Heb. 12:14), but knows full well that there may be times when others will not let us live in peace. Turning the other cheek will avoid many conflicts. Others will be forced on us.

So at times, fighting back may be the only or the best option. A child may need to fight to protect a younger child from a bully. Or a child who is being hit may need to hit back to protect himself. It's certainly reasonable for parents to tell their children they are never to hit another person *first*. But it may be just as important to help them see when fighting back is acceptable.

One thing that we may also want to consider is the well-being of the aggressive child. If fighting always wins him his own way, because no one is willing to fight back, he may be deprived of an important lesson. He needs to know that when we hurt others, they are likely to strike back and hurt us. We can never hurt others safely, and must learn other ways to relate to them.

My own older son never wanted to fight as a child. I told him how much I appreciated his peacefulness, and told him he should never hit another child first. But if a child hit him, not once but several times, he was to hit him back, harder. In this way he would help the other child learn that it's not good for him to hit others or to fight.

17. *What kinds of peer pressure will my children experience?* Children, like adults, find that the price of acceptance by other children is paid in the coin of conformity. With younger children it's conformity to the kinds of things the group wants to play and do. It's hard for the third-grader not to throw snowballs (or even stones) at passing cars, when the neighborhood boys do it on the way home from school. Older children experience other pressures. Girls may become clothes-oriented, and even boys may be terribly embarrassed if you want them to wear a different kind of winter footwear than the other kids.

In general, however, children who come from homes in which mom and dad supply plenty of love and companionship, along with consistent but mild discipline, are more adult-oriented than peer-oriented. They want to please the important adults in their lives, and are more likely to choose adult than peer values when there is a conflict. Peer-oriented children are more dependent on relationships with other children, have lower self-esteem, and generally come from an inadequate home environment. They are more likely to play hooky from school, smoke, or do something illegal, and tend to feel less happy with themselves.

Two points here are important. The desire to fit in is natural and is important to children. When it's a matter of the kind of clothing a child wears to school or a particular toy all his friends have, it's not harmful (if we are able) to supply him or her with similar things. The best way we can protect our child from unhealthy peer pressures—to do something they know or believe is wrong—is to invest the continuing time our children need to feel loved and supported and appreciated at home. As we maintain our good and open relationship with our children, and talk about it when peer pressures bother them, we can insulate our boys and girls from developing the need to join friends in wrong behavior.

When your children feel pressures from friends to do what they know is wrong, the *talkable Bible stories* on pages 215–218, 237–240, 258–261, 313–316 will help.

18. *What about friends who are a bad influence?* Even when the home environment is excellent, children may be troubled by friends who are a bad influence. Sometimes children will be shunned or picked on by groups of friends. A child may pick up bad habits if teased into smoking, or if he plays with others who constantly use bad language. Often the friends who are a bad influence on nine- through eleven-year-olds are older than they. The behavior that bothers us fascinates because it is associated by our child with a more grown-up, exciting world.

For most children, school and neighborhood provide choices of different friendship groups. Usually our children will pick a group that has similar values, and will choose not to associate with children who do things that are wrong. But sometimes the only playmates available are the troublesome influences. What can we do then?

One option is to forbid our child to associate with the children whose influence we distrust. If these are the only children available for play, this option may not be best. We might instead recognize that misbehavior among children is often linked with *settings* and with *numbers.* Children will be more likely to misbehave when off somewhere on their own, and when with others who reinforce the group choices. We might then try changing the setting and the numbers of boys or girls with whom our child plays. For instance, helping our child set up a clubhouse in the back yard or basement may lead the neighborhood children to play in our environment, where there is a sense of adult supervision. Limiting the number of friends who can play—"You can have two friends in, but no more"—may keep things below the "critical mass" needed to trigger bad behavior.

Another option that ought always be exercised is to talk through the problem with your child. Younger children will already know it is wrong, and feel an internal conflict between their desire to fit in and their own moral standards.

Punishment is an option, of course. Several principles of discipline can help us correct our own boy or girl (see paragraphs 62–66). But what is most important is to maintain the good relationship we already have with our child, and to help him or her make the difficult choices he must make about his friends. In childhood as well as in adolescence, we can only supervise a child's behavior while he's in our presence. We have to help children build internal values and controls, so they will make right choices when we're not there. The *talkable Bible story* on page 215 can be of particular help here.

Play

19. *What does play do for our children?* Play makes many contributions to the healthy development of six- through eleven-year-olds. Play with friends develops social skills (see paragraphs 7, 13). Imaginative play stimulates creativity (see paragraph 20). Playing with objects and certain kinds of toys stimulates development of physical skills. Games and sports exercise growing bodies and develop coordination. Play often involves fantasy and pretending. These stretch mental development. Imaginative play will often involve pretending to be grown up. This kind of play helps boys build a sense of masculine identity, and girls develop a sense of feminine identity. Children play with others and alone; opportunity for both kinds of play is important.

Family play is also enriching. Sharing in games and backyard sports can build a sense of comradeship between children and parents, enriching family warmth and closeness.

As children grow older, competitive forms of play (see paragraph 115) let children test their expanding abilities, establishing a sense of personal competency and achievement.

Play is far more than a pastime to boys and girls. It's one way our children grow, expand, and explore the world as well as their own potentials.

20. *Is "pretending" and "make-believe" bad for our children?* Preschool children may think Santa is real. But some parents feel that, by school age, boys and girls ought to make a clear distinction between what's real and what's pretend. So when a second grader talks to an imaginary friend, some moms and dads may panic.

The same feeling of panic may come if an older child tells fantastic stories about experiences at school or adventures on the way home. One day he says a gangster took a friend away in a big black car. Another day he tells of being chased all the way home by teens who want to hurt him. Or he comes to your room at night and insists he saw a flying saucer outside his window. To many parents this seems much like lying. It's a moral issue now, and moms and dads wonder if they shouldn't punish their child for telling fibs.

The child with a make-believe friend needn't cause us much concern. We don't really have to teach the child the difference between the real and make-believe. It's enough to observe at times, "It's fun to pretend sometimes, isn't it?" Or at other times you might explain, "When you go to school, it's not good to play with your imaginary friend. Then it's time to play with real boys and girls." As time passes, and more activities attract our child's interest, fantasy play will grow less and less.

The child who makes up stories and presents them as if they were true, is likely to cause more concern. Without overreacting, explain that people need to treat make-believe and reality as separate worlds. Other folks need to know when we tell them something if we're talking about the real world or about make-believe. If we don't make this clear, people won't be able to trust us. They may not believe us when we need to tell them something important. The "Little Boy Who Cried Wolf" is a familiar children's story which illustrates this point well.

Our goal here is not to blunt our child's imagination. It's to help him make a clear distinction for others between his make-believe and reality. We might actually encourage his fantasizing. "You have a fine imagination, Tim. Have you thought about writing your stories down? You would make a fine story writer."

Guiding our child to use his imagination acceptably, and win praise, is a very positive way to help. If writing isn't something he or she can do, try setting aside a "story time" at supper. Let the child tell his stories to entertain the family. Others can even join in and make up stories of their own. Redirecting imagination is usually more effective than confrontation. And it avoids stunting a gift which God may intend our child to use as he matures.

Most children will outgrow the habit of telling fantastic tales as truth if we're patient with them, explain, and redirect their imagination. And, if necessary, if we set limits, we should insist our boy or girl tell us when a report is made up. Only when the child himself is unable to separate the world of imagination from the real world would a visit to a professional counselor be indicated. See *talkable Bible stories* on pages 156–158 and 247–248.

21. *How do parents respond to a young child's curiosity about sex?* Boys and girls between six and eleven usually express growing contempt for the other sex. Children choose friends of the same sex, and the groups that form spontaneously will be made up either of boys or of girls.

Still, there will be times, typically with younger children, when "playing doctor" has a special fascination. Children are curious about their own bodies and those of the opposite sex. How do we react if we discover a "doctor" incident, or if we find our child toying with his or her genitals?

It's important to set firm limits on play with others. Children should be told that some parts of each person's body are private. We don't ask to see the private parts of others, or show them ours. These private parts are very special and wonderful. When children grow up, and become adults, they will marry. Then those special parts will be used to love a husband or wife, and to make a family together.

Today there are many fine Christian books and booklets, written to help our younger and older children understand sexuality. These books give simple, clear answers to the questions children ask. And the books help children see their sexuality as a gift from God. If we become aware that our boy or girl is curious about sex, or find one "playing doctor," one of these age-graded books can be especially helpful. "I know you wonder about how boys and girls are different," we might say to our six- or seven-year-old. "Let's look at a book I bought, and see if it answers your questions."

Children also should be taught not to play with their own bodies when others are present. But there is little value in making an issue of normal self-exploration. Such exploration will not have a significant role in the life of a normal, active child, or have a negative effect as he or she grows into adolescence.

In fact, what is most important is for us as parents to take exploratory sex-play in stride. If we become overly excited, or embarrassed, or angry, we'll communicate an impression about sexuality that we do not want to give. Sex isn't dirty or wrong: it is one of God's good gifts, to be appreciated in its place and in its time. When we deal with emerging situations with calm firmness and understanding, we make a significant contribution to our child's developing personality.

22. *How can we enrich our children's play?* We've seen (in paragraph 19) some of the reasons why play is important, and some of the kinds of play that are important to children. What can we do to enrich the play of our children, so the important benefits play offers can be realized?

One thing we can do is organize space so children will have room for different kinds of play. A plywood sheet made a "desk top" divider in the closet of one of my sons. On it he stored his favorite toys and games. A couple of pillows and a reading lamp made the lower half a private den, where he could retreat when he wanted to read or play alone.

We can provide play and work materials. It's better to provide raw material than the precision, detailed, battery-driven toys advertised on TV for Christmas. Children can make their own creations with tinker toys, and stretch their imaginations. A sand box can become a fantasy kingdom. Even the cardboard tubes on which wrapping paper comes are valued as swords—until battered apart. Family games should have high priority and definitely be on our "buy" list, along with "things to do" idea books.

Sometimes we'll need to help our children organize their time so they'll have time to play. Most boys and girls can use suggestions on organizing time so lessons, chores, and practicing can be done and time still be reserved for play.

And of course, we also need to be sure that we understand the importance of play for our children. Let's not so overload them with organized clubs and groups and lessons and choirs that they have no time for their own important business—play.

Sleep

23. *How much sleep do our children need?* We all know that getting enough sleep is a basic need of children. But how much

is enough? There are individual differences; some children need more sleep, and some less. It's hard to measure these differences because tiredness gives us no clue. In fact, the more tired a child is the less likely he's going to feel sleepy or find it easy to go to sleep. So we can't tell how much sleep our child needs by waiting at night till he or she is ready to go to bed.

In general, children of six need about twelve hours of sleep. This drops to ten or ten and a half hours by age twelve. Some children may need more or less than this average. But ten to twelve hours is where we ought to start our thinking about bedtime.

If we find that it's hard for Jimmy to wake up, or that when Beth goes to bed at nine she's always awake by five, we'll be able to make adjustments. Sleep deficiency is a serious thing. A bedtime pattern which leads to long-term sleep deficiency can affect a child's general health and school performance.

24. *Why don't children want to go to sleep?* Getting children to go to bed and to sleep is the number one problem reported to pediatricians by parents these days. It's not difficult for us to understand the reluctant child's point of view. Boys and girls feel hungry when it's time to eat. They don't feel sleepy or tired at bedtime. It's hard for them to accept our assurance that they need to go to bed—especially when sleep means giving up so much. The TV has to be turned off. Friends and games have to be abandoned, and books put away. Older children and adults get to stay up, and younger boys and girls lie awake listening, wondering what they're missing, and feeling left out. More than one child purposely leaves homework to the last minute just so he can argue, "But, dad. I can't go to bed *now*. I've got to do my homework."

There's no great mystery to solving the bedtime problem. The solution begins when we recognize the fact that getting the kids to bed is our responsibility: they won't turn in at night because they want to! If we accept this fact, it relieves us of the frustrated feeling that our kids *ought* to get themselves to bed. We'll find it easier on everyone if, instead of waiting and waiting for Jim and Beth to go to bed when they know it's time, we take the initiative. Actually, there are several things you and I can do to help make the nightly bedtime struggle easier on everyone.

*Regularity. This is the first step in solving what is a major problem in many homes. Determine a bedtime and stick to it, with a (very) few exceptions for special events. It's good to involve our children in bedtime planning. In my home, we asked our boys what time they wanted to get up for breakfast and get ready for school. We worked backward, figuring the number of hours of sleep they needed. We then added in time for our nightly reading and talk time (see paragraph 25). Letting the kids do the figuring, we asked, "OK, what should your bedtime be?"

Since the boys were part of the process and had some choice in setting times, they never felt that bedtime was an arbitrary thing which adults decided nightly on the spur of the moment. Reestablished at the beginning of each school year (and sometimes renegotiated in the middle of the year), "bedtime" was an understood and accepted part of the regular pattern of daily life.

*Scheduling. Sometimes giving children help in scheduling after school activities is a key to a peaceful bedtime. After school in our house was playtime: there was whiffle-ball or football or basketball in the back yard, or a trip to the swimming pool. But school work needed to be done within the hour before or after supper.

*Snacking. We need to watch what children eat before bedtime. Sugary snacks pour quick charges of energy into the body, and make settling down for sleep almost impossible. Especially if a child is highstrung, Twinkies and other sweets should be ruled out after supper. If a child complains of hunger, a snack of fruit or a piece of toast (without jelly) will do.

*Bedtime rituals. Building a pattern of things we do as bedtime approaches helps significantly. Quieter activities should predominate in the evening, so "slowing down" can take place. A pattern for bedtime rituals is given in paragraph 25.

Taking these measures won't necessarily solve all bedtime problems. They will help. In time the complaints and delaying tactics will gradually disappear. But it does take firmness on our part, and a self-discipline necessary to set up and maintain the procedures that help our children get their needed rest. I remember when one of my boys would complain after being in bed a while, "But I can't sleep!" I told him, "That's all right, son. You don't have to go to sleep. You just have to go to bed when it's bedtime. You can lie awake and rest there just as long as you want."

The calm assurance of moms and dads who know that they set the pattern of daily life for their children, rather than being ruled by childish whims and passions, provides children with a sense of security which brings them rest.

25. *How can we make the most of bedtime?* Bedtime is prime time in the Christian home. It's the time when children need a bedtime ritual to prepare them for sleep. And it's the time when we are best able to give our boys and girls the individual attention

so important to building closeness and intimacy. Three things can play an important part in your family bedtime rituals. Talk. Singing. And stories. We staggered bedtimes in our family, partly because the boys were five years apart in age, and partly because we wanted each one to have his own personal time with mom or dad.

*Between the ages of six and eight all three features can be important. Singing songs our child has learned in church or Sunday school, or from a favorite record, may take up five or ten minutes. Talking about what happened at school, what friends said and did and other events of the day, takes up another ten minutes or so. Then there's a story. Sometimes we may read to him or her from a Bible story book. Often it's a chapter from a missionary biography tale, or one of C. S. Lewis's books for children. This is prime time, because it serves children as a "quiet time" to focus on the Lord, as well as to share with mom or dad. As a child nestles down to sleep, remembering God also helps to reduce fears and the incidence of bad dreams.

Bedtime is prime time in the Christian home.

*Between the ages of nine and eleven the singing is likely to drop away. Children will want to spend more time talking or reading. Visit a Christian bookstore and select bedtime reading together. Older children need to feel that they have more freedom to choose what they hear and do. I kept up the tradition of reading and talking at bedtime into my youngest's junior-high years. Often we'd extend the time, talking about the book we were reading and questions it suggested. Taking time to be with your children at bedtime will do more than help them rest well. It is one of your major opportunities to give Christian nurture to your boy or girl.

Making the most of bedtime does cost a parent. It costs us our time, and often the surrender of a favorite TV show. But it's one of the best investments we can possibly make in our child's future.

26. *What do we do about bed-wetting?* About ten percent of all children still wet their beds at the age of six. Some four percent will continue to do it as late as twelve. So bed-wetting isn't abnormal.

It does, however, cause stress, for the child and the parent—to say nothing of extra work changing bedclothes.

While bed-wetting may at times be a sign of some troubling problem or stress, this is not necessarily the cause. If your home life is stable, and the bedtime patterns discussed above are followed, it's much more likely bed-wetting simply is a matter of growing into better bladder control. A medical exam will indicate if there is a special physical cause. It's important, especially if the habit persists at age eight or beyond, not to make an issue of bed-wetting. Most children already feel ashamed and frustrated. Parental pressures are likely to make a child more fearful, and anxiety will make it more difficult to achieve control.

There are a number of things we can do to turn the problem into an opportunity for positive nurture. We can communicate our confidence that he's growing up, and will succeed in time. The *talkable Bible story* on pages 137, 323 will help you here. We can also take practical steps to help him or her gain control. First, limit the intake of water or other drinks for several hours before bedtime. Second, make going to the bathroom the last thing that happens before settling down to sleep. Third, try providing an alarm clock to wake him up in the middle of the night so he can visit the bathroom. You may need two clocks, one set around midnight and the other at three or so. Plan these steps with your child, helping him see them as ways he can act responsibly to take control of his problem.

If you continue to show acceptance and confidence, and avoid expressing annoyance or overconcern, the problem will be overcome in time. But punishment, verbal or physical, only makes this problem worse.

27. *What about nightmares and bedtime fears?* Bedtime fears, of the dark and of imaginary things the dark may contain, aren't at all unusual. Nor are nightmares that may cause a child to wake up screaming. How do we deal with them?

Nightmares are quite common for the six- or seven-year-old. Intense bad dreams in many cases seem to be a part of growing up, and will disappear in time. By the age of eight or so, bad dreams are often correlated with a frightening TV show or event. When a bad dream comes the best thing to do is to go to the child to reassure and try to calm him or her. You may want to take the child to a different room. If possible have the child tell you about the dream. But don't be surprised if he or she can't remember it or talk about it. It may be helpful to sit with the child until he or she has fallen asleep again.

Persistent nightmares may be related to special stress. It's possible you'll want to take your child to a child psychiatrist. These practitioners help normal children as well as those who are mentally disturbed. But there are also things you can do that reduce the likelihood of bad dreams, and at the same time reduce nighttime fears.

The bedtime ritual described in paragraph 25 helps reduce tensions and bring relaxation. Leaving the door of the child's room open a crack, or providing a night light will also help. We put pictures from Sunday school take-home papers on the wall by the bed, and talked about the Bible story just before sleep came. Awareness that God is present, and thoughts of his love, provide images to fill a child's mind. One of our sons had a favorite picture of Jesus the Good Shepherd placed just below the night light, so he could look at it if he felt afraid, and be reminded that Jesus was with him.

Limiting the frightening images a child may receive watching a horror show, and providing warm positive images which affirm love and security instead, is a basic way to relieve nighttime fears and limit nightmares. *Talkable Bible stories* on pages 164–167, 221–223, 273–275, are particularly helpful.

Security

28. *How can parents help children feel secure?* One of the basic needs of children is a sense of security. This doesn't mean that our children will never be anxious or uncertain or fearful. At times

all human beings find themselves in situations where they are anxious. We can't insulate our children from normal stress, and we shouldn't try. Learning to cope is important: everyone needs to learn and relearn overcoming fears to grow toward healthy maturity. What is important for you and me, and for our children, is to have an underlying security base: a source of confidence that we can meet life's challenges even when they are uncomfortable for us.

Two factors are particularly important to help a child build this sense of security. One is the assurance that parents are there—loving, protective, willing and able to help. This is one reason why divorce or death or parental fighting places special stress on children (see pages 54–56, 89–92). A single parent can provide the relational base for a child's security. But mom or dad, and preferably mom and dad, need to be there, their love unquestioned. In homes where children are loved, and communication is open and warm, this important relational foundation for security usually exists.

The second important security factor is a growing awareness of adequacy. A child needs to have successes as he grows, to learn by experience that he can solve his problems and overcome difficulties. There are ways mom and dad can help a child build a sense of personal competence (see paragraphs 48–52). As we help our boy or girl achieve, we're helping to provide him or her with a sense of security.

Helping to meet the need for security won't free our children from experiencing fears and anxieties. But it will make it easier for them to deal with normal fears—and easier for us to help them.

29. *What is the nature of children's fears?* It's natural for a child to be frightened when he's confronted with a situation he doesn't understand or one in which he doesn't feel able to cope. At such times a child will become tense, uncomfortable, upset, and anxious—in short, afraid. These very real physical symptoms can lead to tears, flight, paralyzing terror, or panicky screams. Children who have fears aren't abnormal. They do not necessarily lack the foundations for security discussed in paragraph 28. They may simply need our help to learn ways to cope with the real or imagined dangers.

It's almost impossible to catalog the fears of well-adjusted children. There are so many things children may fear. There is fear of wild animals (these are the most common objects of fear between the ages of five and twelve), fears of monsters (usually up until seven or so), and the ever-common fear of the dark. Images from

TV or movies, and newspaper accounts of crimes, may be picked up and exaggerated by children. Fear of storms is quite common at eight or nine. Children may fear not being liked by others, or taking tests at school. A household pet may be feared, or discovery of a locked door may throw a child into panic.

Many fears are helpful. They are based on reality and cause us to avoid danger. Being afraid to run into the street because a car might hit you is a realistic fear, and one we'd like our boys and girls to have! Being afraid of lighting matches in the house surely isn't all bad. Being afraid to get into a car with a stranger who offers candy is another realistic fear. Realistic fears can lead children to avoid situations in which they or others might be harmed.

Usually what bothers parents are the unrealistic fears their children have, or the panic reaction children sometimes exhibit. It's hard for some parents to take children's fears seriously when they are clearly imaginary. Yet children's fears are very real to them and need to be treated wisely. We need to remember that perfectly normal children may at some time express major or minor fears about almost anything at all. See *talkable Bible stories* on pages 203–205, 240–244.

30. *How should we react to children's fears?* There's no single prescription for dealing with fears, although paragraphs 31–34 illustrate several typical approaches you can adapt. There are, however, general principles we need to remember:

*We need to respect the fears our children have, whether they are realistic or unrealistic. Fears are very real to the child and he or she needs our help, not our ridicule or punishment.

*The first thing we need to do is to help our child feel protected from the feared object or situation. The way to treat fear of the water isn't to throw a child in the pool. And the way to reduce fear of the dark isn't to turn out the lights and close the door, so he'll find out for himself there's nothing to fear.

*After dealing with a child's immediate need to feel protected, we want to develop a plan to help our child overcome his fear. Children's descriptions of their fears typically include (1) a dangerous object—a person, place, or occurrence the child considers harmful or unpleasant, (2) an assumption that the child is actually in danger, and (3) an assumption that the child is helpless or unable to cope with the danger. We can help by focusing on any or all of these elements. We may help a child discover that the kitten he fears actually isn't dangerous at all. We may help a child realize that the wild tigers he fears don't live in our neighborhood. We may help a child practice taking tests at home, so when he's at school he knows he will be able to cope with the tests he takes there.

*It's important, too, to help children realize we're not angry or ashamed about their fears. God isn't angry either, for it's times of anxiety that give his children the opportunity to learn trust. We need to let children know that we accept them, will protect them, and that God loves and protects them too. Many stories in the Bible deal with fears and trust, and will be particularly meaningful for children with fears. *Talkable Bible stories* to use with anxious children include those on pages 150–153, 164–167, 206–208, 223–226, 228–231, 267–269.

The first step in dealing with childhood fears is to be sure our boy or girl feels protected. When the child feels safe, we can move on to help him overcome his fright.

The next paragraphs discuss the most common fears of boys and girls six through eleven, and illustrate ways we can help our children overcome their real and imagined terrors.

31. *How can we help children with fears of real things?* Unlike fears of imaginary monsters and such, fears of concrete objects or situations seldom go away with time. The boy of three frightened by a neighbor's dog may still fear animals at seven. A girl afraid of elevators or high places at five is likely to have the same fear at nine or ten.

The basic approach to helping a young child with such fears will involve "familiarization." This does not mean dragging a child into the fear-producing situation. It means gradual, protected exposure. Stay with your child by the window and watch another child play with a pet dog. Talk about the way the animal plays, and how it barks to show excitement and happiness rather than anger. At another time you may step outside a screen door and pick up a pet dog. Stroke it, and ask your child if he'd like to pet the dog too. Promise you will hold the dog as he does. Later talk about how the dog's fur felt. Also give information about dogs. Tell why their noses are cold, why they pant, that one year of your child's life is six or seven years for a dog, explain how to recognize different breeds of dogs, and so on. The more information a child has, the more he feels a sense of mastery. Your child may never romp with a Great Dane. But helped by the process of familiarization, the chances are he won't panic or run hysterically away either.

The same principle is applied when you talk about how it feels riding in an elevator, and act out going uuuuup! and dowwwn! while your tummy stays where it was. Liken the feeling to that of an astronaut going up in a rocket. Pretend the buttons are different planetary destinations and let your six- or seven-year-old pilot you on your next visit to a department store.

The game of "What If . . . ?" provides another variation. When a child feels upset or threatened, play out the disturbing situation with a number of imagined outcomes. Usually a child will work out options himself. Or he may need help and information to work out a solution. The "What If . . . ?" game can be used when children fear being lost or locked out of the house or chased by older children, or being kidnapped or hurt in an accident, and so on.

Familiarization as an approach to helping children with fears can both change the child's perception of the potential danger, and/or change his feelings of being able to cope. With the familiarization process, you can use the *talkable Bible stories* on pages 240–244, 267–269.

32. *How can we help children with fears of imaginary terrors?* Fears of monsters and terrors and things that go bump in the night are common in children. I well remember listening to a Saturday night radio show, "The Hermit's Cave." Buried in my blankets, after the tale of vampires or mummies, I'd lie there petrified, afraid to turn over, and especially afraid to glance toward the dark closet in the corner. Today images from TV and movies join the scary ghost stories children sometimes hear, and may reappear in dreams as well as in the imagination.

In time, fears of imaginary monsters usually go away. In the meantime a child may need reassurance, or for mom and dad to sit him in his room for a time. Sometimes parents of younger children find that acting out the scary fantasy will help. In the dramatization the vampire cringes away from the little silver cross, or the space aliens are driven off with a laser gun.

Christian moms and dads may find the best solution is to fill the child's room with God's love. A night light focused on a picture of Jesus with children, a bedtime ritual shared by parents and children with singing and stories just before sleep (paragraph 25) creates a bedtime climate of comfort and love. This, with limits placed on viewing the fantasies that bring fright, usually is enough to help. The *talkable Bible stories* on pages 150–153 will also help.

33. *How can we help children who are afraid of the dark?* This most common of children's fears can be met directly or indirectly. A night light, a radio or tape playing quiet music, a crack in the door—all will help to relieve nighttime fears.

When my oldest son Paul showed fear of the dark at about the age of eight, we didn't talk about it directly. Instead I suggested he and I write a book together. He had a younger brother and sister, and I told him about fears that were common for children their age. We were going to write a book to help them, about being afraid and trusting.

The first evening we looked up verses in a Bible concordance containing the words "fear," "afraid," and "trust." We marked phrases Paul thought were promising. The next evening we looked up the marked verses. Paul underlined in his Bible the verses he liked and I typed them out on three by five cards. The third evening we went to the local drugstore and bought a composition book, construction paper, and colored pens. That night Paul titled the book and completed the first page. It was "Paul's Not Being Afraid" book. The first page showed arrows and spears breaking against a construction paper shield. The Bible verse on the page read "Fear not, Abram: I am thy shield and thy exceeding great reward" (Gen. 15:1, KJV).

We added a number of other pages. One featured a verse from a psalm of David: "What time I am afraid, I will trust in thee" (Ps. 56:3, KJV). We talked about fear being all right, and a special opportunity for us to learn to trust God. Paul remembered a Bible story about a time when one of God's people might have been afraid. He drew a picture of Daniel being thrown into a den of ferocious lions, with God's angels there to keep them from hurting him. On the next page we listed things that Paul's school friends might fear. There were things like being kidnapped, fear the Russians would fly over the North Pole and bomb Chicago (where we lived at the time), and of course there was fear of the dark.

We never did quite finish "Paul's Not Being Afraid" book. I never did confront Paul with the earlier evidence of his own fears of the dark. Somehow during the two weeks or so we worked on the project, God worked in Paul's life and the fears went away. Paul had thought about fear, and thought about God, and the sense of God's protecting presence had become more real than his fear of what might be hidden in the dark. See *talkables* on pages 221–223, 267–269.

34. *How can we help children who are shy?* Shyness is a common form of childhood fear. The shy child feels self-conscious and embarrassed, fearful of how others may react to him or her. Shyness may be expressed by blushing, stuttering, talking as little as possible, and by nervous mannerisms. A shy child may be unable to talk in front of strangers or in class at school. Or he may not take leadership in play, and tend to withdraw from others. Shyness, as we all know, often persists through childhood. It's common among young teens, and many adults know the shy person's feelings of insecurity.

Not every quiet or reserved child suffers from shyness. Some simply are less talkative and outgoing, reflecting their own individual personalties or the ways of their parents.

But for those who are shy, shyness isn't easily or quickly overcome. It usually takes time, and a number of positive experiences, for a child to develop self-assurance. It takes a series of events which allow the child to discover self-assurance. It takes a series of events which allow the child to discover that he or she can cope to build confidence and self-esteem. Surely we can't overcome shyness by insisting our child get out there and mix. We can't tell a nine-year-old to *be* confident when she doesn't *feel* confident. What we can do is to help our children gradually develop self-confidence.

We should never tease a shy child or draw attention to his shyness by referring to it in front of others. In fact, if we know our child has trouble reciting in front of class, it's not out of line to ask the teacher to hear your child privately if there is time. Both you and the teacher can let the child know that sometime she will feel confident enough to recite in front of others, but till then you'll not insist. In general, letting a shy child go slowly, knowing that you understand his or her feelings, is most likely to bring progress.

If Ken is physically small and embarrassed by his inability to play sports well, he may have another ability or skill you can encourage that will help him feel good about himself. If Cindy is afraid of going to a party, inviting one or two of the other girls who will be there over to lunch, with games to play or cookies to bake afterward, may help her feel more comfortable about going. Following suggestions given in paragraph 49 to help build self-esteem may be the best way to build the inner confidence which will, gradually, overcome a child's shyness. Also, *talkable Bible stories* on pages 174–176 and 187–190 will help a shy child explore his or her feelings.

As we work to meet our children's security needs, and help them with the problems faced by other normal children, we need to remember that growing up is a process. Growth always takes time. A child's progress may seem slow to us. But let's not be discouraged. Gentleness, warmth and love, and the sure belief that with God's help, our boys and girls will work through each stage of life successfully, can take the pressure off you and me. And take *our* pressure off our children, releasing them to grow at their own pace, working through their fears successfully.

Self-Control

35. *How do we help children develop self-control?* Self-control, or self-discipline, is a basic need of all human beings. In Scripture self-control is associated with maturity and with the work of the Holy Spirit in our lives. While we can't expect children to be self-controlled in a mature, adult sense, we can expect them to be self-controlled for their age. We can expect a two-year-old to

have a temper tantrum when he doesn't get his way. But we shouldn't expect it of an eight-year-old. We might expect a three-year-old to want to take home a toy from a friend's home. But we should not expect an eleven-year-old to steal from the corner store. So one of our important ministries to our children is to help them develop the inner control they need to become self-disciplined.

In another section we'll look at discipline, the development of conscience, and overall moral growth (see paragraphs 64–66). Here we want to focus more narrowly on times when children's emotions or impulses seem out of control—times when they succumb to the temptation to steal or cheat, times when they become angry, or throw a temper tantrum, or fight. We want to look at running away, and at the control of bad habits. What links these topics is the simple fact that each situation calls for the child to stand in judgment of his feelings or impulses, and to choose not to give in to those passions.

The key to helping children develop self-control is expressed in a single word: responsibility. As children grow we need to let them do as much as they can for themselves. And we need to let children experience the consequences of their actions.

*Overprotected children seldom develop confidence or self-control. The mom who does everything for a child, from putting on his galoshes for him when he's four, to working out his math homework when he's nine, guarantees his immaturity. Sometimes a parent's motive for not letting a child take on responsibility is impatience rather than a desire to protect. "Here, let me tie your shoe," mom might say to her four-year-old. "You're taking too long." Or to the eight-year-old, "You're setting the table wrong. Go on out, I can do it quicker myself." If we're to help our children feel and be responsible, and to believe that they have the capacity to control themselves, we need to wait while Joey ties his shoes, and explain as often as necessary until the table is set right. Girls need to help mom cook, and now and then prepare dinner for the family. And, if parents are wise, boys need the same kind of kitchen experience. Both boys and girls need to have assigned chores, and be given whatever training is needed to help them do their jobs well. By giving our children the chance to accept responsibilities we help them develop self-confidence and self-control.

*Parents who let their children avoid the consequences of their actions actually erode self-control and self-discipline. God has made our world in such a way that effects follow causes. This is true in the physical universe with its laws, and true in the moral universe with its laws. Children need to learn early that they will be held responsible for their actions, and that certain unavoidable consequences will follow when they choose to follow their impulses instead of doing what they know is right.

In specific self-control problems discussed in the following paragraphs, we'll often return to the principle of natural consequences. What you also need to remember is that the specific suggestions on how to use natural consequences need to be backed up by a family practice of giving children responsibility. It takes both for a child to develop a confidence in his own ability to accomplish.

36. *How should parents respond to a child's anger and temper tantrums?* Eight-year-old Kim burst into tears and shouted "I hate you!" at her father. Then she ran out of the room. How should dad respond? And how is this different from the situation described by the woman who wrote, "My seven-year-old daughter has violent kicking and screaming fits when she doesn't get her own way. Frankly, her tantrums frighten me!" How should mom respond?

Anger is something all of us experience. The Bible recognizes the inevitability of angry feelings, and warns us not to attempt to justify our anger (cf. Gal. 5:22, 45). In the meantime we are taught, " 'In your anger do not sin': Do not let the sun go down while you are still angry" (Eph. 4:26). The feelings of anger may come. But we're not to let those feelings provoke us into sinful actions. And we're to work on the situation so that anger will not be harbored. Both these guidelines show us how to help children with anger. We're to help them work through the anger so they do not harbor angry feelings.

There are many reasons why children get angry. Anger may be an expression of frustration. It may be a response to opposition: a way children have found effective to get others to do what they want. Sometimes anger is a desire to hurt another person who has hurt us. Parents have tried many different ways to deal with children's angry outbursts. One study recorded the following parental reactions: scolding, reasoning, threatening, coaxing, soothing, spanking, ridiculing, depriving of privileges, isolating, bribing, granting the child's demands, and putting to bed. None of these responses were particularly effective. And in every case where adult responses were inconsistent, the outbursts of anger became more frequent.

Keeping in mind our goal of helping children work through

their angry feelings, and helping them learn not to express their anger in wrong or sinful ways, there are several principles that will help us.

*Much depends on our response to children's anger. If we can remain calm and quiet rather than becoming angry or anxious, we'll be much better able to help. And our children will pick up from this cue that we expect them to learn control.

Verbal expressions of anger (like Kim's "I hate you") are better than physical expressions. We should recognize them for what they are: a child's expressions of her feelings. One of the best things about emotions is that they do change. Kim didn't choose to have that feeling of anger. It just came. That feeling is uncomfortable for her as well as for dad, and doesn't change the fact that she loves dad as well as feeling angry at him.

Normally expressions of feelings like this should not be punished, and certainly not evoke an angry retort. It's best if dad goes to Kim's room a few minutes later (giving her a chance to cool down), and talks. "I know you're disappointed that you can't go to your friends' party, and that you feel angry. It's hard when we're angry with someone we love. There are times when I feel angry at you, but you're my girl, and even when I feel angry I still love you. I'd never want you to be anyone else's girl but mine."

Taking the lead in making peace isn't "giving in." It's teaching children how to follow Jesus' pattern of forgiveness and reconciliation. An understanding parent can help a child's angry feelings change, and relieve him or her of a great burden.

*Temper tantrums should be dealt with calmly but firmly. Temper tantrums are common in two-year-olds. They may persist in some six- or seven-year-olds. Most experts recommend that if they continue by eleven or twelve, or are frequent, professional help be obtained.

Most look at temper tantrums as a way of getting parental attention or manipulating mom and dad. The kicking, screaming seven-year-old mentioned earlier had wrested control from her mom. Mom was scared, and so the daughter threw a tantrum whenever "she doesn't get her own way." The suggestion to ignore a tantrum, most common in the literature, is inadequate here.

Ignoring is offered as a response because it does not reinforce a tiny child's demands for attention by either punishing or giving in. With twos and threes, ignoring may be effective. If the tantrums don't pay off, and mom and dad keep right on doing what they're doing, most preschoolers won't repeat the action too many times.

But when we're dealing with older children, more help is needed. Possibly the best course is to establish a clear policy with the child before he or she has a tantrum. Explain that many two- and three-year-olds have tantrums because when babies are very tired they can't control themselves or act grown up. If your child has tantrums, you're going to assume that he or she is overtired, too, and not able to act grown up. So if he or she does have a tantrum, you will put him or her to bed to rest for an hour.

Now the ground rules are established, and the child understands the consequences of his actions if he has a tantrum. He also sees that the consequences aren't just punishment, but are appropriate to the act.

When he has his next tantrum, remain calm. Ignore the behavior while he kicks and screams (or restrain him if he seems likely to harm himself or others). Then, calmly but firmly, put him in bed for his nap. You must be consistent in your response, and remain firm. If he tries the tactic on a shopping trip or a visit, cut the trip short and take him home for the nap. The chances are that when the consequences of a tantrum are firmly established, your child will discover that he can control himself after all.

A number of *talkable Bible stories* will help you explore anger with your children (see pages 167–171, 211–214, 337–340). It's best *not* to use them immediately after an incident. Wait a day or so, and then you can talk together about the incident as past history.

37. *How do we help a child overcome the temptation to steal?* It's not unusual for a preschooler to pick up a candy bar while mom's shopping in the supermarket. Usually mom explains then: "That belongs to the store, honey. It's not ours until we pay for it." By seven or eight, when a child takes the property of others he knows he's stealing.

There are many reasons why children might steal. Sometimes it's an impulsive act. Sometimes a few children will shoplift for adventure. If the home is stable and warm, and children are developing naturally, stealing is unlikely to be a symptom of rebellion or of a more serious problem. Yet any stealing incident is serious and calls for parental attention.

What parents need to do is to make it clear—whether the theft was from a friend, or in the home, or in a store—that stealing is wrong, and that restitution is required.

Restitution is the natural consequence prescribed by Scripture and by good sense. In the Old Testament the thief was not only to return what was taken but was to pay back at least double (Exod. 22:1–4).

When a child steals he should take the item back to the owner, apologize, and acknowledge responsibility for his act. Mom or dad may come along, but the child himself should be there. It may not be out of line when an object is taken from a store to follow the Old Testament pattern and pay for it as well as return it, in case there has been any damage or loss of value. Payment should come from the child's allowance.

Parents who pay for the object themselves, or in other ways let children avoid responsibility for their actions by acknowledging and returning stolen objects, make a tragic mistake. *Talkable Bible stories* related to stealing are found on pages 226–228, 285–288.

38. *How do we help a child overcome the temptation to lie?* There's a difference between the stories children tell when exercising their imagination (paragraph 20) and lies. Telling untruths involves that proverbial "fib." Even when boys and girls know better, the temptation to avoid a punishment, or get even with someone, or to gain some momentary advantage, will get the better of them at times. Lies are serious, even though few grownups are unswervingly truthful. Most children of six or seven know what lies are, and that they're wrong.

As with other control problems, we want to help the child develop a habit of telling the truth. What can we do to help that pattern develop?

*We need to be sure that we are truthful with him and with others. If we tell him, "I'll take you to the store when daddy comes home," and then do not do it, it's hard for him to see our failure as less than a lie. If we tell him, "The cookies are gone," to stop him nagging for another, and he discovers later they aren't gone, he's likely to adopt our pattern of lying to avoid unpleasantness or inconvenience.

*We need to avoid overreacting. Rather than showing horror when we catch a child in a lie, it's better to express our disappointment. "If you aren't going to tell me the truth, I won't be able to trust you. If you tell me something is true when it isn't, how will I know when you're telling me the real truth?"

*Check your discipline approach. If you typically use harsh punishment for wrongdoing, a child may begin to lie to avoid being punished. Children can't be forced to be truthful. But our approach to discipline shouldn't be such that it motivates a child to lie (see paragraphs 62, 63).

*When we suspect a child of lying, but are not sure, it's better to assume he's telling the truth than to try to force him to admit he has lied. Later events will make things clear. If the child has lied, your earlier kindness and trust are more likely to help him break down and talk about why than are suspicion and accusation.

*If lying is repeated or persistent, work out ground rules that will help the child break the pattern. One reasonable set of ground rules is:

—Mom and dad are going to trust you to tell them the truth.

—If you do slip and tell a lie, you can confess it and you won't be punished.

—If you tell a lie, and we find out about it later, we will have to punish you. If you lie about something you've done wrong to get out of taking responsibility (if you lie about hitting a sibling because you're afraid you'll get sent to your room) the lie will double the normal punishment.

If the child understands ground rules like these, and accepts them as fair, then you need only follow through consistently. As with other self-control issues, you can expect your child to grow out of the wrong behavior in time. Don't overreact, but do maintain standards of right and wrong, and respond with the calm, firm support that helps your child choose what is right. The *talkable Bible stories* on pages 156–158, 247–249, 313–316 can help with this problem.

39. *How do we cope with a physically aggressive child?* It's one thing when our child is fought with (see paragraphs 15, 16). It's another if he is the fight-er. How do we help children who react to frustration by striking out?

In general, when children have fights with their friends, it's best if moms and dads stay out of it. As noted earlier, quarreling is common among friends, and sometimes will break out into a fight. Normally children make up quickly and will be great friends again the next day.

If your child starts fights often you probably need to step in to help him. The social-skills training approach described in paragraph 13 can make a contribution.

Some parents help a child redirect anger. One provided a "kicking place" where her son could go and kick on some carpeting attached to a plywood frame. Playing the "What If" game described in paragraph 31 might also be used to help him work through alternatives to fighting.

Of course, you'll want to talk about the experience with your

Running away doesn't necessarily mean a child does not feel loved at home.

child so you can understand his fears and feelings. *Talkable Bible stories* on pages 337–340 will help.

40. *How should parents respond to a child who wanders off or runs away?* Most children who are loved and wanted won't be runaways. But any boy or girl may run away at times, or wander off. Children have a natural curiosity and desire for adventure. I must confess that, while I always felt loved and comfortable at home, and had no desire to abandon my parents, I marked my first day of kindergarten with one adventurous runaway, and at times during my early years found the woods near our home far more attractive than school.

What can one do with wandering children? If we're upset and worried about what might happen to them, we need to explain our concerns. Sixes and sevens can begin to understand why we worry. We also should establish ground rules. No skipping of school. Check to find out what time you're expected home. Have a clear understanding of off-limits areas. And, always travel with a friend. When time gets away, and a child doesn't make it home by suppertime, follow the "natural consequences" principle. You're sorry, but supper's over. He knew when supper was to be served, and that he needed to be home. The next meal is breakfast. He'll have a hungry evening, but he won't starve. And he may remember the next time to be home on time.

We can also organize some of the adventures that children find so exciting. Your six- through eight-year-olds can tent in the back yard, and nines to elevens can take part in scouting, church clubs, and camping. *Talkable Bible stories* that relate to running away are found on pages 290–295.

41. *How do we help a child overcome bad habits?* Children's habits are often more annoying than "bad." Perhaps that is why so little is written about them. That, and the fact that habits are hard to break, may explain why even *Parents' Magazine* seldom dealt with bad habits in the past decade.

What are "bad habits"? They may range from nail biting, to forgetting to wash hands when appearing at the meal table, to neglecting to make the bed or flush the toilet, to letting dirty clothes lie around one's room. Most habits aren't moral issues. So it's hard to claim that a child "ought" to do this or not do this or the other. Mom and dad may nag, but nagging doesn't do much good. And usually the fault doesn't call for punishment.

One of the things that wise parents will do is to think very carefully before making a childhood habit an issue. Most kids will outgrow their bad habits. Many parents feel they need to limit their intervention to things which are significant. This is probably wise. But if something a child does really bothers one or both parents, it's better to try to deal with it.

Many habits can be treated by recourse to natural consequences. Dirty clothes are spread around the child's room? Don't pick them up, mom. Get a plastic basket or hamper. Tell the child you will wash clothes he placed in the hamper, but you won't pick up for him. When he suddenly needs that baseball shirt, or she doesn't have a thing to wear for school, too bad. Next time put it in the hamper where it will get washed.

Bad tasting nail polish can go on an often-bitten nail. Dinner can wait while hands are washed. A child can be called away from play to flush the forgotten toilet. If you keep calm and treat correcting such things as just a matter of course, the child will usually find it is to his advantage to do it right the first time.

In all self-control issues, then, it's important for us to remain calm and confident. With our support and love, our boys and girls will develop the inner control they need to make right and good choices in life. Let's never lose our confidence—in them, in God, and in our ability to help them—just because progress may be slow.

Health

42. *Keeping children healthy and happy.* The emotional climate of the home, and the sense of security loving parents provide, is our most important contribution to our children's health. Still, most of us will have a few problems with picky eaters, childhood illnesses, and sometimes times of stress when there is serious illness in the home or a child must visit the hospital. There are also some religious questions that moms and dads have. When a child or a child's loved one is sick, should he pray for healing? How do we treat the Bible stories of Jesus' healing miracles? Another related problem has to do with handicapped children. How should moms and dads relate to them, so that they're able to reach their full potential too—whatever that potential may be?

As in other issues affecting our six- through eleven-year-olds, you and I will set the tone for our home. We can help our children most when we've thought through the issues, and planned how best to respond.

43. *What about children's diet and eating habits?* Dr. John Powers, in his helpful book *Food Power: Nutrition and Your Child's Behavior* (St. Martin's Press, New York, 1978) begins his first chapter by introducing Mary Sue. "Almost ten, she continually tormented, teased, and struck her playmates. At home she wandered restlessly from room to room, handling forbidden, fragile articles, and throwing objects. In school she had a short attention span, wouldn't finish her work, dawdled, and talked endlessly. Her penmanship, never very good, deteriorated. She was a fourth grader, doing third-grade work." Mary Sue and other children whose stories are told in Dr. Powers' book, aren't "bad" boys and girls. Yet some showed hostility and temper outbursts. Many were hyperactive. Most had sleep problems, and many showed prolonged bed-wetting. Unfortunately, following the suggestions given in earlier paragraphs won't help parents of such children.

Despite having plenty of food to eat, these children were suffering from forms of malnutrition, usually linked with carbohydrate overload. Mom and dad let these kids eat what they wanted. And what they wanted was junk food! What they got were malnutrition diseases, that showed up as poor health and bad behavior.

Eating a balanced diet clearly is important, for more reasons than to control children's weight. Providing (and controlling) a good diet for children is a basic need if our boys and girls are to grow naturally toward maturity.

Without going into detail, we all know the solution. Give children balanced meals. Limit between-meal snacking. And don't give in when advertisers insist on TV that their particular sugar-loaded snack is "part of a healthy breakfast."

Maintaining good eating habits is another of those things that calls for more self-discipline by parents than self-discipline by children. When our picky eater won't finish his meal, but complains a half-hour after supper that he's hungry, bring out his half-eaten meal, or give him an apple. But that peanut butter and jelly sandwich, or the ice cream he's begging for, shouldn't be permitted. Set up some ground rules on snacks. It may be all right to have some fruit or beef jerky when he comes home from school. But never a bite should be permitted in the hour and a half or so before meals.

Even if our children don't show the extreme behavior of Mary Sue, setting limits on what and when children eat is important. We can't expect kids to be hungry for the food that's best for them. So we need to establish guidelines for them, and help them live within our limits. Surprisingly, helping a child restructure his eating pattern may do more to bring peace and happiness to the whole family than any other single thing we can do.

44. *How do we help a child face a visit to the hospital?* Every once and a while a child will need to go to the hospital. Most boys and girls will have worked through fear of doctors or dentists by the early grades. But that hospital visit can be traumatic even for older children. Actually, the same approach we take to help a child prepare for his hospital visit can be used with younger boys and girls for a doctor or dentist appointment. Much research has shown that even adults do better if they know what to expect from a hospital visit, and are told honestly if there will be pain. Some hospitals have preadmittance visits for children to meet nurses and see the rooms they may stay in. Bookstores have books designed to help children understand what will happen when they enter the hospital, to familiarize them with X-rays and hospital beds and anesthesia and other probable experiences. Mom or dad needs to reassure the child that they will be there as much as possible, even when the procedure is simple. Children also need to be told honestly if there will be some pain, and assured that the doctor will give them medicine so it won't hurt too much.

Parents who prepare a child for a hospital visit may find in talking about what will happen that the child has a number of questions. Answer as many as you can. You may even want to call the doctor or hospital with questions you can't answer. Find out ahead of time if your child can bring favorite and familiar toys or pictures with him. Something from home is always comforting in a strange place. Many hospitals now permit children to wear their own clothing as they recuperate on a children's ward. See *talkable Bible story* on pages 261–264.

45. *How do we help children face illness in the home?* All boys and girls will have periods of illness, and experience a more extensive bout with the measles or mumps. But sometimes it's mom or dad who is sick. No matter who is sick, extended illnesses need to be handled wisely.

Children who are ill usually have their greatest difficulty when they're getting well again. Then the boredom of being stuck inside or in bed, and their natural energy, make recuperation a problem for everyone. The best we can do is provide as many quiet resources for them as possible: books, puzzle pads, toys, and whatever our child likes to do best. We can't expect a child to take confinement too cheerfully. We'll probably be plagued by calls for attention. But both the child and parent can weather it. It's usually only for a few days.

It's more serious if an extended illness strikes mom or dad, or another member of the family. Then there are several things we need to do to help children with the anxiety they will sense in us, and with the changes in home-life that invariably come.

*Don't try to "protect" the child by not talking about the illness. Instead, without giving details beyond his or her comprehension, honestly express your own concern for the sick person. Explain that the doctors are doing what they can to help mom or dad get well. Share your own trust that God loves you and your whole family, and is with you during this time.

*Don't ignore the child or keep him on the "outside" during this experience. On the one hand, try to take a few minutes to give exclusively to the individual when he or she comes home

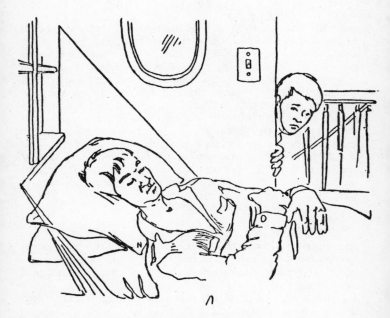

**Children can cope better with serious illness in the home
if they feel they contribute and can help.**

from school. If you have a bedtime ritual, try to maintain it if
possible (see paragraph 26).

It's important to let the child participate, and to share the added
responsibilities illness will bring. The more a boy or girl feels he
or she is contributing, the less helpless and fearful the child will
feel. Hold a family council and ask everyone for suggestions on
how he or she can help. One child may do additional cleaning.
An older boy or girl may take on the washing, or volunteer for
food preparation.

*Give the child a chance to participate spiritually in the family
crisis. Pray together for the sick person. Let your boy or girl call
the Sunday school teacher and classmates to ask them to pray.

Children do not need to bear the full burden of a serious illness.
But they should share in adjustments the family must make, and
feel that they are contributing to make it easier for the sick person

and to help him or her get well. See *talkables* on pages 231–233, 299–302, 346–349.

46. *Should we teach children to pray for healing?* For some parents this is a troubling question. What if the child prays, and the sick person doesn't get well right away? Or if the sick person should die (see paragraph 88)? Won't that disturb a child, or threaten his trust in God?

Other parents have additional theological concerns. They believe that God works through doctors and medicines. They are not comfortable with what they view as a "magical" approach to faith. Contrast this with the view of some believers that all healing is supernatural, and that in fact God is committed to make well whoever really trusts him.

While we can understand the adult theological concerns of parents, such questions really aren't at issue. The Bible pictures prayer as an expression of the relationship between God the loving Father and the human beings who are his children. God invites us to come to him with every concern and with every need. God assures us that he loves us, that he hears our prayers, and that he will do what is best for us. The Bible doesn't promise that what we want is always his best. Sometimes the answer God gives us is "No," or "Maybe." Sometimes the answer is "Yes." But the most important thing for us as believers and for our children is the realization that God does love us, that he cares about what is happening to us, and he invites us to share every need and care with him.

In view of this great reality, how can we hesitate to assure our children that God cares when they're sick, or when someone they love is ill? How can we hesitate to let them tell God their concern, and ask God to make the sick person well?

The Bible gives us added reassurance. We learn in the many gospel stories that God can heal. We also learn that God is wise and loving. He may not choose to make us well now. But he will never leave us, and he will give us what is best.

A number of Bible stories can be used with children in times of illness to help them sense the comfort of God's love, and help them trust him to do what is best. We can safely leave the more complicated theological questions till our children grow up. But we can never leave our boys and girls without the comfort of prayer. *Talkable Bible stories* that will help are found on pages 231–233, 299–302, 307–309, and 346–349.

47. *How do we relate to children with handicaps?* When our daughter Joy was born, my wife suffered a massive placental separation. Joy was without oxygen for five minutes as the doctors worked frantically to perform a Caesarean section. As a result Joy suffered brain damage, and will never grow mentally beyond the five- or six-year capacity she exhibits now at twenty-one. Having Joy in our home did add certain kinds of stress to family life, especially for Joy's younger brother, Timothy. But the lessons we learned during her growing-up years parallel the advice of others in our situation.

*Our attitude toward Joy was critical. Some statistics indicate one of eight families has a child who is handicapped in some way, whether seriously like Joy, or suffering from a minor learning disability. We decided early that Joy must be loved for who she is, and treated as much like other children as possible. She wasn't to be overly protected, but helped to respond and grow to the limits of her capacity. Viewing a handicapped child as "helpless," and treating her that way, is actually holding the child back.

*Achievements need to be recognized and praised. All boys and girls need praise and the approval of loved ones. Handicapped children are no different than others in this respect, even though what a handicapped child like Joy can accomplish will be much less than normal.

*Provide as many normal experiences as possible. Don't keep a handicapped child inside, isolated from others. Disabled children can accept their limitations, but it's hard if mom or dad seem ashamed of them. It took lots of special care when young Joy went shopping with us, or out to a restaurant. Sometimes she received strained looks from others when she was overly enthusiastic. But gradually Joy learned how to conduct herself, and always took great delight in our shared adventures.

Joy is now in a special home/school in Kentucky, where she will probably live out her life. The time came when she herself wanted to go away, where she could live with friends. She lives there happily now, and the school takes great care to help her continue to develop and use her every potential.

Boys and girls like Joy need just as much love, firmness, acceptance, and guidance, focused on helping them reach their potential, as do normal boys and girls. The basic principles that we use in guiding normal children generally work just as well with the handicapped.

Achievement

48. *Why is a sense of achievement important to children?* The desire to do better is an important source of motivation for boys and girls six to eleven. The feeling that they *can* do better is closely linked with children's personality and their general outlook on life.

One of the most significant factors influencing achievement motivation is a child's past experience. Successes strengthen a child's aspirations, and failures weaken them. In fact, a child's successes or failures have a number of far-reaching effects.

*In general, a boy or girl who predominantly experiences successes will become more independent, be more confident, cheerful and happy, and more willing to help others. Successes that come too easily, however, aren't all positive. Effortless success tends to decrease motivation, and may lead to contempt for others. It can

To help a child become more confident, cheerful, and willing to help others, generate feelings of success.

produce an overconfidence that crumbles when a child must face stiffer competition later on. We need to help a child recognize and enjoy his successes. But we need to be careful not to turn every event into a great personal victory.

*In general, a boy or girl who predominantly experiences failures will be unsure of his abilities, feel inadequate and inferior, and will become cautious, easily embarrassed, and self-conscious. Such a child is likely to have weaker motivations, and be less willing to make an effort. He will tend to be gloomy and unhappy, and may well blame others for his or her failures.

Children develop their impression of success and failure from several sources. They have the chance in play and in school to compare themselves with other children. And they have the reactions of mom and dad as a basis for evaluation. In fact, our interpretation of our children's experiences may be the single most important factor in how they feel about themselves and their efforts. What are some things that we can do to help boys and girls develop a healthy sense of personal competence and strong motivation to achieve?

1) We can help when children's aspirations are too high. When our Timothy was nine, he felt great frustration because he couldn't play basketball as well as his teen-aged brother and I. It was hard to help him realize that more growing up was necessary, and that he was really doing very well for his age. Sometimes children plan to do too much for a school project, unrealistically setting a goal they can't reach. We need to help them set goals they can achieve.

2) We can help by adjusting our own aspirations. Often "success" and "failure" are relative terms. A child who studies hard and raises a "C" to a "B" has had a significant success. But if mom shows disappointment that it wasn't an "A," that success may be experienced as a failure! If dad remembers high-school glory days with longing, and pushes a young son who is a slow developer physically into Little League, or shows disappointment whenever he's at bat without a hit, even his success on the diamond won't be enough. We need to remember that our children are individuals, and that "success" is working up to their individual ability rather than someone else's. *Talkable Bible stories* on pages 135–140, 187–190, and 304–307 will help you and your children think about what is "success" for them.

3) The biblical teaching of the specialness of each individual gives us perspective. We parents need to appreciate the particular gifts and the abilities each child has—and not compare one child with others or with our own "ideal." You and I can be assured

that God has a place of spiritual significance for each individual in the body of Christ. But each of us will fulfill different roles. Each of us has the privilege of using our own special abilities to serve others. God's wonderful plan for each of our children will be discovered in time. As they are growing, we need to accept our children as they are, encourage them in their interests, and communicate our own confidence that each *is* a special person, with a place to fill in God's kingdom of love.

49. *How do we help a child develop self-esteem?* A child's self-concept grows and takes shape during the time between six and eleven. It's constructed as the child relates to other people and picks up clues about their image of him. It's added to by his own view of his physical, mental, and social abilities, tested by measurements of his performance against age-mates. But "self-esteem" focuses attention on a particular aspect of self-concept. Self-esteem is linked with how a child feels about the person he sees himself to be. A child with a "good self-image" or "high self-esteem" has a sense of worth and value, and self-confidence. As we saw in paragraph 48, the belief of a child that he has value and can achieve is closely related to his motivation and to his total personality.

The first clues a child has from which to build his self-concept come from mom and dad. We are the ones whose opinion he most values. It's easy to see then that what we do and say is closely linked with our son or daughter's self-esteem. We can see why even a talented child, who does good work in school and is helpful at home, may have low self-esteem . . . if parents are perfectionists who never acknowledge accomplishments, but instead show by remarks or indifference that they think the child should do better. We can also see why a boy who can't compete with his age-mates in sports might have a very good self-image . . . if his parents love music and show warm appreciation for his developing skill with an instrument.

In fact, we can define quite clearly the things that parents can do to help build a child's self-esteem and his feeling of personal worth.

*We can be sure to treat our children with consideration and respect. This means, among other things, listening to children and their feelings and helping them develop personal responsibility (see paragraphs 79 and 80).

*We can help our children recognize their success and set realistic goals (see paragraph 48).

*We can help our children develop the skills needed to be successful in everything from social relationships with others (paragraph 13) to sports (paragraph 115). We can reaffirm our children's value to us and to God, making sure that our boys and girls feel loved. *Talkable Bible stories* on pages 135–140, 187–190, and 244–247 will help our boys and girls sense God's love and approval.

50. *How do we encourage creativity in our children?* There are many kinds of achievement our children may experience. There is social achievement, in which a child is liked and wanted as a friend. There is achievement in sports, so important to boys. There is academic achievement in school, or in hobbies. Then there is the fascination of creativity: that combination of old ideas or things into new forms which brings the joy of unique personal achievement.

Creativity is not accidental discovery or a flashing, sudden insight. It's related to what is called *divergent thinking.* Divergent thinkers don't look for the one right answer; they look for many possibilities. They explore for new information and combine it in different ways, enjoying the fresh and the different. Surprisingly, creativity isn't directly linked with intelligence. A child with high grades or IQ is not certain to be more creative. Of course, a person does need to have enough intelligence to gather and organize information. But creativity has to do with how a person uses the knowledge he or she already has.

Creative children tend to be flexible, have a high need for independence and autonomy, be playful, self-assured, and self-disciplined. They are more curious than others, enjoy fantasy, like to pursue their own interests, and may be somewhat timid socially. We can help our children develop creativity in quite simple ways. We can encourage exploring and curiosity, even though a younger child's constant questioning may irritate. We can encourage the development of individual interests, and be willing to visit the library with him often when he wants more information on his present fascination. We can provide raw materials and toys he can manipulate, avoiding the kits and ready-made mannikins that call for structured, step-by-step construction. Because creativity is not an asset in school (where the learning of prescribed information wins better grades and the teachers' approval), our encouragement at home will probably determine whether children develop or abandon creative thinking in the critical childhood years.

51. *Why is parental praise so important to children?* A child's adult potential is strongly influenced by his achievement motiva-

tion, his positive self-esteem, and his capacity for creative thinking. Achievement motivation will affect the enthusiasm with which our sons and daughters respond to present and later opportunities to grow and reach higher goals. A sense of worth and value, and the confidence that the person can successfully overcome life's challenges, is intimately linked with reaching the full potential which God has built into individual personalities. Ability to think freshly and creatively enables the individual to make unique contributions to others' lives, as well as to avoid the "dead-end" thinking which locks many adults into boring routine.

While many factors contribute to development of these vital achievement-related traits, one common element is parental praise. Children are motivated by the desire for mom's and dad's approval. They gain their first impressions of themselves from mom and dad, and generally continue to grow in areas in which they receive mom's and dad's praise. The warmth of our approval is more important in motivating children than any reward of sweets or money or toys.

52. *How can we believe in our children?* Our attitude toward our boys and girls is so important. Yet at times it's hard not to become discouraged. Bedtime problems aren't resolved. Our child doesn't relate well to children in the neighborhood. He or she whines or pouts. Even though we're doing all the right things, as we understand them, we just don't see a speedy change in our children's behavior.

In times like these we need to trust God for our children, and remind ourselves of how patient God the Father is with you and me. Growing up is a process. It takes time for any human being to change. But change *will* come. The process of growth will take place, and God will use our consistent, loving guidance to help our boys and girls grow toward personal and spiritual maturity.

It is trust in God—not in our parenting skill, or even in our children's potential—which gives us the confidence to keep on loving, and to communicate to our boys and girls the calming assurance that there is no problem so great it cannot be overcome. See *talkable Bible stories* on pages 244–247 and 323–326.

2. YOUR FAMILY LIFE STYLE

53. *Why is a stable family life style so important for children?*
The whole life of most preschoolers is centered in the home. Their only significant relationships are generally with family. As boys and girls reach the school years, their world expands. School and friends play an increasingly prominent role. Even so, home and family are still of first importance. Despite changes in the ways families live today—with more working mothers, greater mobility, many single-parent families, and so on—research has shown that the family is still the primary socializer of boys and girls. Family continues to be the primary shaper of a child's personality, and the primary source of his values.

In the first chapter of this book we explored some of your child's needs—for friends, play, sleep, security, self-control, health, and achievement. We looked at ways parents can help children turn problems in these areas into opportunities for growth. In this chapter, we focus on relationships within the family. We see how your life together can enrich children's growth, and your own.

There are many things about a family's shared life that are important to nurture. We'll look at the most significant: those elements of shared life which have direct impact on communicating values, and on supporting the healthy growth of young personalities. We'll explore communication, discipline, sibling relationships, family responsibilities, and times of stress, as well as holidays and vacations. And we'll suggest *talkable Bible stories* that can help bring your children vital insights from God's Word.

Nothing in this chapter suggests your present family life style is a failure. When you and I love our children, and treat them with concern, we never really fail. What you will find here are ways to enrich family experiences, and ideas that may help you resolve problems that trouble parents of most six- through eleven-year-olds.

54. *What biblical principles should guide family life style?* The Old Testament establishes a simple pattern for family interaction. The pattern is found in Deuteronomy 6, and is reflected often in

Bible history, Proverbs, and the Prophets. In Deuteronomy 6:5–7 we hear God's call to his people to love him and recognize him as God. Moses tells the people: "These commandments that I give you this day are to be upon your hearts. Impress them on your children. Talk about them when you sit at home and when you walk along the road, when you lie down, and when you get up" (6:6, 7). The principles expressed in this core Old Testament passage on home life are simple, yet of ultimate significance.

* Parents model faithful living. As we love God, and build our own lives on the truths of his Word, we are able to communicate faith and morality to our children. We can share what we experience as we grow in faith. We cannot share what is not real to us. So the parent's first obligation is in his or her own relationship with God. As we love the Lord and grow in him, you and I are equipping ourselves to build the character of our boys and girls.

* Parents communicate faithful living. Today, as in Old Testament times, children pick up their values and beliefs from mom and dad. It's our responsibility to build communication bridges: a relationship with our boys and girls over which our own love for God and commitment to his ways can travel freely.

* Parents communicate in daily life. Christian nurture isn't some Sunday kind of thing, in which religious education is limited to a classroom. The situations in which the reality of God is best communicated are found in daily life. This is why the approach taken in this *Handbook,* which links specific childhood experiences with relevant Bible stories, is so important. Here we learn *how* to "talk about" God's words in the lying down, the getting up, and the walking along the road of life that we share with our children.

Communication

55. *What are our communication goals?* There are many ways in which we communicate with our children, and they with us. We all pick up nonverbal messages: we learn to recognize when a child is upset, and children can tell when we're anxious. But verbal communication is most significant. Only when we talk can we learn why a child is upset; only when we talk can a child be reassured that we're not upset because of something he or she has done. It's by talking that the things inside us—what we think and how we feel—are shared.

One basic goal of communication is to develop a family climate in which each person feels comfortable and secure and accepted and supported by others whom he feels he understands. When we examine communication as a nurture factor in the Christian home, we explore how the ways that we talk with our boys and girls will affect relationships, communicate warmth and closeness, and promote personal and spiritual growth. We want the ways we talk together to express how we feel inside, so that neither parents nor children live with uncertainty.

Imagine that dad comes home, deeply upset about something that has happened at work. He's anxious, and angry too. So when he comes in he's not prepared for Joey, who runs up and says, "Dad! Look what I did in school today. I got a gold star!" We can understand if dad brusquely says, "Don't bother me now, Joey," and rushes off to take a shower.

The problem is, Joey can't interpret his father's reaction. All he knows is that he was excited about an accomplishment, and dad didn't care.

Even when the family relationship is good, Joey is going to feel hurt and rejected. If this is just another in a series of such incidents, before long an impression that his folks don't care, or that his accomplishments are worthless, will be firmly imbedded.

But what can dad do? Joey's too young to understand the stress of adult life. Surely dad can't explain.

Actually, dad doesn't need to explain. All he really needs to do is to open a line of communication and share something of what he's feeling inside. "Joey, I want to look at your paper. But right now I'm feeling tense and upset. I need a shower to relax me. Let's look at it in a half an hour, when I'm feeling better."

Just a few additional words transform the experience. Joey may still feel disappointed. But he knows he's not rejected, and that his work is important to dad. He is also learning that other people have feelings and needs, and that living with others means taking their feelings into account. A few words, and the situation is transformed from a possible problem to an opportunity for training. And it was woven so naturally into the family's shared life that it probably was not even recognized as nurture.

Our goal, again, is to develop patterns of communication in the family which help each person feel comfortable, secure, accepted and supported. By building such relationships, we provide a climate for maximum personal and spiritual growth. See *talkable Bible story* on pages 158–161.

56. *What is parental modeling?* The Old Testament words, "these commandments shall be in your heart" (Deut. 6:7), focus our atten-

tion on parents. As you and I build God's values and ways into our personalities, we communicate them to our children.

Looking back at the experience with Joey (paragraph 55) we can see why. Dad's first, brusque reaction was understandable. But it wasn't a very good example of New Testament principles, such as consideration of others or putting the needs of others before our own (cf. Phil. 2:4). But the alternate response was an expression of that concern for others which God in Christ encourages in us all. Joey wasn't brushed aside, but was treated with respect. Dad took the time to explain why he couldn't look now, and to promise that when he was emotionally able, he would.

In this brief encounter Joey heard dad quote no Bible verses. No Bible stories were told. Instead Joey saw dad live one of the values affirmed in the gospel: other persons are important and merit our consideration and love.

Boys and girls like Joey—all our children in that critical six to eleven age-span—imitate their parents. They build parental traits into their own personalities. Without being aware of it, children pick up the attitudes and values of the adults they live with as well as their beliefs. When we live out a Bible truth, and model it in our relationship with our children, we communicate powerfully the Word we are called to teach our boys and girls. As God's Word takes root in our hearts (Deut. 6) and is translated into our lives, it is transmitted by a God-intended modeling process to our children.

Studies have shown what parents can do to encourage the modeling process, and the quiet transmission of biblical values to their boys and girls. In another book (*A Theology of Christian Education,* Zondervan, 1979) I summarized the factors that enhance modeling. Things which encourage modeling are:

1) Frequent, long-term contact with the model(s).

2) A warm, loving relationship with the model(s).

3) Exposure to the inner states of the model(s). That is, models need to share what they feel and are thinking.

4) Opportunity to observe the model(s) in a variety of life situations.

5) Consistency and clarity in the model(s) behavior and values.

6) Correspondence between the model(s) behavior and their expressed beliefs.

7) An explanation (in words) of the model(s) life style. That is, models need to tell as well as show the truths and principles which guide their actions.

How clear it is! The primary models of children—those who

have that long-term, loving contact, who share many common experiences, and whose ways as well as words can be observed— must be their parents! When we add good communication, which includes sharing inner states and teaching those Bible principles which guide daily life, we have the secret of God's plan for the nurture of boys and girls.

It's important to add one note here. Sometimes we make the mistake of thinking that we have to be perfect to model faith. Because we're not perfect, we may feel guilty and anxious. If dad comes home upset and neglects to express his feelings to Joey, won't that *bad* model be catching too? Won't dad's failure to apply his Christian values in this situation harm Joey's personal and spiritual development? Two things help us. First, it's not the isolated incident, but the overall pattern of family life that counts. We all fail at times. Then we need God's forgiveness. If dad later realizes he's hurt Joey, he can apologize and ask for forgiveness. When he does, dad is teaching another great Bible truth: that confession and forgiveness bring reconciliation. Second, you and I are growing, just as our children are growing. We're not perfect yet. The Bible says we "are being transformed" (2 Cor. 3:18). So Jesus' working in our lives isn't seen only in what we do, but in our own growth and changes toward Christlikeness. It's not having arrived, but the fact that we're on the way, which communicates the reality of Jesus.

So if you and I are growing in our faith, and keeping communication lines open with our children, we can trust God to make us a positive force in their lives.

57. *What characterizes ineffective parent talk?* Communication involves how we talk with our children. Some patterns of parent talk open vital communication lines and support growth. Other patterns of parent talk close communication lines and hinder growth.

It's important to understand: what we're considering here is patterns of family communication, not isolated incidents. It is the way we *usually* talk with our boys and girls that has an impact on nurture.

* "Control talk" patterns are ineffective. "Control talk" is marked by the adult continually giving instructions or advice to the child. Control talk focuses on behavior, it tends to be corrective, and it erodes the child's sense of autonomy and responsibility. For instance, listen to this conversation (only mom's words are

"Control talk"—correcting or directing—isn't the only or the best way to guide our children.

reported). It took place during the ten minutes after eight-year-old Jack got home from school:

"Put your books in your room, Jack. Don't leave them on the table. Yes, you can have a sandwich. Jack, put the butter back. And wipe up the crumbs. I don't want ants in here."

"Just a minute, where are you going now? Who? All right, but don't go any further than the end of the block. And I want you home the first time I call."

"Just a minute. Jack, you didn't wipe up the crumbs. Use the paper towels, not the sponge, Jack. Do you have any homework to do tonight? You have to come back earlier if you've got homework."

"Be careful when you cross the street."

There's nothing particularly wrong with any single statement here. But if you look back you see that almost everything mom says *corrects* or *directs* Jack's actions. This kind of talk does not

let Jack know mom as a person on whom to model. And it doesn't
help Jack develop as a responsible individual.

* "Closed channel" talk is ineffective. Look over mom's talk
with Jack again. Her control talk has characteristics beyond its
focus on behavior and giving of directions. This kind of talk does
not explore or expose what we earlier called "inner states" (paragraph 56). We don't know what Jack thinks or feels. And we
don't really know what mom thinks or feels. All we know is how
she wants Jack to act.

It is good for a child to have a clear idea of what is expected
of him. But children need to build a relationship with parents
which includes sharing of thoughts and feelings. Only when sharing
is part of our life together can modeling really nurture.

* "Unresponsive talk" is ineffective. Conversation should be a
two-way exchange. We express ourselves, and listen to others express themselves. We respond to their ideas and thoughts and feelings, and they respond to ours. But look again at the way mom
talked with Jack. We catch no hint of responsiveness. Mom reacts
to what Jack says and does. But she doesn't really *listen,* or respond
to him on a personal level.

One important goal for parents of six- to eleven-year-olds is to
develop good communication patterns, for communication helps
turn problems into opportunities for ministry. As you work with
the *talkable Bible stories,* and with suggestions in various paragraphs of the first three chapters of this book, you'll see that there
are better ways to solve problems than to resort to control, closed-
channel, and unresponsive patterns of talk with your boys and
girls.

58. *What characterizes effective parent talk?* The quality of our
relationship with our children, and our effectiveness in nurturing
them, is usually reflected in the pattern of our talk with our boys
and girls. Effective parent talk supports a child's personal growth
and the development of responsibility. It helps us provide a clear
example on which children can construct personal values and personality traits.

* Effective parent talk is positively reinforcing. Ineffective parent
talk directs and corrects, sending the message that we do not see
the child as adequate, able, or responsible. It's almost certain that
Jack's forgetfulness about school books and wiping up crumbs (paragraph 57) is a direct result of mom's talk, which communicates
her expectation of irresponsibility.

Reinforcing talk picks up positive behavior and encourages it by praise. When Jack was three, mom might have wiped up the crumbs after Jack spread his own bread, and commented, "I like to get all the crumbs wiped up in our kitchen. I don't want little black ants crawling around where we get our food ready, do you?" After a few such experiences, Jack is almost sure to wipe up the crumbs himself, and mom then will praise. "Why Jack, thank you! I'm so happy you want to help me keep our kitchen clean. You're growing up so fast. I bet there are older children than you who don't wipe up their crumbs like you do."

Notice the elements here. Mom overlooked the inadequate behavior. She modeled the correct behavior, with comments explaining why. She then praised when the child responded and mimicked. This simple approach will build good habits and will, at the same time, develop a sense of responsibility and self-esteem.

* Effective parent talk is multi-channel. In effective parent talk we share thoughts and feelings as well as other kinds of information. When dad explained to Joey how he was feeling and why he couldn't listen just then (paragraph 54), dad opened vital channels and shared information about his inner state that Joey—or even another adult—could not have guessed with any certainty. When our talk includes information about what we experience, and how we think and feel about it, we'll be more effective in our nurture.

* Effective parent talk is responsive. When we talk with our children we need to listen to their feelings and thoughts, and respond to them. Good listening, active listening (paragraph 59), characterizes good parent/child communications.

One of the important contributions of the *talkable Bible stories* in this *Handbook* is that the "talkable" suggestions are designed to help you and your children listen to each other, and share with each other on feeling as well as information channels. Reading the Bible stories together and talking about them will help you strengthen the good communication patterns in your relationship, as well as to explore important messages in God's Word.

Talkable Bible stories which deal specifically with communication are found on pages 158–161, 193–196, and 335–337.

59. *How do we listen effectively?* Many names have been coined for the kind of listening which strengthens good communication. It's been called active listening, reflective listening, and acceptant listening, among others. The basic notion is quite simple. We listen not only for what the child says, but also for feelings implied. When the child speaks, we resist jumping in with an adult judgment, criticism, or solution. We listen further, to gather as much

information about the child's thinking and feelings as we can.

We can illustrate effective listening quite simply. Jack comes home from school and throws his books down on the table. From the action and the look on his face, mom picks up clues to his feelings:

"You seem to feel upset," she observes.

"I'm not upset," Jack responds. "I'm mad."

"What happened?"

Sitting down in the kitchen, Jack is quiet for a minute. Then he says, "It's that Mrs. Hedley. She's just not fair, mom. I think she hates me."

"What makes you think that, Jack?"

"Oh, she wouldn't take my homework. Just 'cause it was a day late."

"And you feel that was unfair?"

"Well, she let Jenny turn hers in late."

"That doesn't seem fair, Jack. Did your teacher explain why she wouldn't take yours but did take Jenny's?"

"Yeah."

"But you don't think her explanation was a good one."

Jack is quiet for a moment. "Well, I guess—she said it was because it was the second time for me."

"I see."

"Well, I forgot and left it home once. And then I, well, I didn't get it done last weekend. I did it last night. But she said it was too late, and that I'm too good a student not to do my work on time."

"That doesn't sound like she hates you, Jack. It sounds like she thinks a lot of you. You know, when you told me Mrs. Hedley isn't fair, I thought you were mad at her. I guess you were feeling angry, but maybe not at your teacher."

"Yeah. I guess I was just mad."

Mom nods. "I know I get mad at myself sometimes when I do something I don't want to. Like when I yelled at you the other day. I felt ashamed after that, and really mad at myself."

Jack nods too. "Yeah. I guess maybe I'm mad at myself too. Mom, can I have a sandwich? I'm hungry."

Glancing back over this conversation we see several important things. Mom didn't take sides, either with Jack or Mrs. Hedley. Mom didn't ask many questions, but when she did they were honest requests for information, not disguised messages. For instance, "Don't you think you should have done your homework on time?" isn't an honest question. It's a disguised message that not too subtly says, "It was all your fault, son. Admit it!"

When it came to probing Jack's thoughts and feelings mom didn't ask questions, she made statements. "But you don't think her explanation was a good one" is an example. Mom restated what Jack has been saying. Now Jack knows mom has heard him, and he has a chance to modify his statement any way he wants. As the conversation gradually exposes Jack's real problem (he's feeling upset and angry at his failure to live up to his own expectations), mom continues to accept his feelings and shares her own experiences as well. In this particular situation, once Jack understands his feelings they begin to change. His uncertainty over his teacher's feelings about him, and his own feelings, are relieved. Jack is a responsible boy, and he'll think twice about "forgetting" homework next time.

How much better this listening mother's approach than that of a mom who jumps to conclusions, takes sides, and very possibly uses the occasion to lecture Jack on responsibility or angrily calls Mrs. Hedley to ask why she's persecuting her son.

Effective listening is a vital element of good communication with our boys and girls. It is a vital element of good Christian nurture.

60. *How much can our children really understand?* One of the concerns we have as parents is: How much of our communication can young children understand? Research has made it plain that boys and girls don't have the ability to think in adult ways. It's hard for our six- and seven-year-olds to take the role of another person, and see things from his point of view. During the junior years (nine to eleven), children have a strong sense of fairness but little grasp of grace. They simply may not be able to grasp some of the things we want to help boys and girls to understand.

Establishing good communication patterns for talking and listening in the family will not automatically overcome such problems. But good communication gives us two great advantages. First, we'll understand more about how our children do think, because we will listen closely to them as they express their thoughts and feelings. We'll be much better able to evaluate how to reach them on their own level.

The second advantage is a vital one. There are times when children have to simply accept our judgment. They will not be able to grasp the reasons behind some of our values and choices. In a home where communication lines are open, a child knows that mom and dad do listen to him, and share with him. It will be much easier for such a child to respond to adult guidance. He may not understand why we make a particular decision. But he will know his thoughts and feelings are not ignored. He can trust us more easily, because the way we communicate with him says unmistakably that he is loved.

61. *Making time for good communication.* None of us have time for extended exploration of thoughts and feelings every time our child comes home from school, or dashes in breathless after play. Mornings can be hectic. There's breakfast to eat, lunches to pack, teeth to brush, books to be gathered, and a bus to be caught. Active listening probably will not be part of our family's morning routine! It is to be hoped, though, that there will be quiet times when we're with our children. We may share an evening meal, or the half hour before bedtime (paragraph 25). At times like these, or when a child is clearly upset and concerned, enriching conversation with active listening and good parent talk is important.

It may not even happen every day. But when we know how to share and to listen, and use these skills at appropriate times, our family life will be enriched.

Discipline

62. *What is good discipline?* The word "discipline" is a little confusing. To some folks it is just another word for punish. When someone speaks of disciplining a child, the first question may be, "How? Do you spank him, or send him to his room, or what?" But "discipline" doesn't mean "punishment." When Jesus told his followers to go and "make disciples," he went on to explain. Making disciples involves "teaching them to obey everything I have commanded you" (Matt. 28:20). So "discipline" for the Christian has a clear goal. It is to produce a person who willingly responds to God's Word, and chooses to live by it.

When you and I "discipline" our children in Christian nurture, we teach and train them, with the long-range goal of developing individuals who will not need our control, but will have the self-control and motivation needed to choose a godly life for themselves.

Here's where discipline-as-punishment breaks down. You can force a child to do what is right. But someday your child will grow up, and move out. Then he or she will do what he or she wants. Our nurture goal must be that when he or she does move out, our child will *want* to do what is right.

Good discipline, then, is discipline which helps a child understand and choose good ways. It is a discipline which builds self-control and the motivation to choose good. Poor discipline may get a child to make right choices now. But poor discipline will use techniques to obtain obedience which hinder the development of self-control and inner motivation.

There are a number of factors involved in good discipline. We look at them in the following paragraphs.

63. *How does good discipline use punishment?* Punishment does have a role in discipline. Both Testaments view the hardships of life as a form of discipline. Also, the natural consequences of human sin are divine punishment, intended to warn us away from wrongdoing. So both Testaments quote Proverbs 3:11, 12: "My son, do not despise the Lord's discipline, and do not resent his rebuke, because the Lord disciplines those he loves, as a father the son he delights in" (see Heb. 12:5, 6).

Punishments are valid when they "fit the crime." When I ran away several times as a six-year-old, dad finally hauled me off and put my dog's collar and chain around my neck. "Ezra doesn't run away as much as you do," he announced, and left me sitting miserably outside. I got the message. It was punishment. But it fit. And I learned from it.

When a child steals, he should take the item back himself, and/or pay for it from his own allowance. This is punishment. But it fits. And a child learns from it.

When we moved into a new home in Illinois and my kids couldn't remember to shut the front door, I had to help them. Their mother had allergies, and leaving that door open in ragweed season was serious. Despite explanations and requests, the kids trooped in and out blithely, forgetting to close the door every time. So I got out the Ping-Pong paddle (used to administer infrequent spankings) and put it by the door. "I know you don't want to leave the door open and let the pollen in that hurts mom. So this will help you remember. When you leave the door open the first time, you get one whack with the paddle. If you do it again, two whacks. Three times, three whacks. It's important to mom's health to close the door. This will help you remember." In this case the threat of punishment was enough. That paddle by the door did help the kids remember, and the door-closing problem was solved. I never had to give my six-year-old a single spank.

When isn't punishment appropriate? When it's too harsh, used too often, and doesn't fit the wrongdoing. Punishment is also ineffective when it's used as a threat to force compliance. It's all too easy for us to resort to threats of punishment when there is a conflict of wills. "Judy, I told you four times to go to bed. If you don't do it *right now* I'm going to whack you good!"

What's wrong with this? First, there are much better ways to motivate a child to good bedtime habits (see paragraph 24). Second, the threat shifts the issue from going to bed on time to a conflict of wills between mom and Judy. Now the issue is very personal. Mom is mad, and she's going to win this battle and make Judy go to bed. Judy may give in and go, but now doing the right thing feels like losing, and losing isn't something anyone likes. Judy goes, but she doesn't want to and she didn't choose to— she was "made" to. Third, mom's got herself in a box. She's really made a threat, and she's got to follow through. But does mom really want to hit Judy for not going to bed when asked? Or is spanking better reserved for a much more serious infraction?

How much better it would be if a bedtime pattern had been established (part of that "teaching" process Matthew mentions) with its own built-in rewards (time with mom or dad for a bedtime ritual) and penalties ("Sorry, no reading or talk tonight. We don't have the time. Remember, I reminded you twice it was time to get ready for bed").

Punishment will be used in good discipline. At times. But we'll never be able to rely on threats or punishments to replace the training and parental planning that help a child choose what is right.

When you do have to use punishments and other negative forms of discipline, the *talkable Bible stories* on pages 143–147, 244–247, and 290–294 will lead to helpful discussions with your children.

64. *How does good discipline teach right from wrong?* There are several factors to consider in helping our children understand right and wrong.

* Setting limits is important. This involves making clear what behavior is permitted and what is not. Limits are simple for a little child. "No, don't touch the stove. It's hot." Limits are more complex for an older boy or girl. "Yes, you can bake some cookies, but you have to clean up afterward." Or, "Yes, you can go play, but not until you finish cleaning your room." Setting limits is important because it helps children understand what is expected of them, establishes areas of freedom, and builds awareness of standards by the use of multiple examples.

* Reasoning and explaining is another way we help our children understand right and wrong. Boys and girls may not always agree with us, or even understand our reasoning. But talking things over

gives parents and children a chance to practice good communication skills (see paragraphs 58 and 59), and gradually builds awareness of common principles which underlie our standards.

* Setting a good example by our own behavior also teaches our children right from wrong. Boys and girls naturally mimic parental behavior, and pick up our attitudes and values. The example we set in our daily life is one basic way we train our children (see paragraph 56).

A parent using these methods will build sensitivity to what is right and wrong, what is appropriate and what is not.

Just because sixes to eights are sensitive to right and wrong does not necessarily mean they understand why a particular action

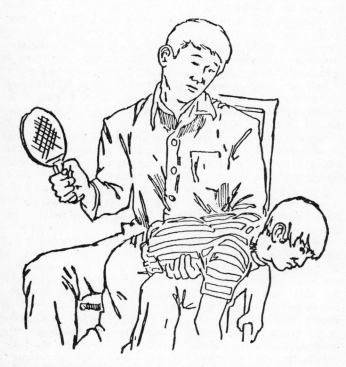

"Discipline" is not punishment. But at times punishment will play a part in good discipline.

is right and another wrong. Children's thinking is bound by particular circumstances. They are not able to take an abstract idea, like being kind or resisting temptation, and then apply that concept to the situations in which they find themselves. Instead, children build an intuitive understanding of appropriate behavior by receiving guidance in a number of situations. Our boys and girls may not be able to explain just why something isn't right, or relate it to an overarching biblical principle. But as we help them build a moral framework by setting limits, reasoning and explaining, and providing an example of good behavior, our children *will* learn right from wrong. See *talkable Bible story* on pages 171–174.

65. *How does good discipline develop conscience?* Conscience involves more than knowing right and wrong. It involves caring about doing right, and feeling badly when we do what we know to be wrong.

God has built the capacity of moral awareness into human beings. Every culture knows standards of right and wrong, and sensitivity to failure to meet standards. Children learn the specific content of their conscience—what acts they believe to be right, and what they believe to be wrong—by the process outlined in paragraph 64. Our children also develop sensitivity and strength of conscience through interaction with us.

Two dimensions of conscience are important to us. The first we can call pre-conscience. If you and I relate to our children in ways that build their sense of responsibility and self-esteem (see paragraphs 35, 48, 49), they will have a desire to please the persons who are important to them. As we express our approval and communicate praise, they will be strengthened in their desire to do good. Their motivation to please us, and to please God, will be healthy and strong.

We want to be careful about the development of what I've called post-conscience. On the one hand, a sense of sin is necessary if a child or adult is to turn to God for forgiveness, and make things right with others. But too powerful a sense of guilt may create fear, which can keep a child or adult from coming freely to God. Too powerful a sense of guilt may instill a fear of God which is inappropriate in view of the gospel message that God is eager to forgive us and to work within us to make us truly good. In general, harsh punishments inflicted for every infraction of mom's and dad's rules distorts the conscience. If a child fears punishment for every failing, he's likely to try to hide wrongdoing by lies or in other ways. Fear is likely to blind him to the great fact of forgiveness, and mask its healing power in human relationships.

Children will have a more sensitive and responsive post-conscience if our discipline is consistent, but mild. Use of natural consequences, expression of disappointment, and the gift of forgiveness all combine to develop a healthy conscience in our boys and girls.

Talkable Bible stories on pages 218–220, 140–147, and 258–261 will help you and your children think about choosing to do right, and what to do if we make wrong choices.

66. *How does good discipline use obedience?* The Bible has much to say on obedience. Children are to honor their parents and to obey them (Eph. 6:1, 2). As adults we are to give our allegiance to God and choose to obey him. There can be no doubt that obedience has a role in good discipline.

But there are several things about the nature of obedience, as explained in Scripture, that we need to understand. Obedience is in essence responsiveness, or willingness to respond. Obedience can not be coerced, but grows out of a love relationship. We can force a child or another adult to behave as we demand, if we have sufficient force. But we cannot make him *responsive* to us. Jesus put the issue succinctly: "If anyone loves me, you will obey my teaching" (John 14:23). Only the power of love can create that inner responsiveness which issues in freely chosen obedience. "He who does not love me will not obey my teaching," Jesus went on to add (John 14:24).

It is important that children obey us for the same reason that we obey God. Children lack the experience and the judgment to know whether a particular course of action will be good or bad for them. You and I lack God's wisdom and his judgment. So we make a personal commitment to live by the Word of God, even though sometimes we may not understand just why following a particular precept is best for us. Ultimately, it is because we trust God and love him—and know that he loves us—that we are willing to take his word about the things that are helpful and the things that will hurt.

Obedience, understood as responsiveness, comes as our children love us and trust our love for them. We can use force and punishments to make them do what we demand. But this is not "obedience" in that inner, dynamic biblical sense. Everything we've suggested in this chapter about communication and discipline, and everything in the sections on self-control and achievement in the last chapter, are directly related to building the kind of relationship with our children in which they obey out of love and trust, rather than because they feel they have to. When our children choose what is right to please us and God, even though they may not want to do it, and are not quite sure why we say it's the right thing in the first place, we experience the rewards that come from having truly obedient boys and girls.

Talkable Bible stories that help you explore obedience with your children are found on pages 184–187.

67. *How does good discipline help a child choose rightly?* I noted earlier that children's thinking is bound by particular circumstances. Boys and girls do not take an abstract concept and apply it to evaluate situations. They would if they could. But many studies have shown that children just have not yet developed this capacity. Instead, children experience a number of situations, and develop an intuition. They realize that a certain thing is right or wrong, even though they can't quite understand or explain why.

Helping a child make the right choices, then, calls for more than reading a Bible story with him or her, and saying, "Debbie, I want you to be honest." Debbie will want to be honest. But without our help, she won't recognize as dishonest peeking at a friend's paper at school, or telling you her school work is done when it's not, or "borrowing" a neighbor's toy.

It certainly isn't fair to punish a child for an action he or she hasn't linked with a trait we've talked about. Our task in helping children make right choices is to help them learn to recognize a situation in which they will have to make a moral choice, and think ahead about what they will do. Earlier we looked at using a "What If . . .?" game to think ahead about how a child might act if something he or she fears happens. We also talked about giving social training by using cut-out figures or role playing (see paragraph 31). We can use such methods to help children recognize situations in which particular actions are right or wrong. Most of the *talkable Bible stories* have some suggestions for doing just this kind of thing to help apply truths the story teaches. You can sharpen your own ability to help your child make right choices as you explore these stories with him or her.

In general, however, if you explain and talk about those situations which occur over and over again in your child's home and school experiences, your child will build a good understanding of the choices he or she needs to make. If good communication marks our relationship with our children, just talking about the things that happen will provide the guidance they need. See *talkable Bible stories* on pages 171–174 and 237–240.

68. *How does good discipline utilize rewards?* For years educators have debated the value of extrinsic and intrinsic rewards. Will children do better if they get a gold star on a paper, and a lollipop for being on time all week? Or will children do better if adults simply express approval and praise for achievements, and the boy or girl begins to feel good about his or her own accomplishments? The general consensus is that, in the long haul, intrinsic rewards are better. Children don't have to be bribed to do well, or promised material rewards. If doing well is rewarding in terms of the approval of significant adults and in terms of that good feeling which comes with doing well, motivation will grow and extend into adulthood.

In general also, focusing on right behavior, and expressing approval for it, is far more helpful than focusing on wrong behavior and punishing for failures. We don't even need to reward with a smile or praise every time. Now and then will do . . . if the tenor of our relationship is positive and approving.

This is perhaps the most important question. Is the general tone of our relationship approving or disapproving? Are we most likely to notice the things a child does right, or the things a child does wrong? When you and I are predominantly approving, and notice and praise what is done right rather than concentrate on failures, our children will be much more likely to choose what pleases us, and to choose it gladly.

69. *How does good discipline utilize forgiveness?* Forgiveness is one of the most dynamic of all biblical concepts. When speaking of God's forgiveness, the Old and New Testament words chosen both mean to "send away." Jesus' self-sacrifice on Calvary laid the basis on which our sins could be cleansed, and we could be perfected by God. The Bible even teaches that the sin of believers is the one thing that God literally forgets. "Their sins and lawless acts," the writer to the Hebrews quotes from the Old Testament, "I will remember no more" (Heb. 10:17).

When God deals with us now, it's on the basis of a fresh and new relationship. Even when we continue to fail, the Bible tells us we need only confess our sins, and God will forgive us our sins and keep on cleansing us from unrighteousness (1 John 1:9).

Fresh offenses are met unstintingly with fresh forgiveness, and the past is never held against us. The blessing of numberless fresh starts is extended freely to the people of God.

The concept of "confession" also has a distinctive biblical meaning. It does not mean "feel sorry," or even "say you're sorry." It means to "acknowledge": to agree with God in his evaluation of our wrong acts. It is true that biblically, repentance—as turning away from sin—is intimately linked with confession and forgiveness. But nowhere is it suggested that we are allowed only one failure, or two, or at the most three. Instead, God will continue to forgive us when we acknowledge our sin, and continue to nurture us toward the maturity it takes not to fail.

When the Bible speaks of forgiveness as something which God's

A sensitive conscience can help our children seek forgiveness.

people are to extend to each other, there is a delicate change in word choice. In the original language the word is no longer "send away," for only God can forgive sin in that decisive, cleansing sense. Instead the word is "be gracious." And this you and I can do. Like God, we can forget the faults that are acknowledged, refuse to hold past failures against our children or others, and give each person the wonderful gift of fresh starts.

Underlying the Bible's teaching on forgiveness is an amazing and wonderful truth. God has chosen not to relate to you and me on the basis of what we do or do not do. He does not love us more when we are good. He does not love us less when we turn from him, though he will let us experience the natural consequences of disobedience. God's love is practical. He knows that a person who experiences forgiveness will be more responsive to him, and more open to change, than a person who lives under the terror of constant threat. Love is more effective than fear in helping our children choose the way we help mark out for them.

As parents, you and I have an example in the way God treats us to show us how to treat our children. When a child fails, and acknowledges his fault, we forgive him freely and encourage him to try again next time. When he fails again, and again confesses, we forgive him freely and encourage him to succeed. Boys and girls will not take advantage. If combined with the other elements of good discipline, repeated forgiveness will free our children from a sense of failure, and encourage them to try again until they succeed.

Talkable Bible stories linked with forgiveness are found on pages 218–220, 234–237, and 244–247.

Brothers and Sisters

70. *What kinds of sibling relationships can we expect?* One father's complaint reflects the feelings of many moms and dads: "Our two boys fought so much it used to drive my wife and me out of the house. They fought over who was interrupting while they did homework. They fought over who got more privileges and who was doing more chores. They fought about who started fights. But we finally found the solution. The older went off to college."

I can't guarantee the accuracy of that quote. But I can guarantee that what's called "sibling rivalry" is a reality. Boys and girls in the same family will bicker and argue. They'll tease and tattle, get upset and angry, shout and sulk. There will be jealousy and resentment, hurt feelings and tears. Whenever people live close to one another, there are frictions. When the persons are children six to eleven, still immature, with feelings and emotions they don't understand and can't control, there's bound to be much friction. In fact, a family that is always peaceful would be unnatural—and probably unhealthy!

At the same time, the healthy family isn't at constant war. Brothers and sisters will show love, play together, help and share as well as fight. It's likely the younger will at times exhibit a bit of hero worship for the older—at least when talking with outsiders.

A certain amount of sibling rivalry is all right. But if rivalry and antagonisms dominate brother/sister relationships, the situation isn't healthy, and isn't necessary.

How do we tell if sibling rivalry has gone too far? The situation is unhealthy if siblings are always unwilling to help each other, always unwilling to share, won't play together unless forced to, make aggressive physical attacks on each other, are constantly tattling, and will destroy each other's property. Generally if we've established good communications with our children (paragraphs 58, 59) and are working to help each develop a sense of personal achievement (paragraphs 48–51) we won't see the excesses. Even if things should get out of hand, there are steps we can take to reduce friction to acceptable levels.

So if you've envisioned that ideal of an ever-calm home, adjust it. Your children can be each other's playmates (particularly if they are close in age). They can take the roles of teacher and learner, or protector and dependent if they are older. They need not be adversaries and rivals. But there will be frictions. And those frictions in your home provide opportunities for your children to learn and to grow!

71. *How do we help a child adjust to a new baby?* The first weeks do a lot to set the tone of sibling relationships. In general, preschoolers needed the most help with the birth of a new family member. But the same principles apply for preschoolers and young children.

We need to recognize that the coming of a new family member means readjustment for adults and children. The pattern of relationships in the family will change. There will be new demands on your time and attention. This readjustment is likely to be difficult for children, and may feel like rejection to them. If six-year-old Carrie comes home from school expecting mom to have a cookie and juice ready and to sit down with her, but mom is busy with the new baby, Carrie may feel resentment. She may feel less secure, less certain than before of mom's love.

What, specifically, can we do to help our older child, and get the sibling relationship off to a good start? Here are some suggestions:

* Prepare your child before the baby is born. Explain how the unborn child is growing. Look over your older child's baby book with him or her. Let your child help pick out clothes or other things you're buying for the new baby. Get small gifts for him or her too. Don't send your child to a relative's during the first days the baby is at home.

* Involve your child in care of the baby. But don't overdo responsibilities for nine- to eleven-year-olds. Children need time to spend with age-mates, for the sake of their own development.

* Find special time to be alone with your older child while the baby sleeps. Some younger boys and girls may regress when the new baby comes. They'll want to be held, or be read to as

Children can be helped to feel the new baby is *theirs*, not just yours.

they were when younger. Don't be concerned about temporary regression, and don't ridicule the child for acting like a baby. Instead, give the warmth and support he or she may temporarily need. It's especially important if your child has enjoyed some special private time with you—as in a bedtime ritual or when coming home from school—to continue it whenever possible.

Frictions will develop as both children grow. But you can reduce sibling antagonism by helping your older child or children to adjust at the time of birth.

72. *How should we react to bickering and arguing?* "You did so!" "I did not." "Daddy, he touched my crayons!" "I did not touch your stupid old crayons."

It doesn't take too many repetitions of arguments like these to set a parent's teeth on edge. Especially when the tone of voice is so grating. That scornful, contemptuous tone is aimed like a sword at the younger. And the younger whines! Sometimes it seems like the bickering goes on all the time. What's a parent to do? There are several principles that can guide us.

* While quarreling is a source of irritation for us as parents, it's not necessarily bad for the children. Children who are relatively close in age will tend to compete with each other, and feel resentment. At the same time, they may be best friends. As we discussed in paragraph 13, children need experience in relating to each other to work on their social skills. Bickering in the family may not sound like healthy learning, but it often is. Mom and dad don't need to intrude with appeals to be kind or love one another. Bickering isn't necessarily evidence of a lack of affection.

* Disputes should be permitted within limits. But the acceptable range should be clearly defined. For instance, no hitting or physical abuse. While we don't need to step in all the time, protection of life and limb is recommended!

Consequences of fighting should be clearly defined and applied to both children equally, no matter who was the "aggressor." Isolation in one's room is often helpful, and it permits the child's emotions to cool as well as interrupts play.

It is also helpful to provide "safe territory" for each child, where the individual can go to be alone and unbothered when he or she wants. This can be a child's own room or, in a more crowded situation even a special chair in the living room. The idea here is that a boy or girl who has had enough arguing can retreat there, and the other can't follow verbally or physically. (Of course, the safe territory must work both ways. A child in the safety zone can't stick out his tongue at the other!)

* Much of children's bickering may be aimed at getting mom and dad involved—on their side. We need to be very careful that our children don't manipulate us into unnecessary intervention.

Go back for a moment to that first bit of dialogue. The younger's cry, "Daddy, he touched my crayons!" is typical both of the insignificance of most sibling arguments, and of the child's attempt to get a parent to take sides. Some parents will jump in with a command. "Ken, don't touch Sue's crayons." But in the continuing rivalry between the children, Sue has just scored a point! Now Ken is going to feel additional resentment and need to figure out a way to score a point for his side.

How much better if dad simply ignores the call to take sides, or comments, "You kids can work out a fair way to play," and continues his reading. Or, if the bickering becomes intense, comments, "You know, if either of you aren't enjoying your quarrel you can always go to your safety zone."

Knowing about sibling rivalry doesn't always help us deal with it. But when we can, benign neglect is usually the best way for us to handle bickering.

Several of the *talkable Bible stories* in this *Handbook* focus on sibling relationships, and can help your boys and girls explore their own relationships (see pages 153–155, also 167–171, 278–282, 329–337).

73. *What can we do about jealousy between brothers and sisters?* Some view even normal sibling rivalry as a competition for attention and recognition by parents. As such, there is going to be some jealousy, rooted in the desire to be the most loved.

Jealousy can be extremely destructive in the family, and harm growth toward godly maturity. We can't make jealousy go away by saying it's wrong, or labeling it as sin. But there is much that parents can do to minimize the flashing of that destructive monster's green eyes. Ways that we as parents can help children and reduce the threat of possible jealousy are:

* We can avoid making comparisons between our children. "I wish you'd come when I call like your sister does" isn't going to make Junior come more readily. And it is going to make him resent the sister you're praising.

Each of our children has his or her own talents, attributes, and accomplishments. To minimize rivalry, we give each individual praise and encouragement fitted to his or her own individuality. A child who does something well should be praised for that accomplishment, not for doing it better or quicker than a sibling. No child should be compared unfavorably to his brother or sister.

* Don't treat each child equally. Treat each fairly. Children who are older will need less sleep. They may be responsible enough to go out for longer periods of time, or to go further away, than the younger. Older children may be ready for more complicated toys. You wouldn't give a chemistry set to a six-year-old. But it might be just the right gift for your eleven-year-old. Children with different amounts of homework will have different amounts of time available for play. Older boys and girls may have more chores, or more responsible chores.

These differences are bound to generate feelings of jealousy, and claims of unequal treatment. It will be hard for younger children to understand, but repeated explanation, with repeated reassurances of your love for each individual, will keep feelings within bounds—particularly if you take the relationship-building steps outlined next.

* Perhaps the basic resource you and I have to head off jealousy is love for and sensitivity to our children. All we need to do is to express that love in ways our boys and girls can feel.

For instance, one of the most important things a parent can do is to spend private time with children. One couple I know tries to arrange a day every month or so when one of their children can be an "only child" and go out with mom or dad. Another dad has breakfast out at a restaurant every Saturday with a different one of his five children. When my own kids were young, staggering bedtimes gave each of our three a half hour or so alone with one or both parents—and gave the older children the extra time up that is the rightful privilege of age.

Finding ways to reassure each person that he or she is loved can reduce the pressures on children. This will not eliminate the existence of jealousies. But it can keep jealousy from becoming a dominant theme in family relationships.

Several *talkable Bible stories* can help your boys and girls explore jealousy as it was experienced by biblical people, and help them discover God's better way to live together in love (see pages 167–171, also 208–211, 278–282).

74. *How about shared rooms and toys?* When it's possible, it's best for children to have their own rooms, at least after age eight or so. Of course, it's not always possible. The next best thing we can do is to provide some safety zone area where a child can have privacy when he or she wants it (see paragraph 72).

Sometimes parents make a mistake by emphasizing sharing. There are many things that boys and girls will share: games, toys, and backyard play equipment. But children also need to have things which are their own. And children need to learn to respect the special property of others.

Generally family games, books, and toys which are suitable for use by all family members, might be held in common. But an older child's chemistry set, or a favorite teddy bear taken to bed by a six- or seven-year-old, should be respected by all, as private property. See *talkable Bible stories* on pages 285–288 and 335–337.

75. *What does it mean to be "family"?* We all have an ideal image of the happy home. We can envision shared laughter, hugs at bedtime, a filled cookie jar, children playing noisily in the back yard, their joyous shouts punctuated by laughter. All too often we have to confess that our family falls short of that ideal. In fact, the more fervently we wish for the perfect home, the more frustrated we might become by bickering and teasing, by whines and complaints and angry words hurled by children who seem to hate rather than love each other.

There are several things that help us put family in perspective. Family is the place God designed for growing to take place—not for maturity to be exhibited! All those years we have with our children, from birth on through adolescence, are years when they are most imperfect. We don't see the final product till our children near their thirties! It's hard sometimes to realize that the bickering eight-year-old will be a loving father at twenty-eight. But it's true. The way we live with our children's imperfections, the ways we encourage their personal and spiritual growth, will have a great impact on who they become.

What it takes from us to nurture healthy growth is a great fund of love and a great reservoir of patience. As we apply the nurture principles outlined in this *Handbook* and draw on the resources provided in God's Word, we can be confident that our children *will* grow, and will become all that God intends them to be. See *talkable Bible story* on pages 329–331.

Adoption and Foster Parenting

76. *Why do some parents adopt or become foster parents?* Adoption is an option chosen by some couples because they can't have children of their own. Others, with a child or two, decide to adopt one of the unwanted older boys and girls who might become available. Other couples take children into their home and serve as foster parents. While government agencies pay foster parents, studies show that the motivation of many foster parents is religious, and/or concern for the well-being of the children, who otherwise would have no family life.

Today some 200,000 children are in foster homes, 80 percent of whom have experienced rejection by at least one parent. While there is, understandably, additional stress caused by the foster child's background, adults with adoptive or foster children express general satisfaction by the end of the first year with the child's improvement and with their own role.

There are no special or "different" nurturing guidelines for parents with adoptive or foster children. The same supportive love, building of responsibility, with good communication and discipline, is needed by all boys and girls.

There have been studies showing the kind of couple who will

Adults with adoptive or foster children express general satisfaction with the child's improvement and with their own role by the end of the first year together.

make good foster and adoptive parents. The desirable qualities include: familiarity with children (their own, or growing up in a large family), good parents of their own, skills in dealing with children, an ability to relate to "difficult" children, a sensitive adoptive father who sees things from the child's point of view, and closeness of the couple.

77. *What special concerns do parents have about adoption?* Adoptions dropped off in the United States during the 1970s. One reason was the increased cost of seeing children through high school and college. Another was the rising number of abortions, which in the past decade has taken the lives of millions of unborn children. Another factor is fear of adopting a two- or four- or seven-year-old child. Some are still convinced that if the first, critical years go wrong, the child will be warped for life. Thus, many parents are simply afraid to take older boys and girls. Add this to the fact that there are many more black and Hispanic children than Caucasians available, and that few want to adopt across racial lines, and the drop in the number of adoptions isn't surprising. Add one last factor, that many are unsure how much heredity may influence the kind of person a child becomes, and we can understand why there are fears, even when two people want children to care for.

Actually, the years have proven that older children taken into stable, loving homes generally become well-adjusted adults. They do well in school. And they seem particularly responsive to their adoptive parents.

The decision to adopt shouldn't be taken lightly. But as you love and nurture, you can do so with the confidence that God will use your love to bring out every potential of your adoptive children.

78. *Should children be told they are adopted?* An older child will already know. A younger child is likely to find out sometime. The discovery of a hidden adoption can have far worse consequences than growing up hearing the word "adopted" used casually by mom and dad, and realizing that it does not mean the child is any less loved.

It's not a bad idea to have an adoption day, like a birthday, with a party and presents, from the very beginning. "When we adopted you . . ." and "Before you were adopted . . ." are phrases that can be commonly used in your home.

But who are an adopted child's "real" parents? Not the biological pair, but the couple who invests years of daily love and care. The real parents, the parents to whom the adopted child belongs, are those who have developed the warm bonds forged by shared lives.

It's comforting for an adopted child to realize that mom and dad are also adopted. You see, God chooses individuals who respond to Jesus to be members of his own family. We are adopted, the Bible says, and become God's sons and daughters (cf. Eph. 1:5). It's a wonderful thing to know that the parents, too, share the privilege of being chosen to be loved.

Responsibility

79. *How can parents encourage a sense of responsibility in children?* In life each of us is responsible for many things. We're responsible for our own choices. We're responsible to other people. We're responsible to care for our possessions. But the sense of responsibility doesn't just appear at a certain age. It's developed gradually. While we do not want to give too much responsibility to children at an early age, a child denied the opportunity to exercise responsibility will fail to develop that trait. So we need to provide our boys and girls with responsibilities appropriate to their ages—responsibilities that fit their ability level. With those responsibilities we need to provide appropriate guidance.

There are many traits linked with responsibility. There is sensitivity to others. There are good work habits. There is willingness to do disagreeable tasks. There is the willingness to stick to a task until it is completed. There is making the difficult choice when responsibilities conflict with fun or pleasure. These traits develop gradually as our boys and girls are nurtured. The little things we do with our children—teaching them to bring a toy inside to protect it from the rain, to come home before going next door to play so mom will know where they are, to bring back the change when they go to the corner store for dad—all are part of the pattern of a family life style which builds responsibility.

In the next sections we'll look at many opportunities you and I have to gradually build a sense of responsibility. We'll explore chores and allowances and pets and hobbies and lessons and even time management for children. Our goal is to suggest simple ways that we can help our boys and girls grow toward responsible adulthood. *Talkable Bible stories* on pages 304–307 will help you explore aspects of responsibility with older boys and girls.

80. *What about chores for children?* Slavery is out. But boys and girls need to be taught to pull their weight in family living. Jobs have to be done around the house. Children should have

their share. While younger boys and girls often enjoy helping clean or polish, by school age the fun is usually gone, and the things boys and girls do to help is "work." A number of guidelines help us with the complaints that are likely to come from our children now and then.

* Check our own attitude. If one spouse has to grump at another about undone tasks, we can expect a negative attitude in our children. Dad never gets up the screens, dust bunnies breed under the beds, and the living, family room and kitchen are always piled high with debris? Then we can be pretty sure our kids won't do much better. A major factor in building attitudes and traits in children is modeling. The example we set is likely to spill over into their attitudes and behavior.

* There's not as much work to do around the home today as there was when most families lived on the farm. But there's still plenty of work to go around. It's a good idea to sit down and list all the chores that need to be routinely done. List seasonal jobs as well. Include the traditional "do the dishes" and "take out the garbage" as well as cleaning and polishing, helping prepare meals, yard work, and so on.

Once the list is made, it's possible to post a "duty roster" that rotates weekly. Or set up a "job bank," with each job written on a card, to be drawn by adults and children. You can organize your tasks by age, or preferences. You can set up a time schedule in which each family member contributes two or three hours of work on Saturday—after which the family does something special together.

Chores needn't be a burden, grudgingly done. But it will take a little planning and cooperation, and some self-discipline on your own part.

* Some parents pay children for the chores they do. There is nothing necessarily wrong with this approach. But most folks seem to feel that it's better to pay for special extra work, and keep the family chores on a different basis. Chores are a child's contribution to family well-being, and thus are a work of love.

Several things can nurture the feeling of contribution. One is expressions of appreciation by parents. Another is a very simple thing: working together. There is a vastly different impact in "Go rake the lawn" and "Jim, it's our turn to rake the lawn. Will you get the rakes? And I'll get the plastic lawn bags." Working *with* our children can lighten tasks, communicate our own positive attitude toward work, and give us a chance to chat casually about many things.

* Some families make a division between "women's work" and

"men's work." The women get inside duty, and the men outside duty. Or the women do cleaning, and the men do things that take more muscle. It's probably better if we avoid sex-stereotyping family chores. Most young people these days stay single for more years than earlier generations. Many today choose a single life style. Men as well as women need to know how to do the household chores and the cooking that once were considered the province of mom alone. Because more women than ever are working outside the home, the caring husband will accept more responsibility to help in the home than was usual in the past.

81. *What about children's allowances?* One opportunity we have to teach responsibility and values comes when children are given money of their own. But many parents have questions about allowances. How much should children have? Is it really theirs, or should

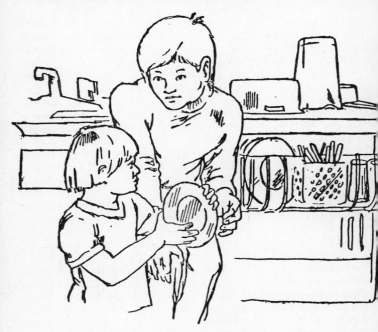

Household chores become meaningful when we help each child feel he or she is contributing to family well-being.

ground rules be laid down? Should allowances be earned, or simply given?

When our son Paul was a young eight, he got a small amount as an allowance. He rushed out the moment he got it and spent it foolishly. One day he and I talked about his allowance on the way to school. I talked about different things he might do with his money. There was giving, at Sunday school. There were larger things he might want to buy. There were birthdays coming for his younger brother and sister. At the end of our drive Paul just sat there in the car, pouting. Then he named a particular amount and asked grumpily if that was enough for giving to the Lord.

I explained to Paul that I wasn't trying to tell him what to do with his money, or how much he ought to use for any purposes. When he got the money from me, it was his own money. He could use it any way he chose. I only hoped he would think about the best ways to use his money.

That evening Paul wanted to talk. He'd been figuring. If he was going to set money aside for presents, and money for church, and money to save, well, he needed a larger allowance! Paul was right. And he got it. He immediately prepared several little boxes in which to put the differing amounts he'd set aside for different purposes.

There is nothing wrong in talking with a child about the use of his money. But to have any value in developing personal responsibility, that money we give him must be the child's, and he must be free to spend it, even unwisely.

* Children from a very young age need the opportunity to handle money. By school age—or about seven—money can be provided on a weekly basis. How much a child receives will depend on what he's expected to use his money for. Younger children might just be given pocket money. As children get older, funds and responsibility can be increased. The allowance you determine together can include money for minor school expenses and bus fares. Older children may get an allowance that involves purchase of some of their clothing.

Expense money and responsibilities will be increased gradually, of course. We shouldn't expect too much of our sixes and sevens, nor should we increase responsibilities until children show ability to use what they already have with some self-control. When we see a young child begin to save part of his weekly funds for a more costly toy, rather than rush out to spend it all on candy and comics, we have evidence he or she may be ready for added financial responsibility.

What is particularly important is that at each stage of growth in financial responsibility, children and parents work out just how much a child will receive, and what that money is expected to cover. It's also important that the agreed-on allowance be provided when due.

* It bothers some parents when children use their first allowances foolishly. At that point they may step in, tell the child how to spend the money—and defeat the purpose of giving allowances in the first place.

There are, of course, natural consequences of foolishness. The amounts aren't increased. And when an appeal for more comes, it's not out of line to explain why a child is not considered ready yet.

* Learning to save and to budget is an important part of a growing child's experience with money. There are a number of ways this can be encouraged. Many suggest a child open a savings account when he or she begins to earn money. While the allowance probably shouldn't be earned (and certainly should not be taken away as a punishment), there are tasks a boy or girl can do to earn extra. Washing and polishing the car, or giving the garage a special cleaning, aren't really normal family chores (see paragraph 79), and might merit pay.

There are other things parents can do to encourage saving too. It is difficult for boys and girls to work toward goals that are distant in time. Six months might not seem long to an adult. But it can seem like forever for a child. The solution is to set a series of goals that will ultimately mean achievement of the longer range goal. For instance, a younger child who wants to buy a $15 baseball glove might be promised that the folks will contribute half if he can save half. So when allowance time comes and he puts a dollar in a savings jar, you might contribute your dollar immediately. If he puts away 75¢, then you contribute 75¢ immediately. Of course, the money saved can't be dipped into for other purposes—unless your child gives you back your matching contribution at the same time.

* Much of the value children will attribute to money, and their patterns of use, will be set by us. So we want to share our priorities and spending patterns with children as they grow. One way we tried to help our children with giving involved not only open conversation about finances, but a special "missions jar." Loose change was dropped in the largest glass jar we could find. As Christmas approached we explored several missions to which the money might be given. The kids shared in the process of choosing the mission, and in counting and rolling coins Christmas week. Each year several hundred dollars collected this way was given as our family's special "birthday gift" to Jesus.

Long ago Jesus said, "Where your treasure is, there will your heart be also." Money isn't our treasure. But how our money is used demonstrates our personal priorities, and what we do view as treasure. See *talkable Bible stories* on pages 285–288 and 302–304.

82. *What about family pets?* Pets are part of the family in many homes. They're loved and played with, taken on trips, and they can help meet children's needs to give and receive affection. Pets can also give children an opportunity to develop a sense of responsibility to other living creatures. But if "they'll learn responsibility" is our motive for getting a pet, and if the children are too young, mom and dad are likely to be disappointed! We end up feeding and caring for the pet.

If children are older, say eight or so, and they want a pet of their own, it's reasonable to explore ahead of time with them responsibilities they must accept. A child of eight can even get a book on how to train dogs, and learn much about responsibility by working to housebreak the pet, to feed and clean him, and so on.

83. *What about hobbies and special lessons?* During childhood years boys and girls are curious and exploring. They develop many interests, most of which will be pursued for a few weeks or months and then exchanged for others. Our youngest became intensely involved in rock hounding, fossil collecting, astronomy, and a dozen other interests. He purchased (with some help) an expensive telescope, subscribed to an astronomy magazine, worked out sky charts, and spent many a night one summer watching the moons of Jupiter, and using charts to locate particular stars. The passion passed, to be supplanted by fencing and survival books.

It's difficult for moms and dads to know when an interest is simply part of a growing child's exploration of his world, and when it will grow into a lifetime interest. It's hard to know when an initial interest in music should be encouraged with lessons, and if it is, how long mom and dad should insist on continuing lessons after the interest wanes.

We have similar problems with lessons for sports, like tennis, and skills such as skating or ballet. Where does the need to build responsibility by sticking to a commitment and seeing difficult times through begin and end? When does the need to provide children with many different enriching experiences suggest release from obligation is in order?

It's hard to come up with specific guidelines for every child and family. My nephew started violin lessons at eight. Now in high school, after years of disciplined daily practice, he wins scholarships. But when my folks gave me piano lessons for one birthday, for the next birthday they wisely let me stop. We need to recognize individual differences and be responsive to them.

In general though we can suggest:

* Don't begin lessons or expect serious follow-through on interests of six- and seven-year-olds.

* When an older child asks for lessons or becomes involved in a hobby that incurs significant expense, talk together about the nature of the commitment he or she is making. How much practice will it take? What might have to be given up to meet practice requirements? Only when the personal costs are completely understood by the child should we go ahead.

* It's best when a child is willing to make a commitment that we set a time limit. "We'll try the lessons for six months. Then we can talk about it again." If the ground rules have been understood and commitments to practice, and so on, made, then our boy or girl ought to be held accountable even if the reality of commitment brings a change of heart in a couple of months.

Helping a child evaluate what is called for in terms of his or her commitment to a hobby or to lessons, setting a reasonable length of time the commitment should run, and then helping our son or daughter hold to his promise for that time, is one way to develop responsibility.

84. *What about children's clothing?* Boys and girls of school age are often sensitive to what others are wearing, and motivated to be like their friends. As much as possible, we need to let our children participate in choosing their own clothing.

Often it's good, as children show a sense of responsibility, to provide a clothing allowance. We can expect our boys and girls to make some mistakes. But mistakes can be an opportunity to learn. The more children's clothing is their own, by purchase and by preference, the more we can expect them to take care of it as well.

Care for clothing and other possessions is important if boys and girls are to build a sense of personal responsibility. A child who loses possessions, or leaves toys outside to be spoiled by the weather, shouldn't have those things replaced automatically by mom and dad. The natural consequences of such irresponsibility is to do without. Or to spend one's own earned or allowance money to buy a replacement.

85. *What about children's time management?* Life is complicated for adults. And it's becoming more complicated for children. Boys and girls have obligations to school work and home tasks. They need time to spend with their friends. Often children have extra lessons, or sports. Usually church clubs or choirs add more items to children's agendas. But children also need time just for growing: time to read, to play, to talk with mom and dad about their world. Children need time to play with pets and to enjoy their own hobbies: time simply to be a child, with no schedule to meet. Children need time to dig worms and go fishing, to collect bottles to return for deposit, and to set up a lemonade stand in their front yard. They need to sleep out in the back yard in a family tent, draw pictures, and lie on the floor to watch TV. Childhood is for growing, and growing requires time to relax as well as to work.

We want to remember this about childhood. If we become too concerned about developing responsibility, we may push our children too rapidly. In our society there are already many pressures on children and youth. We push them too quickly into activities and relationships that are really appropriate only when they are older. So in helping our children with their schedule, we need to help them set aside plenty of time just to be boys and girls, growing in a relaxed and natural way.

We'll find that children aged ten through eleven need just as much help as six- and seven-year-olds in working on schedules. At every age we need to help them develop flexible patterns for their waking hours, and good sleep habits (see paragraph 24). Much of our help will be in terms of constantly reviewing priorities. What do you *have* to do? When will you do those things? How much time do you have left? What are some of the things you like to do that fit in that leftover time? What will you need to cut out, just because there isn't enough time for everything? If we help our children follow this process whenever life presses in—and make sure that the "want to" activities fit in *after* the "have to" activities are completed—we'll help our children become responsible in a very significant way. And we'll help protect that very precious privilege of being a child.

Times of Stress

86. *How do we deal with times of exceptional stress?* All of us live with tensions, as well as with joys. Stress is part of a child's life too. A friend refuses to play, or won't speak at school. Siblings fight. One runs to his room in tears, convinced that he's treated

unfairly, and that mom always sides with his older sister. A promise dad made has to be broken, and no explanation can console. Teacher gave a low grade on a writing assignment. A chore that's been put off has to be done *now,* before going out to practice with the team. These and hundreds of other incidents create stress for boys and girls. Learning to cope with the problems and the disappointments of life is simply part of growing up. No matter how down a child may feel we know that, with our love and support, his feelings will change and the next day everything will be all right again.

But there are some times when the next day doesn't bring change. There are some kinds of stress that deeply affect the network of relationships which provide a child with his or her basic security. There is moving. The thought of leaving the house that has been home, and all one's friends, can be terrifying to a boy or girl between the ages of six to eleven. There is the tragedy of death in the family. When a parent is taken, great readjustments are required. Today many homes are shattered by divorce. And it's not only the divorce which brings stress. There is the time of deepening crisis, while mom and dad experience their relationship breaking down. There are special stresses later, too, as adjustments are made to become a single-parent family. If remarriage comes, stepfamilies have new stress developing their own pattern of relationships. Finally, in some families, children suffer a physical injury or handicap, and again adjustments must be made by all.

In this section we want to think together about special stress which affects the whole family system. We want to explore ways that adults can help children cope with these times, as well as cope with the normal stress dealt with in other sections of this *Handbook.*

Resources in Scripture are particularly significant for times of special stress—significant to adults as well as to children. *Talkable Bible stories* are linked with each of these stress situations.

87. *How do we help children deal with moving?* For younger children, a major move may generate a number of fears. His or her room is as familiar as a friend. The thought of leaving it can create anxiety. This is particularly likely if moving creates stress for mom and dad, and they feel anxiety as they rush to get the old house sold. Older boys and girls are likely to feel a deep sense of loss at the thought of leaving best friends and schoolmates. There will be new friends to make in the new city, of course.

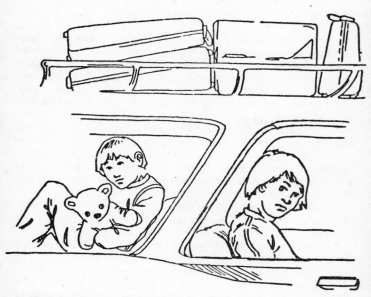

Moving, usually so difficult for children, can become a family adventure.

Yet fear and uncertainty about social relationships and new schools will lurk in the hearts of the most well-adjusted children.

No research shows that moving, in and of itself, creates disturbances in children. Supported by a stable family unit, individual boys and girls can work through the sadness of leaving one home, and the challenge of establishing a new one. But children do need help from mom and dad. What are some of the things we might do that can help?

* Let your children know about the move from the beginning. The more a boy or girl participates in the process, the easier a move will be for him or her. Be sensitive to feelings during preparation, and be ready to talk about your own feelings as well as encourage children's expression of their emotions.

* Gather as much information as possible about the new area to which you're moving. This might include pictures and a diagram of the new house, snapshots of neighborhood children, schools, playgrounds, and other neighborhood features of interest to boys and girls. A map of the community, and information about special

things to do there (zoos, lakes, and so on) will help too. Bring back several newspapers from the area, and make a game out of a paper search. Let each family member work through the papers and make a list of discoveries about the community. Try to surprise each other with the things you find out. Getting into the spirit of exploration can add the positive flavor of adventure which will balance the natural feelings of loss of the familiar.

* Let your boys and girls help with packing and preparation. They will want to be sure that all their precious things will be brought along. They can also work with the family's possessions. Taking on responsibility for listing all household items in various rooms, to use as a preparation check list, can help a child feel grown up and involved in the move.

* Younger boys and girls may need to take some favorite belongings along in the car. The younger children might also play at moving with dolls, some small boxes, and a wagon.

* Before the move, you might also help your children plan their new room or rooms. When possible let children select their room from a layout of the new home. We gave each of our children a room allowance of over a hundred dollars when we moved to Arizona. The children were excited to plan what furniture or decorations they'd buy to fix up the new room. The children also picked out room colors, and we painted together before moving them into their new rooms.

* When you come close to the departure date, some families plan a series of farewell events. There may be a special day for a trip with a best friend, and an exchange of gifts. There should be an exchange of addresses, and promises to write. Sometimes plans can be made for children to make exchange visits on vacations.

* When you arrive in the new city, it's good to plan family half-day or day trips to get to know the locality. And to explore all the things you've read about in preparation. Inviting neighborhood children in for a cookie can help get new friendships off to a good start.

* It's particularly important as you plan a move together to encourage exploration of children's feelings and concerns. The *talkable Bible stories* on pages 147–150, and 190–193 can stimulate this sharing and help build confidence that God will be with you, to help make moving an adventure that will enrich your lives.

88. *How do we help children deal with death in the family?* Death is difficult for children to understand. Partly because children do

not understand, and partly because the loss of a family member threatens the child's security, death of a loved one or even a friend can bring unusual stress.

Children between six and eight are usually concerned about dying as a process. They do not know what is happening, and are likely to ask such questions as: "What makes people die?" "How do you know you're dead?" "Can they come back to life?" For young children neither the universality of death, or its irrevocability, is understood. But some studies of children this age from homes of believers showed that most of the children saw death as the beginning of a life in heaven, full of love and happiness and peace.

Children between the ages of nine and twelve do understand the finality of death, and the fact that death comes to all living beings. This does not make the death of a loved one easier. But it does mean that a boy or girl can deal with death more realistically.

Parents who have death touch their family—whether the death of a friend, a grandparent, or a member of the nuclear family itself—often have many questions. Should children go to the funeral? Should we talk about death with children? Should we mention the person who had died afterward? What fears may children have, and how can we deal with them? There are guidelines to help us with questions like these.

* When death comes, grieving over our loss is natural and healthy. Even Christians, who know that death is not the end, grieve—but not as others who are without hope (1 Thess. 4:13).

The reality of death and the reality of hope both require that we share honestly with our children. We need to express our own sense of loss, and our confidence. When my mother died, I brought our nine-year-old Paul with me to Michigan. He sat, strained and silent, in the home where he'd spent many happy vacations. He sat just as silent as I gave my mother's funeral sermon. Later that night he finally cried. Then I hugged him, and I cried too, and told him I had brought him with me just so we could cry together. We would miss grandma very much. But I also told him of the great sense of joy I felt as I had spoken that afternoon, and looked over at the coffin, to realize that mom wasn't there. She was with the Lord she had loved, far more alive now than ever before.

* When death comes, speak about it openly without using confusing euphemisms. Grandma didn't "go away" (a young child will wonder where, and ask when she's coming back). Grandma didn't "go to sleep." Although this term is used in Scripture, its symbolism is for adults. A young child is likely to fear sleeping, concerned that like grandma he may not wake up again. Grandma did die. Her body was buried. But her personality—all those things we loved about her—are now in heaven with Jesus. In God's good time we'll all be together again. Then we will live forever, and death will have no more power over us.

* Children who have experienced the loss of a loved one are likely to feel anxiety. When will they die? Will mom or dad die? What will happen to them if mom dies? Questions like these are not selfish, as a grieving adult might at first feel. They are very important questions, which reflect the fact that a boy's or girl's sense of security has been shaken. The child needs information and reassurance.

It is fair to point out that today most people are quite old when they die. Sometimes a child dies in an accident or from a sickness, but most grow up to have families of their own and see them grow up. Most moms and dads will grow old, and be with the children as they go through grade school and high school and college, and as they begin homes of their own. If you've made a will that identifies caretakers for your child should something happen to adults in the family, you can explain this as well.

It is often hard to judge from a child's questions the exact nature of his feelings or fears. We need to listen sensitively and give simple answers, being ready to go on and add more information if a boy or girl appears to want more.

* While death is a shattering experience for those left behind, it is healthier if the family talks together about shared experiences with the deceased. It's good if children hear the adult talk of his own feelings of loss and sadness. And it's important to remember the good times shared. If we shy away from mentioning the lost loved one, as some do, children may feel a deepening sense of "wrongness" about the death. They may fear that if they die, no one will remember or talk about them.

* At times a child will feel that the death of a loved one was his fault. Younger children typically have "magical" notions about cause and effect. If a boy or girl was angry with the person who died, the child is likely to feel guilty, and may believe that somehow he or she caused the death.

Talking about death and dying, and answering questions children have is very important. Several *talkable Bible stories* will help you explore both the sorrow and the Christian hope with your boys and girls (see pages 349–352, 179–181, 326–329, and 340–343).

89. *How do we help children when their parents divorce?* Divorce is all too common these days. Many thousands of children between

the ages of six and eleven will know the trauma caused by separation of their parents. How harmful a divorce may be varies from child to child. But mental health specialists agree that divorce is always harmful. At the same time, divorces which are an outgrowth of constant conflict in the home may do less harm to children aged six to eleven than if the parents stayed together "for the sake of the children." We can't generalize and say that divorce is always more harmful than keeping the family unit together.

One nine-year-old wrote, "At the beginning, it seems really awful, but then in three or four weeks, you realize that it's not all that bad. When my mother and father told me about the divorce they said it was for my good, too, and I didn't believe them. They thought divorce was good, but I thought just the opposite. But now that my father has moved out, it isn't all that bad. But I still think that divorce is dumb." Children do have the capacity to adjust and to cope. When divorce comes, all we can do is to minimize the stress and try to build a new, stable home life. What are guidelines that can help?

* When the decision to divorce is made, children should be told. Boys and girls are sensitive to family crises, and may be more concerned if the cause of tensions they sense are kept secret. It's good if parents can explain that they feel a divorce is necessary, with as little blaming of each other as possible. Also children need to be reassured that mommy will still be their mommy, and daddy will still be their daddy, although they won't live in the same house any longer.

It is extremely difficult, while mom and dad feel the anguish and grief that usually accompanies divorce, for them to be sensitive to the feelings and needs of the children. But children will need as much reassurance as adults are able to give. Especially boys and girls need to be assured that the divorce is not due to their fault or failure. All too often young children do feel guilty, and blame themselves when a divorce comes. It is best if parents acknowledge that *they* have failed, not the children.

* After the divorce, the custodial parent will have the primary responsibility for developing the stable, secure home context children need. This is often a great strain. Mother is usually the custodial parent and has her own great adjustments to make. There are also likely to be financial needs. The custodial parent and children need some 80 percent of the before-divorce income to maintain their earlier standard of living. Few shattered families have that much money available.

It helps if the family home can be retained for the children. Its familiarity, and the familiarity of friends and school, help. It also helps if mom is careful in talking about dad. An adult's own needs can lead him or her to attack the other spouse, and try to get the children to take sides. This is generally a tragic mistake, and should be avoided if at all possible. If, on the other hand, dad was a tyrant who abused mom and the children, they are likely to express relief. "Boy," one might say after a week or so, "I love dad. But, it's sure good not to have him around!" In such cases, honesty about your own feelings can affirm the right of the child to feel "disloyal." Expressing feelings honestly, without an attempt to manipulate the loyalty of the children, will be part of the healing process.

  * Children need both parents. Moms and dads each have something special to contribute to young lives. It is to be hoped that

Divorce, which creates so many one-parent families, does damage children. But God can redeem our tragedies, and the single parent can nurture successfully.

a good relationship can be maintained between the divorced parents and their children. Visits and shared custody arrangements can help maintain the child's realization that he is loved by both parents.

There is no easy way to work through the pain of a divorce, and no sure way to minimize damage to the children. But boys and girls are growing things, far tougher and far more able to adapt than we might believe. God can redeem every tragedy, and healing can come to adults and children alike. *Talkable Bible stories* on pages 162–164 and 343–346 may be adapted to stimulate sharing during or after divorce.

90. *How do we help children cope with life in the one-parent family?* In the great majority of cases, single-parent families are father-absent families. At least seven million children today are growing up in such fatherless homes.

The parenting skills needed in the one-parent home are not significantly different from those needed in the two-parent family. So the suggestions given for dealing with specific problem or nurture situations in this *Handbook* are just as relevant for a mom alone as for a mom and dad. Yet there are special concerns that the single parent must also consider.

* Fathering and mothering differ, and children gain from contact with both parents. (Of course, some dads may be so involved with work, or so often on the road, that their children experience paternal deprivation.) Children whose fathers are absent may fill the gap with a father surrogate, and have their special fathering needs met. Finding a father surrogate may not require remarriage. A grandfather can fill the bill, or a neighbor who takes time to be with the children. Some church club programs, and community programs like Big Brothers, can also make a contribution. A father who is faithful in visitation or shares vacation months with the children may also meet this need. But single parents need to be aware that both boys and girls need significant time with parents or surrogate parents of each sex.

* The greatest difficulty a single parent is likely to have comes from the overwhelming additional emotional load and from time pressure. Many single mothers must work, take care of the house, solve financial problems with insufficient funds, and still find time to listen to and be with the children. Often such pressures create special needs in mom's life—needs which can only be met by other adults who will help her and minister to the children.

A single parent will need to talk over what's happening in her home with others in a similar situation. She needs a chance for

social contact and support from other adults. She needs to participate in church activities where she can minister and be ministered
to. Finding time for herself and building supportive relationships
with others is particularly important for the parent alone. See *talkable Bible stories* on pages 162–164 and 282–285.

91. *How do we help children adjust to stepparents?* Nearly thirteen
percent of children under eighteen live with a remarried parent
and a stepparent. Most of the stepparents would agree with the
woman who wrote, "My adjustment to the stepchildren has been
more difficult than I ever expected." The new adult coming into
the home, ready to love the spouse's children, may be disappointed
that the children not only fail to respond to him or her, but may
show resentment, may ignore the stepparent, and may actively
engage in a campaign to make the parent prove loyalty to the
child by taking sides against the stepparent!

There are multiplied reasons for the stress of readjustment. Accepting the stepparent may seem like disloyalty to the dad or mom
who has left. The children, already shaken by death or divorce,
may be afraid that the new partner will steal the remaining parent's
love and leave them isolated. What's more, the new family unit
will not have had years and years of living together, during which
each member has the chance to come to know the others. There
will be differences in priorities, differences in ideas about discipline.
When the reconstituted family has children from both partners,
there will be competition for love and affection. There will be mis-
understandings, as parents and children misinterpret each other's
responses.

Once again, as in the single-parent situation, the nurture principles outlined in this *Handbook* do apply. But putting them into
practice will generally be much more difficult, and it will take
time for most "blended" families to achieve mutual love and unity.
In addition to taking special care to use parenting skills and be
patient, what guidelines are specifically applicable to those parenting in stepfamilies?

* A strong and healthy bond between the adult couple is a
necessary foundation for a strong stepfamily. This means time to
be together. It means much communication between husband and
wife. It means talking through nurture issues on which husband
and wife may differ. It's not a bad idea for stepparents to read
through a book like this *Handbook* together, and talk about each
paragraph, sharing past experiences and the ideas about child rear-
ing each has. Also, use the paragraphs to kick off conversation
about individual children in the new family.

* It's important to be aware of how difficult adjusting to a new person or persons in the home will be for children. Several things can help. Expecting adjustments to take a long time is important. Accepting the children as they are—rather than launching a program to change them to fit your expectations—is wise. To demonstrate caring, be willing to wait for a response. Caring relationships always take time to develop. We shouldn't expect instant love from stepchildren.

* Children between six and eleven will generally be more responsive to stepparents than are adolescents. It's valuable for a stepparent to take the lead in caring and building communication bridges. At the same time, the process should not be pushed. Using the *talkable Bible stories* in this *Handbook* as the basis for biweekly family devotions, with mom and dad and children together, is a low-pressure way to encourage sharing of feelings and getting to know each other.

92. *How do we help children adjust to handicaps?* Boys and girls born with handicaps are less likely to feel their difference as intensely as children whose handicaps come from a sudden illness or accident. Still, the way we relate to our handicapped boys and girls is important. We can help children deal with the stress handicaps generate in several specific ways:

* Establish realistic limitations and expectations for our children. As much as possible, expect of the handicapped child the same things you expect from other children. If your normal boys and girls have chores, handicapped children should have similar responsibilities to make a contribution to the family. The specific things they do may differ. But each child should have duties that fit his or her capabilities.

* Look for ways to provide the environment and training needed to give the handicapped child as much freedom and responsibility as possible. This will help your handicapped child build that achievement motivation and positive self-esteem discussed in earlier paragraphs.

* Try to help your handicapped child with the growth and mastery of emotions and social skills. Today there is increasing emphasis on legal and economic rights for handicapped individuals, and the trend of positive changes gives solid reason for hope. If your handicapped child will be able to work and to care for himself, your preparation of his personality may be as important as the job training he may receive later.

We can share our conviction with the children that each human being is significant. Because of this conviction, we believe in the worth and value of our handicapped boy or girl. We express our belief by our attitude, and by our commitment to give them the same loving nurture we give every child in our home.

Holidays and Vacations

93. *What is the nurture significance of annual festivals and holidays?* The calendar was one basic means of the nurture of God's Old Testament people. Each year God's people relived the great redemptive experiences of history, recalling how God acted to make Israel his own special people.

There were a number of yearly festivals. One festival recalled deliverance from slavery in Egypt, and featured the Passover meal. Together families acted out the night of departure from Egypt, standing to eat a traveler's meal, waiting for Moses' word to leave. They told again the story of God's judgment on their oppressors, and the price paid for their freedom.

Another festival saw families camping out under the stars. For a week they lived outside in lean-tos, remembering the years of wilderness wanderings.

The annual reenactment of Israel's relationship with God gave families a chance to affirm together their own personal relationship with God.

Some of the holidays we enjoy are similar in character. Probably the most enjoyable is Christmas. Easter commemorates the crucifixion and resurrection. For the early Pilgrims, Thanksgiving was also a Christian holiday: a day of celebration and appreciation for harvest gifts from God. Many Christians find building family traditions into holidays and vacations makes a great contribution to family unity, and to the nurture of their boys and girls.

94. *How do we make Christmas and Easter spiritually meaningful?* Special music, decorations, and gifts make Christmas exciting for boys and girls everywhere. We found that nightly Christmas ritual was exciting for our children. During Christmas vacation, everyone got to stay up late. The first day of vacation we decorated the tree, and cast a small plaster crèche, with figures of Mary, Joseph, the baby Jesus, shepherds, and sheep. (Hobby shops carry such kits around Christmas time.) The children helped us paint the figures, and we set them up in a place of honor. Each night we sang carols and lighted one more candle around our manger scene. We read Bible stories and talked about them, culminating

67270

Christmas eve with the birth story, as the manger was brightly lit by several burning candles.

Easter was similar, with late evenings spent together. The Bible stories focused on Jesus' arrest and crucifixion and his resurrection. Sometimes on these holidays we read missions books or acted out the life of early believers in the catacombs.

Developing special family traditions, which focus on sharing the meaning of these two central events of Christian faith, supplements whatever training our children might receive in church—and builds family unity.

There are books and booklets of family ideas for Christmas and Easter available in Christian bookstores. A series of *talkable Bible stories* for each holiday can be found on pages 249–258 (Christmas) and 309–323, 326–329 (Easter).

95. *How do we make other holidays special?* Not every holiday needs to be linked with faith to be significant to the family. Halloween can be special if we make the children's costumes to their own design, rather than buy packaged plastic witches and spacemen costumes. Thanksgiving can be a special "review of our family year" time, with family prayers of appreciation and worship. Valentine's Day can provide an opportunity to make valentines together, creating our own special expression for other family members, and finding some rhyming or other way to say just what we feel about the ones we love. A family valentine made for God can give a similar expression to him. Such shared times of fun, as they are repeated annually when the special times of year roll around, can make a lasting contribution to family unity and intimacy.

96. *How do we make family vacations special?* When children are younger, unpressurized vacations are desirable: not too much travel, less organized activity, and more time to explore. Simple vacations at a rented cottage, or camping outdoors, can be an exciting adventure. Planning for such vacations can involve the children too. Working on the route, planning meals the kids can make, and picking up inexpensive books on plants or birds the family may see, can stretch vacation fun and family closeness. It's sometimes a good idea to let an eight-year-old use a simple camera and be the official vacation recorder. Pictures, with a diary the family writes together, can build a child's sense of responsibility and provide a family record for later review and remembering.

By the time children are nine through eleven, they are more likely to be interested in seeing places and things. Planning longer trips, with built-in sightseeing, can be fun now. Again, the more children participate, the more meaningful vacations will be for all. An East Coast visit can explore origins of our nation. Another might feature Civil War history and battlefields. Some of our best vacations featured national parks of the West, and ruins of Southwest Indian culture. But children do need to be older, and to share the interest, if this is to be a truly "family" experience.

Sometimes parents wonder if they should take vacations without the children. Certainly husbands and wives need time alone to enrich their relationship. If grandparents are available, time with them can enrich the children's lives. So the idea of the family vacationing apart isn't all bad. What is important is that *some* vacations should be shared. And those vacations that are shared need to be organized around the children's interests and needs, rather than those of the adults.

97. *Should children six to eleven go to camp?* Being away from home, at camp with counselors and other children, can be significant growing-up times for boys and girls. Not every six- or seven-year-old is ready for camp. Readiness is a matter of individual development. For those who are ready, though, a week at camp—or even two weeks—can be very helpful.

Many churches and religious organizations sponsor camp programs. Some of these are excellent. Others are highly regimented, and not as beneficial. Check on the kind of camp program that is offered before signing up your children. A *decentralized* camp program, with activities organized around cabin groups, is superior to a *centralized* program, in which all children do activities at the same time. Many Christian educators are convinced that camp experiences are spiritually stimulating, for children between eight and eleven especially.

Several guidelines will help you think about providing a camp experience for your children. The guidelines are expressed in questions you'll want to ask.

* Do the children show an interest in going to camp when friends at church or school talk of camp experiences? How ready are they to take the plunge?

* Will the children go to camp with friends? Camp may be an adventure shared by two neighborhood buddies. Or an event sponsored for all fourth graders at your church. It's easier for children when they're going with friends.

* Has there been recent stress or a loss of a loved one in your family? Might the children interpret being sent to camp as a desire to get rid of them? If you've talked through any loss or stress with your children, so they are sure of your love, it's possible a camp experience may be just what's needed.

* Do you know the camp and its staff? Are the facilities good, and leaders well trained? What experiences have other parents had in sending their children to the camp you're considering?

If you and your child feel comfortable with your answers to questions like these, camp can make a contribution to a boy's or girl's self-confidence and social development as well as to spiritual growth.

3. Your Child at School and Church

98. *Why is school so important to children?* Boys and girls spend most of their waking hours in school. After parents, a child's teacher is likely to be the most significant adult in his or her life. The attitude of the teacher, and the atmosphere of the school, can oppress or exhilarate. Achievement in school work can help build self-confidence and motivation. Failures can shake a child's self-esteem. The boys and girls whom children come to know best usually are their classmates, and it's at school that many social patterns are set. Some children will be liked and accepted; others will feel painfully shy and left out. After the home and family, school will likely have the greatest influence on your child's growing personality.

It's important then to explore crucial factors that relate to a positive school experience. And to see ways that parents can help boys and girls live successfully in this important environment.

Choosing a School

99. *How do we recognize a school that is good for children?* Often you and I have options as to what school our children will attend. Some public school systems provide options. In many localities there are private or Christian schools in which our children might be enrolled.

What's best for our child? Perhaps the first factor to consider is the general atmosphere or climate of the school. Visit the school and several classrooms. Do the children seem happy and involved, or bored and resentful? Do the children talk with each other, or does the teacher maintain such strict control he or she must give permission for any act? Does the teacher appear warm and involved, or tired and tense? Does there appear to be a friendly relationship between children and teacher—with smiles from each—or is there a feeling of judgmentalism and fear? Do you hear any laughter? Do people in the halls talk with you? Is the school clean, and is care taken with materials and books? Or do the kids scatter paper

A visit to your local schools will help you sense the quality of life there.

and show little respect for materials? Do children talk with the teachers individually? Do the children seem to work together, or only compete with each other? Is discipline strict, and does the teacher threaten? Or do the children seem cooperative and enthusiastic, and at ease with the teacher?

It shouldn't take many visits to get an impression of the quality of life in a local school. When you do visit, simply ask yourself, "Would I enjoy spending several hours a day here?" If you would not, it probably would pay to look at alternative schools for your children.

100. *What educational approaches do schools take?* Today schools are returning to an emphasis on teaching basics: reading, writing, and math. Yet there are different theories on how the basics can best be taught. You are likely to find one of three underlying philosophies expressed in your local public or private school.

* Individual instruction usually features programmed learning materials, which may or may not be linked with teaching machines and computers. Some Christian schools stress individualized instruction, with children moving at their own pace.

However, rigorously individualized programs have serious weaknesses. They fail to take sufficient account of the need of children to learn from each other in discussions, and learn from interaction with their teachers.

* Open classroom systems promise flexibility, with children in a single classroom working together or alone on different projects at the same time. In general, the climate of the good open classroom is excellent, and children have the chance to learn cooperatively rather than alone. One key to effective open classroom teaching is the time individuals get with their teachers, to go over work and to plan. Typically, open classrooms stress availability of resource materials, so children have many sources for enriching and broadening their learning.

The effectiveness of the open classroom depends on the skill of the teachers, and on time to develop personal responsibility in children. This approach is particularly valuable for children who are gifted or are highly motivated for learning.

* The traditional classroom features a single teacher who guides the learning of a group of students. There is less individualization of learning, and more stress on working through the curriculum in an ordered way. An attempt is made to bring all children along at the same pace. The traditional classroom may be boring for the gifted child, or for average children if the teacher slows to the pace of the least quick learners.

A good teacher can use many group and other learning techniques in the traditional classroom. But it is important in this system to keep the teacher/student ratio in balance. A teacher with eighteen to twenty-two children in the public schools has a reasonable load. If the classroom is packed with up to thirty children, the quality of education will suffer. Some of the better private schools work for a teacher/student ratio of under one to ten.

Each of these learning systems has advantages and disadvantages. But generally parents should hesitate to commit a child to a completely individualized system. The open classroom and traditional systems can each provide good education—if each is well done.

If you're still not sure which would be best for your children after visiting possible schools, check overall scores achieved on standardized state tests by children in the different schools. Talk with parents of children about their impressions of each school.

101. *Should your child go to a private Christian school?* Christian parents have a number of reasons for paying tuition to send children to a Christian school. Their motives range from concern for what a child might be taught at the public school, to fears about safety and the bad influence of children in the public school, to the conviction that public schools no longer provide quality education, to the desire of parents that their children be taught the Bible, to the belief that a Christian environment is important.

But should our children be sent to a Christian school? There is no hard-and-fast rule, but consider these issues when you evaluate:

* While a Christian school can make contributions to your child's spiritual development, the influence of the home has been demonstrated to outweigh the influence of the school. You set the tone for your child's growth. Good parenting is the most important single nurture factor.

* Not all so-called Christian schools provide quality education—nor express the loving climate of Christian community. If you visit a Christian school, and sense an oppressive or regimented atmosphere (paragraph 99), don't send your child there.

* Not all public schools provide inferior education. There are many excellent public schools that teach well, maintain a healthy climate and good discipline, and are sensitive to the concerns of Christian parents in the community. Public schools, like Christian homes, vary from community to community. Public schools, like Christian schools, should not be stereotyped. Each school should be evaluated on its own merits.

* Children's individual differences should be considered. One of our children may profit from a Christian or private school environment, and another may do better in a neighborhood public school. For instance a shy child, who is frightened of bigger boys who might ridicule or threaten him on the way to school, may do better in a private school. Or a gifted child who is held back by the traditional structure of your local Christian school may do better in the open classroom of your local public school.

Because there is no universal "right" or "wrong" choice for all Christian parents, each family must evaluate the options and make its own choice. It's good to know that God will lead in making this decision. And that whatever decision is made, the nurture of your boys and girls remains your own great privilege and responsibility.

102. *What is the parent's relationship to the school system?* Whether your child is in a public or private school, there will be

opportunities for you to be involved. Read school notices, attend fairs and activities. Attend and speak up at public meetings. Be a school booster. Be available to help with transportation on field trips. Send notes of appreciation for extra efforts a teacher or staff member may make. You'll not only contribute to the general quality of the education your child receives, you'll become known, and have greater influence if problems occur.

103. *What characterizes a good relationship with your child's teacher?* Few teachers and parents know each other well. There really isn't time to develop close relationships. But if you follow the booster suggestions (above) you will be recognized and build a reservoir of good will.

Parent-teacher conferences are scheduled periodically by most schools. At times a parent or teacher may initiate a conference to discuss a child's problems. But the periodic conference will probably be your most significant point of contact with the teacher.

To make a conference meaningful, review your child's school performance and his current concerns. Talk with him or her about such things as "What do you like best?" "What's hardest for you at school?" "How do your friends like school?" Questions like these help you know what to explore at a conference.

Both you and your child's teacher are concerned about your child's development. Each of you knows your child, but in a different setting. You want to compare notes and find ways you can help each other encourage the healthy development of your child. This calls for open communication and mutual respect. It also calls for planned follow-up in areas in which either parent or teacher believes the other can help. For instance, if assigned homework is not being done, it may help if the teacher sends home a list of each week's assignments. If a child complains at home that he doesn't understand the assignments, this can be shared with the teacher. Or the teacher may suggest that a parent drill a child in spelling if this is the child's weak subject.

Periodic face-to-face meetings do help, as can a well-timed phone call to a teacher to talk over a concern, or express appreciation. Taking the time to communicate with your child's teacher can help your child in several different ways.

104. *When should a parent see the principal?* There are times when you may want to talk with the school principal, who is charged with the overall operation of the school. These are times when you or your child are worried about something that affects

your child's school experience. Visits to the principal should not be made to accuse, but to seek or give information and to share concerns. What are typical problems that might indicate a visit to the school principal is in order?

* Your child suddenly dislikes school. He complains of stomach pains in the morning, or reverts to bed-wetting.

* Your child begins to show bad habits, such as stealing or lying or using bad language.

* Your family is working through a major crisis, and you feel a need to let the school know.

* Your child complains of being bullied in the school yard or on the way to and from school. Or gangs of kids are hijacking children's lunch money.

These, and other events which might suggest a serious problem in the operation of the school itself, should be taken up with the administration. Questions about homework, tests, and in-class treatment are best taken up directly with the teacher.

105. *How important is PTA anyway?* Working through a local Parent/Teachers Association is probably the best way to influence policy matters at school. Leaders in parent-teacher organizations can influence curriculum, help set educational goals and discipline policies, and help to establish school priorities. They can also have an influence in negotiations between school boards and teacher's unions. The role the PTA takes in a particular school district is often shaped by individual parents, who are willing to become involved and work toward goals they feel are important.

Setting Our Goals for Our Children

106. *What are reasonable expectations for our children's school performance?* School has many values for children beyond whatever they achieve academically. In a good school boys and girls will develop social skills as well as the academic. At the same time they do need to develop the basic reading, writing, and math skills foundational to achievement in a modern society.

Yet boys and girls have a different individual pace in their physical and mental development. Typically girls are some six months ahead of boys in development during childhood. Just because one child is behind others at one stage of his development does not mean he won't catch up later.

Other things can affect school performance. Sometimes gifted children are bored with school, and their motivation and grades suffer. A child may be suffering from an undiagnosed learning disability. One of my nephews jumped five grade levels in performance in one year: his folks discovered an allergy to milk products which affected his learning and his behavior. They corrected the problem with a restricted diet!

Because so many complex factors are related to children's school achievement, it's best to avoid setting generalized expectations. Report cards and standardized tests do not measure many intangibles about a child's abilities and potential. We don't want to let our children feel we expect them to get all As or Bs. What we really want is for our children to make an honest effort, to experience successes as a result, and to gradually develop the learning skills and knowledge they need to mature. Special concerns related to this kind of growth are discussed in the following paragraphs.

107. *What about learning disabilities?* Awareness of learning disabilities is relatively new. It was stimulated by the discovery that approximately half the children identified as underachievers are learning disabled. This works out to some seven or eight percent of our school population between the ages of six and eleven!

Because there are so many different types of learning disabilities, it was even difficult to come up with an acceptable definition. Since 1968 the definition of the National Advisory Committee on Handicapped Children has been the standard. That definition, given in the Committee's 1968 report to Congress (page 4) is:

"Children with special learning disabilities exhibit a disorder in one or more of the basic psychological processes involved in understanding or using spoken or written languages. These may be manifested in disorders of listening, thinking, talking, reading, writing, spelling or arithmetic. They include conditions which have been referred to as perceptual handicaps, brain injury, minimal brain dysfunction, dyslexia, developmental asphasia, etc. They do not include learning problems which are due primarily to visual, hearing, or motor handicaps, to mental retardation, emotional disturbance, or to environmental disadvantage."

Learning disabilities may be difficult to diagnose. But if your child is performing poorly in school, the possibility should be explored. Your school system will either have professionals who can help with diagnosis, or be able to refer you to others. Typically the following stages will mark evaluation:

  * Determine if the child has a learning disability.
  * Measure present achievement to determine areas where special help should be given.

* Analyze how the child learns, and his strengths and weaknesses.
* To define the contributing factors, explore why the child is not learning.
* Use the data gathered to formulate a diagnostic hypothesis, defining just what the child's problems are, and to develop a plan for teaching guided by this hypothesis.

Generally a school's teaching, testing, medical, and counseling staff members will be involved in this process. Some school systems have learning-disability specialists who combine many skills.

When an underachieving child has been diagnosed as learning disabled, and a pattern for working with him established, then mom and dad can set realistic goals for achievement. Parents may also have their own contributions to make at home as support teachers.

108. *What can we do to help our gifted children reach their full potential?* While "giftedness" may refer to special talents, such as in music, to most parents it is a concept linked with high intelligence. A checklist of characteristics of gifted school-age children would generally include:
* superior reasoning ability and capacity to grasp abstractions
* intellectual curiosity
* capacity to concentrate and persevere
* wide-ranging interests
* superior vocabulary compared with children the same age
* can work independently
* responsiveness to new ideas
* memorizes quickly
* has unusual imagination
* reads rapidly and with comprehension
* has wide reading interests
* has several hobbies.

Giftedness is not always an advantage in school. Children in the traditional classroom are often bored. Teachers may not appreciate the gifted child, who does not fit in regimented groups. Other children may resent gifted children, who are likely to be critical of those who think more slowly. So giftedness may create adjustment problems in the classroom and in social relationships with other boys and girls. Gifted children will often wrestle at a young age with questions about God and the meaning of life.

Giftedness is not always the result of a hereditary head start. Stimulation and encouragement in the home, with a great emphasis on reading and talking, seem to be the common background of children with measured intellectual giftedness. The more we invest in interaction with our children, and stimulate their interest in reading, the more a child's intellectual development will be encouraged.

One issue raised by giftedness is very basic. Should gifted children be placed in special classes and programs? For some boys and girls such placement provides the challenge they need to stimulate maximum growth and learning. Gifted boys and girls are stretched by interaction with ability peers, and less academic frustration is experienced. On the other hand, some boys and girls are more comfortable in the society of friends who are not gifted. They receive their intellectual stimulation by reading at home, by hobbies, and by imaginative exploration on their own. So there is no simple or universal answer concerning how to provide for gifted boys and girls.

Perhaps the most important thing for parents is to realize that school is not the only place that intellectual challenges can be

There are things besides A's which can make our child's report card praiseworthy.

provided. By encouraging our children at home, we may do more to equip them for their future than will our local school program.

109. *How should we respond to children's report cards?* It's satisfying to mom and dad when children bring home good grades. And it's satisfying for children when they feel the teacher recognizes their good qualities, and that mom and dad are pleased.

But there are several things to consider when responding to report cards. Good grades are not the only criterion. This is because grades are only a measure of your child's performance compared with that of other children. Comparison is not perhaps the most significant thing. For instance, some children get very good grades in school, but never have to work for them. They may not develop the work habits that will be important in later schooling and in adult life. Other children do work hard, and show slow but steady improvement. A child who works hard to raise his grade from a C to a B— may have done something more significant and praiseworthy than the child who brings home all As. So our reaction to children's report cards shouldn't be based simply on grades. We need to consider each individual, his or her effort, his or her improvement, and other factors as well. We need to respond supportively to our children, talk about their cards, give individual praise where it is due, and be just as enthusiastic over a B— that shows improvement as over another child's A.

110. *Should children always be promoted?* We've noted before that children the same age differ dramatically. Some children develop more rapidly; some less rapidly. It's almost certain that in every school there will be children who would do better a grade lower or higher than the one they are in.

Part of the problem with grading is that schools have found the most practical approach is by age. Generally social and mental characteristics of the same-aged children are close enough. No better system—at least no better system likely to be accepted by parents!—has been developed.

Yet no child is really described by some statistical average. Each child is an individual, and his or her special characteristics merit consideration. Children whose development is slower than that of age-mates will be closer physically, socially, and intellectually to younger boys and girls. If a child doesn't seem comfortable in school, and his or her work is not up to the standard of others, holding that child back a grade may be a very helpful thing to do.

Children do compete and measure themselves against others,

even when parents don't stress comparisons. A boy or girl may suffer a loss of self-esteem and self-confidence if he is unable to grasp work other children his age seem to understand.

Some schools will encourage holding a child back a grade when this seems beneficial. Other schools will resist, and try to keep everyone moving lock-step. If you believe your boy or girl would benefit by re-grading, it would be wise to make your case to the school administration.

111. *What about homework?* Through much of the '60s and '70s many schools eliminated homework for children under ten. Increasing concern about the failure of schools to adequately educate children has placed great pressure on schools today to return to the basics. As a result homework is becoming more common.

The homework may involve extra reading, doing math practice problems, writing out answers to questions about a social studies chapter, and so on. In general, encouraging children to study individually, beyond the classroom, is healthy.

What is our part in helping a child with homework? Well, we're surely not to do the work for him. If he has questions, we can talk them through with him, and listen. Often thinking out loud helps a child clarify his understanding. We also may need to help a child with the scheduling of his time (see paragraph 85), so the homework can be completed on time. We may also want to help by freeing him of distractions: providing a quiet place without TV or other interruptions.

There should, however, be a limit on time committed to homework. Our boys and girls need to be involved in the other activities so important for their development. They need time to talk, to play, to be involved in hobbies and interests of their own.

It's probably best if we communicate with our child's teacher about homework. What assignments does our child regularly have? How much time does the teacher expect to be spent on homework? If our child is taking significantly longer, it would be good to let the teacher know. Homework can be a part of the growing child's school experience. But it should not dominate at-home time.

112. *How can we encourage a love for reading?* The basic skill needed by a person in our society is reading. Boys and girls who read well are well prepared for high school, college, and later life. They are well prepared for spiritual growth, for they will be able to read and explore God's Word with greater facility than those who do not read well. During the grade-school years my sons

didn't bring home the highest grades. I was never concerned, because each of them read constantly and widely. I remember my own high school years, when I was bored with school, but read eight books a week from our local library. The person who reads is equipped for a significant future.

We build a love for reading into our children by our own attitudes and practices. The youngest preschoolers should have books, and be read to often. As boys and girls grow, their books should grow with them. Many preschoolers exposed by parents to books and magazines of their own will begin to read even before they enter the first grade. Regular trips to the library during grade school are important. Comic books have a role in building a love for reading in young children. An inexpensive encyclopedia is a valuable resource when there are family discussions and arguments.

As children grow and develop various interests, making sure they can read about those interests is important. When reading is a part of the parent's life, and we encourage it in our children, we are doing the single most important thing to ensure their success in school and in later life.

Sports

113. *How important are sports to children six to eleven?* Boys and girls play ball, tag, run races, jump and climb. Most learn to ride bicycles, and many swim. As far as physical development is concerned, these natural play activities of children generally provide plenty of exercise.

In our society, however, boys often measure themselves and each other by athletic ability. The children who run fastest, who can hit the ball furthest, catch the football and dribble the basketball, gain status and self-confidence. The boy who wants to play, but whose development is slightly behind that of other children, is at a disadvantage. So is the child thrust into Little League before he's had a chance to practice throwing the ball or swinging the bat.

Whenever skill enters in, the twin factors of maturation and practice become important.

Some boys and girls develop in a very positive and healthy way without showing any interest in athletics. If such children have our support, and are successful in areas in which they are interested, we needn't worry that low athletic achievement will be detrimental.

114. *What can parents do to help?* Both my own boys are more than competent athletically. Sports have helped to build their self-

confidence. Most of this has grown out of what happened in the family rather than in the school or organized teams.

When Paul was in second or third grade we started tossing a football. He dropped it at first. Frustrated, he'd begin to cry and want to go in. I told him it was all right to drop the ball, and all right to cry. But he couldn't quit. Before long Paul was holding on to the ball. Soon neighborhood children were coming over, and we organized offense/defense games in the front yard. Every day when I got home from teaching, the neighborhood assembled, and we played football for an hour or more. As Tim got older, he joined in.

When spring came, a whiffle ball and bat were featured in our daily workouts. Great bald spots appeared in our front yard, at

Building skills, not organized competition, is the truly significant role of sports in a child's life.

home plate and the bases. By the time Paul began to play softball at school he was a skilled batter. He soon won a reputation as a home-run hitter.

A little later a basketball hoop went up on the garage. When we moved to Arizona, a cement half-court, poured in the back yard, became our very first home improvement. Every day we found time for an hour or two of basketball together. Paul went out for wrestling in high school. His first two years he wrestled in three weight classes, and did not lose a match. But he quit the third year. Practice took too much time away from our family sports activities, and winning wasn't all that important to him.

It was harder for Tim, always behind his older brother in the development of skills. But now Tim has surpassed his brother in several sports.

Today, nearly twenty years after beginning play with my boys, we still spend up to two hours together daily in sports activities. Paul and I have daily Ping-Pong contests to determine who mows the lawn. We have a weekly family tennis tournament in the summer. And when winter comes, we go over to the college Tim attends and play basketball.

There was never pressure on the kids to win during the childhood years. There was the fun of playing and being together. For the boys there was the chance to develop athletic skills, which helped build their confidence and self-esteem. I trace many positive traits in the children to the benefits of playing and building skills together.

115. *How about team and competitive sports for our children?* Little League and other sports organizations have a generally good reputation. They do meet a need for some children. But they can also be harmful.

Children, as we have already noted, develop at very different rates during the years between six and eleven. Some boys will be bigger and much better coordinated than others. These boys generally will excel in organized sports, and the others will have little chance competing against them. But even some of the more athletic children may not have a chance to practice and develop skills. If the team sports in which we enroll children are highly competitive, and if great stress is placed on winning, they are likely to have an extremely detrimental impact on individual boys and girls.

On the other hand, if adult leadership does not emphasize winning to the exclusion of other values, and if a child wants to participate, being part of such a team can be a good growing experience—particularly if we help children practice needed skills at home.

Television

116. *What impact does television have on children?* Probably the most common statistic quoted is this: by the time our children graduate from high school, they will have spent some 11,000 hours in school. And 15,000 hours watching TV. Breaking that down, the typical American household uses its TV set about 43 hours a week. Depending on the time of year and their age, children watch TV from 17 to 30 hours weekly, most heavily during the prime time hours of 7:30–11! Our six to eleven-year-olds generally watch only 2.6 hours on Saturdays during the "kiddie hours."

A number of studies have focused on the impact of TV violence on children's behavior. The results indicate that children who see violence—especially realistic violence enacted on adult programs—are more likely to engage in antisocial and hostile behavior. On the other hand, children who observe positive social behavior are more likely to act in a positive way. The argument of some, that the cumulative effect of viewing repeated crime and violence has led to an overall increase of violence in our society, cannot be proven or disproved. But it surely is likely.

However, there are other issues linked with TV viewing. While TV can be an educational as well as an entertainment media, the kinds of thinking and reasoning it calls for are different from those called for by reading. If TV curtails reading in the family, it's a problem.

Another issue TV raises relates to family communication. Research suggests that while TV programs are on, families do not talk with each other—except perhaps during commercials. If TV watching habits cut into family time, intrude on mealtimes, and cut out the bedtime rituals (paragraph 25) so important for relationship building, then television definitely harms.

Video games have raised other family issues. How does sitting in front of the screen manipulating flashing objects affect our children? The testimony is mixed. Some speak of dangers; others note advantages in developing better hand-eye coordination and quicker reactions. But as with other TV issues, it may be the extent of the activity rather than the activity itself that is the issue with video games. If, and this is unusual, video game playing dominates your child's free time and pushes out other outdoor and physical kinds of play, then a problem certainly exists.

A few parents I know have become concerned enough to throw out their sets. Others realize it is necessary to establish guidelines—for themselves as well as their children.

117. *What realistic limits can we set on TV watching?* There are two different issues that parents will want to deal with. One issue has to do with the content of the programs watched. The other has to do with the amount of time children spend in front of the TV set.

Normally, the second issue is easier to resolve. The folks at Mr. Rogers' familiar children's TV program did a survey of young boys and girls, and found that in a list of fifteen activities, watching TV ranked fourteenth! Only petting the dog was of less interest. The point is that if boys and girls have friends to play with, hobbies to work on, and other activities to fill their days, TV's passive appeal can't compete. Of course, it's not surprising that TV wins out over doing homework and going to bed. So if moms and dads use TV as a cheap baby-sitter—to keep the children quiet evenings so they can watch their own favorite programs—it's not surprising that most of children's viewing is during prime time. But TV will not be used as a plug-in drug if our children are really important to us—and if we accept our responsibility for their nurture.

One way to get a handle on TV viewing is to use an "hours per week" time limit, or "hours per day" limit. The limit can be used flexibly: if there's a special everyone wants to see, or a program assigned by a teacher at school, that limit can be stretched. Here are different guidelines used by parents in their effort to control hours of watching:

1) Establish the number of hours, starting with one hour a day maximum on school days, and more for weekends.

2) Establish the rule of no viewing during morning "get ready for school" hours, during mealtimes, or until chores/homework are completed in the afternoon.

3) Establish a number of hours for the week. On Sunday afternoon, go through the TV guide to help the children work out where they will invest the time they're allowed.

The other question may be more sensitive. What are children allowed to watch? The violence issue is only one of many. We also want to consider how the characters on the TV show talk to each other. What view of moms and dads is implied? What values are held by the characters? Are these the values that you hold as a family—and want to learn how to act out?

A number of TV programs deal sensitively with life, and have positive messages for children. Both "The Waltons" and "Little House on the Prairie" were praised for their treatment of real-life problems, and for showing a family's sensitivity and concern for others. While TV cartoons have been attacked for their violence component, the unreality of cartoons is easily grasped by school-age children. They are far more likely to try out violence when it's acted out by real people in adult TV shows. The more realistic the violence, the more likely it is to be imitated—whether its used by the "bad guys" or by the "good guy"!

Understanding the power of the media to communicate values and provide models which affect the behavior of children, it's clear that we need to exercise some control over the programs which our children watch.

What is best? Probably working with our kids, to give them a voice in selecting the shows they will watch. If children are limited to a maximum number of viewing hours, it's easier to let them engage in the process of setting priorities. Only if our kids pick

Both the content children see and the amount of time they spend watching TV will concern careful parents.

out a show which has clear violations of our values and standards should we intrude. When a bad choice is made by a child, it's good to watch the show together once, talk about what we specifically object to, and ask our boy or girl to mark this one off his "to watch" list.

118. *How can we help children use TV in a positive way?* Television is here to stay. Despite the potential dangers, there are also advantages. Choosing good programs to watch can enrich children's lives in many ways. Some programs encourage curiosity. Others provide fascinating information. TV programs can stimulate research and reading: the TV program "Little House" led to a revival of the fascinating Laura Ingalls Wilder books. Often, too, programs will stimulate conversation. A death portrayed on "The Waltons" stimulated children's questions in one family.

Even television commercials can be useful. When an ad makes various promises for a product, the next trip to the store can be used to check out its claims, and to compare price and label with similar products. Deceptive phrasing can be pointed out, and the family can make a game out of "catching" honest and dishonest commercial content. Teaching skepticism can help make our children more discerning and responsible.

In the long run, probably the most significant factor in TV's positive or negative impact will not depend on the individual programs the family watches, but on the pattern of TV use in our family. When we limit use, teach discrimination, and keep TV from squeezing out important family experiences, TV can add to our children's growth and development.

Going to Church

119. *What should we seek in a local church?* Coming together to worship God has always been important to God's people. The New Testament places great stress on a community of believers which lives together as an extended family. We are to come to know our brothers and sisters in Christ, share our lives and needs, and draw strength from each other's prayers. The supportive concern of close friends who are committed, with us, to growth in relationship with the Lord, is vital for us all.

There is no question that the greatest influence on the developing faith of children is found in the home. But there is also no question that it's important for children to grow up feeling and being a part of the larger community of faith. In the local church, children will find other adults who love them, and other children who share their beliefs and values. From their earliest years, boys and girls can sense that they belong in our church, for they too belong to God.

There are a number of things that we should look for in a church home. But perhaps—surprisingly—the most important thing is the ministry the church provides for the parents, rather than for the boys and girls. We saw earlier (paragraph 54) that parents are equipped to share God's Word effectively with their children by taking that Word into their own lives. It is as we moms and dads grow in our relationship with God that we are able to model Christ's character in our families. So if parents find a congregation where they can grow, where they can build supportive relationships with other believers, and where they can encourage each other in mutual commitment to Jesus Christ, this is the kind of local church to which we want to belong.

120. *How can we evaluate a church's programs for children?* Many local churches compete for families by providing a full calendar of activities for boys and girls. There are classes and clubs and choirs, with staff members and adults eager to do things with and for children. Often these programs will provide activities and opportunities to build friendships, which our children need. At times, however, they may simply contribute to the too-busy-ness of our society. Some children would do better to stay at home, play with neighborhood children, and grow through shared times with us in the evenings.

So we don't want to be impressed simply by the overwhelming number of activities a church may have for children. What we want to watch for is the quality of those activities in which our children may become involved.

For instance, when my oldest son was in sixth grade, I took him out of our Sunday school. I attended several of the Sunday sessions there, and watched. The well-meaning teacher of Paul's class spent most of his time trying to keep the boys in order. He read mechanically out of the curriculum materials, limited the participation permitted the children, and in short ran a very regimented class. He did talk about the Bible story. But there was no exploration of how the Bible might be linked with the present experience of the boys, except for a moral hurriedly tacked on at the end of the hour. To top it all off, he kept getting the names of the boys mixed up. I am sure he was a well-meaning and nice person. But I really didn't want my son to learn about God in that kind of an atmosphere.

You can contrast this with other classes you've observed or taught. The boys and girls participate. There is a Bible story, and there is time to talk about God and what we learn about him. The teacher shares personal experiences from his or her own life, and we quickly realize that God is very real to this teacher, and that the Bible is an exciting book. We not only want our children in this kind of class, we enjoy being there ourselves!

What I'm getting at is this, the quality of relationships between adults and children in a church's ministries is the key to the effectiveness of those ministries. When we visit a local church, and sit in on children's programs, we quickly sense if these are the kinds of people we want our boys and girls to associate with God. And if this is the kind of learning that makes God seem as real and exciting as he truly is. So when you're looking for a church, visit children's classes. Visit children's weekday programs. And see if you can sense the presence of the vital, loving Christianity to which you want your children exposed.

121. *How much can we expect boys and girls to understand about God and the Bible?* It is certainly true that the Bible is an adult book. It takes an adult mind to grasp the meaning of many of its teachings. Those who have studied how children think, and their cognitive development, have been quick to point out that even our eight- to eleven-year-olds simply cannot accurately grasp many abstract concepts. Some religious educators have even suggested that many Bible truths not be taught to children until they are old enough to know what they mean.

But the Bible is more than a book of abstract concepts. One word that both Testaments use to describe Scripture, "Truth," points up the fact that Scripture is God's unveiling of reality. The Bible is true because what it tells us corresponds with reality.

This means on the one hand that we can trust the Bible when it describes the unseen spiritual world and what happens after death. It also means we can trust the Bible when it talks about our present experiences and relationships. We can learn in the Bible that God is a forgiving Person, and that he invites us to forgive one another. We can learn that forgiveness heals, while staying angry breaks friendships and makes us miserable as well. Because God's Word is trustworthy, we can act on the guidance God gives us, confident that doing things God's way is not only right, but is also best for you and me.

This quality of Scripture means that it's not necessary for boys and girls to understand the Bible's teachings in an adult way. What is exciting about the Bible is that, because the Bible is truth, children can put its teachings into practice even when they don't fully understand. They can hear and believe that God is forgiving, and as a result come to him to confess sins. They can hear and believe that forgiving others can heal hurts. Without fully understanding they can act in forgiving ways. Even children can put what the Bible says into practice, and discover that what God says does work. Children can experience the truths of the Word of God even when they do not fully understand them.

This means that in our teaching of the Bible to children, the academic, classroom approach which focuses on giving and mastering information isn't the most important kind of teaching. What we need is teaching which brings the Bible to bear on the present experiences of boys and girls, and helps them to hear God's own loving voice of support and guidance.

Children may not always understand the concepts underlying a Bible story. After all, you and I can't really grasp the meaning of the fact that God is omnipotent, or omnipresent. But boys and girls six to eleven can believe that God is able to help them, and that God is always with them. We can take the great truths of Scripture, translate them in terms which boys and girls can grasp, and then help our children to apply the Bible's message in their own lives.

The *talkable Bible stories* in this *Handbook* are all designed to introduce your children, through stories, to great truths of Scripture by which they can live. Our children will understand these truths better when they mature. But they will learn to put God's Word into practice, and learn how helpful God's Word can be, now.

122. *What about leading boys and girls to accept Christ?* The Bible teaches us that all people sin. This means that all need the forgiveness which Jesus Christ offers us through his death and resurrection. Many, concerned that children become Christians in this "converted" sense, place great stress on child evangelism. They present the basic facts of the gospel to boys and girls and call on them to make a personal decision.

There are advantages and disadvantages to this emphasis. On the one hand, children are unlikely to understand the "decision" they make. They may well respond from a desire to please a teacher, rather than to establish special relationship with God. Often the words used—"accept Jesus into your heart," and so on—are themselves highly symbolic, and it's difficult to tell what meaning they have for children. As boys and girls grow, and their cognitive abilities develop, there will be a number of points at which they reevaluate their beliefs and move on to deeper faith, or away from childhood impressions of Jesus.

On the other hand, it's clear from Scripture that there is a point of conversion. Believers are those who have put their trust in Jesus and been born again by his Spirit. In the words of Scripture and the church, we need to be saved. And a time comes when we do believe, and are saved.

What is not clear is when this takes place, or even that most of us are aware of the moment of conversion. Children brought up in a Christian home, familiar with Jesus and his love from the beginning, may never be aware of a time of conversion. They may simply not recall a particular point in time when they began to love Jesus and to believe in him in a special, personal, saving sense. In a very real way, this is the ideal toward which our nurture is geared. We want God to be a part of our child's life from his earliest years.

During growing up, there will be times when a child feels guilt and a sense of sin. Without pressing for a "decision," we'll be able then to share the gospel's good news. God loves us anyway. Jesus came to earth and died to pay for our sin, so we might be forever forgiven. The gospel facts, shared simply and often, will stimulate conversion as God's Holy Spirit prepares the heart of our boy or girl.

When there is love in the home, and God is part of our shared life and conversation, conversion will come naturally in God's own time.

123. *What do we want our children to understand about the personality and attributes of God?* Probably the most important single thing we can do in the religious training of our children is to help them develop a positive God-concept. We want our boys and girls to have basic ideas about what God is like, and to build their sense of personal relationship with God on these ideas.

Much of a child's impression of God comes from the model provided by his or her parents. It's not at all surprising to learn that a child who can trust mom and dad finds it easier to trust God. Or that a child who is sure of parental love finds it easier to believe that God loves and accepts him too. A child who is forgiven by mom and dad can much more easily accept the truth that God is a forgiving person, than can a child whose parents hold grudges and never let the child forget past mistakes. So one source of a child's image of God is the character of his or her own parents.

The Bible is the other primary source of the idea of God held by children in Christian homes. We not only read about people in the stories which the Bible records. We read of people who made choices because of their trust in God. We see God's love in the experiences they had. We see God most clearly in the Person of Jesus Christ, God's Son. In the life Jesus lived on earth we discover so much about the character of God. In the life which Jesus freely surrendered for our sakes, we have ultimate proof of God's love for us.

It is particularly important, then, in telling Bible stories to children, to pay close attention to what is revealed about the Person of our God. We want to talk not only about our own experiences, but about him. We want to develop our awareness that God is present with us—loving, guarding, and guiding us toward what is good.

Some Bible stories are valuable just because of what they teach us about God. A number of the *talkable Bible stories* in this *Handbook* are included just because they do help our children develop a more adequate image of who God is, and thus draw them closer to him. Bible stories which focus on who God is are found on pages 150, 156, 247, 258.

As we continue, consistent in our love for our children and consistent in our nurture, we'll see God work in our boys and girls. Guided by his relevant and reliable Word, our family will grow together, to experience the very best of what he has planned for us.

4. TALKABLE BIBLE STORIES

The Bible belongs to children as well as to adults. At times we hear, "The Bible is an adult book." In a way this is true. Many of the realities of our faith, expressed in great doctrines of the Scripture, are beyond the grasp of young children. But God's Word speaks powerfully to boys and girls as well as to adults. Truths they can understand—and experience—are imbedded in Bible stories which have been told and retold for thousands of years. The stories of the Bible are a vital part of our heritage. They speak in vivid, timeless images, revealing who God is, affirming his love for us, and teaching us how to respond to him and to one another.

The stories of the Bible capture vital truths and cast them in events which capture the imagination. Bible stories take root in our lives: Bible characters become our companions. The experiences of men and women, as reported in the two Testaments, help us to interpret our own lives and to understand God's work within us. It's no wonder, then, that as children begin to grow, we intuitively realize that the best way to teach them the Bible is to begin with Bible stories.

Reflecting on his own use of stories in treating children, the great child psychologist Bruno Bettelheim writes in *The Uses of Enchantment* (Random House, 1975) that "For a story to truly hold the child's attention, it must entertain him and arouse his curiosity. But to enrich his life, it must stimulate his imagination; help him to develop his intellect and to clarify his emotions; be attuned to his anxieties and aspirations; give full recognition to his difficulties, while at the same time suggesting solutions to the problems which perturb him. In short, it must at one and the same time relate to all aspects of his personality—and this without ever belittling but, on the contrary, while simultaneously promoting confidence in himself and his future" (p 6). There is no greater resource for children than the stories of the Bible. Bible stories express the human condition and probe man's inner problems, yet explore them with a hope offered by their testimony to God, who speaks through them to young and old.

What makes a Bible event a "story"

Not every event reported in the Bible is a story. Every event does, of course, have significance—but not necessarily as a story. The sordid experience of Lot with his daughters after the destruction of Sodom has genealogical significance. It is a record of the origin of peoples who played a part in Israel's later history. But this event is not returned to again and again, to be told and retold by God's people as story. But other events reported in Scripture have been told and retold across the centuries. Why have some been focused on and not others? What makes certain events "stories"?

First, stories are those events which capture great truths about who God is and about our relationship with him. The Bible is God's unveiling of reality. It is his inspired picture of how we can live in this world in relationship with him and one another. We sense the timidity of Gideon, and watch as God encourages him until he becomes the leader of his people. We see Joseph face tragedy. Yet he remains faithful to God's standards and is finally exalted to be a ruler in Egypt. We see David, ashamed, confess his failure to God . . . and find healing in forgiveness. The great truths of Christian faith are explained in the sermons of the prophets and in the letters of the apostles. But these same truths are vividly illuminated, without sermon, in the stories of our Old and New Testaments. We do not build doctrine on Bible narrative. But through the stories of the Bible we teach powerfully the great revealed truths which hold meaning and hope for children as well as for adults.

Second, stories are events which bring us into relationship with Bible people. In the great stories of Scripture we meet people like ourselves. Their experiences help us to understand God's ways. Their faith sets us an example to follow. Their wrong choices stand as warnings. As we see God's role in the lives of believing men and women, we sense his presence in our own. Through the people of the Bible we discover how the great realities of our faith touch emotions, shape values, and guide behavior. The Bible friends that boys and girls make today will stay with them through their lives, continuing to give gentle guidance toward godliness.

Not every Bible story features human beings. Some, like the story of Creation, feature God's direct action. But most of the stories of the Bible feature men and women on whom children can model, whose lives touch them and teach them about God.

Third, Bible stories feature those events which teach us about ourselves. The most powerful Bible stories illuminate our own lives. We can explore our feelings as we sense the emotions of Daniel, pressured to conform to pagan ways in the king of Babylon's school. We can grow more sensitive to others as we see the compassion of Jesus. Through Bible stories the basic values which infuse our lives can be examined, chosen, and become part of our character.

Boys and girls from ages six to eleven are at an exciting time of life. Exploring, they stretch out to understand and to respond. Growing, they make choices which shape the persons they will become. Bible stories can be one of the most effective means that God uses to guide children's personal growth.

All this helps explain the principle of selection which underlies the choice of Old and New Testament stories for this *Handbook.* The stories that have been chosen are each related to childhood anxieties and aspirations. Each story is linked with specific childhood "problems" which are, in fact, unique opportunities for moms and dads to provide distinctive Christian nurture. The index in the back of the book will help you locate paragraphs in chapters 1 through 3 in which particular childhood needs are discussed, and also to identify Bible stories which provide needed insights.

The stories in this *Handbook* are familiar ones. But each is retold in special ways to highlight its linkage with the experiences of your boys and girls. These specially selected, specially retold Bible stories were chosen because of the unique way each may touch the life of your own six- to eleven-year-old.

How to tell Bible stories

We've all seen the gifted storyteller who can hold a crowd of children in rapt fascination. But storytelling at home is not for the crowd. It's for intimate moments spent with a single child, or for warm times when your family is gathered around. At times like these, stories are not for just telling. They are for sharing. In family adventures with Bible stories, children are participants and not just listeners.

That's why this *Handbook* suggests different ways to share Bible stories with your boys and girls. There are ideas here to help you act out stories, living them together in that "pretend" way which is so real to the young. There are ideas for one activity associated with each story; an activity to help you carry the story truths over into daily life. And, with each story, there are talkable suggestions; suggestions for you to pause and chat with your children about what's happening in the story and how it relates to their own experiences.

In a sense the art of family storytelling means joining hands with your children, going together to visit people of the Bible, and then bringing the truths you learn together back to enrich your experience as a family.

This is just the way stories were used in Bible times. We see the principles of family Bible teaching in a famous Old Testament passage. After calling God's people to love and honor the Lord, the writer gives a simple prescription for teaching children. The instructions are directed to parents, and they begin with the adult response to the Lord. God's words to us, the Bible says, ". . . are to be upon your hearts. Impress them on your children. . . . Talk about them when you sit at home and when you walk along the road, when you lie down and when you get up" (Deut. 6:6, 7). We can see three principles in these instructions.

(1) We are to take God's Word into our own hearts. We are to open our lives to the Lord, to let the teachings and the stories of the Bible shape our personalities. As we are being shaped, we have the privilege of sharing what we experience with our families.

(2) God's Word is to be taught in families. The ideal context for responding to the Bible is found in the close, warm, constant relationships provided by the home. As children learn about God from those they love and trust, and sense parents' love for the Lord, they readily respond to him.

(3) God's Word is to be woven into the fabric of our lives together. Bible teaching isn't just for special, set-aside times in which we mimic the school. Instead, Bible stories are to be linked with daily life—related to the experiences of our boys and girls. It's easy to see why this kind of teaching can be so powerful. When we sense fear in a child, we have an opportunity to hold him close—and to share a Bible story which builds trust in God. When we're disturbed by outbursts of anger, we can turn together to Bible stories which help a child explore his own feelings and learn godly responses. When we observe a fault, another story from the Bible helps explore similar flaws in Bible people, and find better ways to live. Only in the family can the use of Bible stories be so intimately woven into daily life, for the needs of a child are best sensed by loving parents.

So family storytelling is unique. It features intimate moments of sharing together the great, life-shaping stories of the Bible. And our closeness to our children helps us select just those Bible stories which our boys and girls most need to help them grow.

How children understand the Bible

Many studies by child psychologists have shown something most of us realize. Children do not think or understand as adults do. Just as a five-year-old's body does not permit him to play ball with the skill of a teen, so his "mental muscles" have not developed to the place where he is able to think as a youth or adult.

Generally, the thinking of children between the ages of four and seven can be characterized as "intuitive." Words are still personal, and represent what the child has experienced and perceived. A child in this stage of mental development makes little distinction between times and places. There is no sense of gap, for instance, between the time of Abraham and of Christ. To young boys and girls, everything seems "now" and "here."

Children between seven and ten are generally found in the stage of "concrete" thinking. Now children can begin to take the point of view of others, and compare others' feelings and perspectives with their own. Now, too, boys and girls can look ahead, and see the consequences of actions. They can decide ahead of time what they will do, and can understand what their choices will mean.

Older children, generally between the ages of ten and fifteen, reach the stage of "formal operational" thinking. Now they can analyze: now they are able to explore relationships between the real and the possible. Now many "adult" kinds of thinking become possible.

Some educators have examined the ways that children think and have concluded that, because of a young boy's and girl's mental limitations, we should not teach them the Bible. These people argue that to "really understand" the Bible calls for kinds of thinking of which boys and girls are not yet capable. They fear that if we teach them the Bible too young, children will actually misunderstand, and build impressions they need to unlearn later.

But these fears are based on a radical misunderstanding of the nature of God's Word. Certainly the Bible presents concepts and ideas children cannot grasp intellectually. But the Bible does more than present concepts. The Bible unveils realities which God's people are invited to experience! A five-year-old may not understand forgiveness. But he can certainly grasp the fact that God loves and forgives him, and experience the release that forgiveness brings. A nine-year-old may not grasp the mystery of incarnation in an adult way. But she can know that God's Son came into our world, lived here, and that because he became like us he fully understands both her joys and her sorrows.

So our goal in teaching the Bible to children is not to help them master Bible doctrine in an adult, schooled way. Our goal in teaching the Bible to children is to help boys and girls grasp the practical meaning of those Bible truths which they can experience in their daily life now.

In teaching Bible stories we are not trying to link doctrines to abstract ideas. We are trying to link the great truths of our faith with the sights and sounds of daily life. Our goal is to communicate Bible truths as realities which will become the framework of our child's world.

How important such Bible stories are. Stories are not abstract statements. Stories are flesh-and-blood expressions of God's truths. Your children may not understand doctrines in an adult way. But as you share Bible stories with them, in ways fitted to their stage of growth and matched to their personal experiences, your boys and girls will come to know God. They will come to know about him in ways that are deeply meaningful to them.

The stories retold in this *Handbook* are shaped in words and phrases which fit the thinking of the ages for which they are intended. *Talkables* and *action ideas* further link the stories to daily life. Told and retold in your home, these Bible stories *will* help your children grasp great Bible truths. And these stories will help them come to love and respond to God.

How to use these Bible stories

Each Bible story is keyed to specific childhood experiences and needs. And each story is organized in a simple, three-part way.

Background. The background capsulizes the story and its key truths, and identifies the times when it is especially appropriate for you to tell the particular story. In addition, the background indicates numbered paragraphs in the first three chapters which discuss those childhood needs to which the story is related.

The Story Retold. Each Bible story is retold in words appropriate to the age-group and the way children think. You can read the story to the children from this *Handbook*. Or you can read the story ahead of time, and tell it in your own way. However, remember that the story is retold to highlight the needs which it meets.

One of the most important features of the retelling is built into each story. This feature is the *talkable*. *Talkables* are printed in *italic* type, and tell you when to pause in telling a story to explore meaning with your children. Sometimes *talkables* focus on values, to help you share what is important to you in a life-shaping way.

Sometimes talkables focus on the feelings of Bible men and women, and on similar feelings experienced by you and your children. Sometimes a talkable explores behavior, to help your children think about choices they will make. Always talkables encourage you and your children to share with each other and with the Lord.

There's one thing that is very important to understand about talkables. Their suggestions are to help your children share. *But they are also to help you share with your children!* You'll often find that you need to take the lead in responding first to a talkable suggestion.

Your personal sharing is a vital part of family Bible teaching. You see, we adults are models for our children. Much of what our boys and girls learn does not come from our preaching but from our example. Thus we want to share our faith with our children, and talk freely about our attitudes and values and our own experiences, so they can learn from us. When we communicate our values and beliefs and our feelings as we, too, respond to the Bible stories, we transmit a living faith to our next generation.

Action Idea. This is another unique feature. With most stories a simple follow-up activity idea is included. These ideas are optional. You don't have to use them when you tell the story. But you can use them if you want.

What responses can I expect?

Growing up is a process. No childhood needs are met in a moment, nor are the problems of boys and girls solved instantly. While we yearn to see progress in the lives of our children, we must remember that growth is a slow process. This is certainly true in the physical realm. We may not even notice how much our child has grown until we compare a picture taken six months or a year ago, and suddenly realize how much he's changed! So we shouldn't be surprised if growth in the psychological, social, and spiritual realms is also a gradual kind of thing.

When you notice something in one of your children that troubles you, look it up in the index of this *Handbook*. You'll find two things. First, there will be discussion of the problem area, and how it can become an opportunity for Christian nurture. Second, one or more Bible stories which have special value in helping a child gain insight and find God's guidance will be identified. You'll find ideas of what to do in the coming weeks or even months to provide supportive guidance.

Sometimes retelling a Bible story may stimulate no response

from our child at all. For some reason he or she simply does not seem ready, or sense its relevance. In this case it's best to wait a couple of weeks, or wait for a particular happening, then sit down immediately and retell the story. This time the incident may create the readiness.

Sometimes children will be able to respond and apply the story insights immediately. At other times the truths shared may germinate for further weeks, and you may talk of the story several more times before you see responsiveness and change. *It is particularly important to be very patient during such germination times.* You and I are not to use the Bible to club a child, or to impose demands that he or she conform. We are to use Bible stories as gentle words from God: loving words spoken by the Holy Spirit, lovingly providing insight and hope. We too must be patient and loving and gentle, and share helpful Bible stories as a doorway to hope rather than a nagging demand for change.

One indication that a Bible story is having an impact in a child's life is his request to return to it. "Tell me again about Moses dying," a child who has lost a grandparent may ask in the weeks following the death. Returning to the story is one of the clearest of indications that God's Spirit is quietly working through the Word, helping the child deal with a disturbing event in his life.

At other times you *will* see changes, soon. The child who was afraid of the dark hears an appropriate Bible story, draws a picture of it for his wall, and in a week or so begins to go to bed without the anxiety which had gripped him before. How enriching that is, to see such quick and clear evidence of the touch of God's hand.

What is important for you and me to remember, whether the response we see is quick or delayed, is that what we are sharing with our boys and girls is the very, living Word of God. God is someone you and I can trust implicitly. We can trust his timing. We can trust his Spirit to work through his reliable Word, to help us nurture the growing personalities of the children that we— and God—so dearly love.

God Creates
Genesis 1

Background

The Genesis message is that we live in a personal universe. Our world was not shaped by mindless forces. It was lovingly designed by a personal God, to be home for humanity. The pattern and order of creation stand as witnesses: the very regularity of day following day, of season following season, show that the world was planned to provide a stable framework for human life, and give us a sense of security.

How important for our children to sense the essential friendliness of God's universe. Despite sin's impact on nature, God's loving hand can still be seen. Every boy and girl can hear in this mighty Genesis passage the wonderful message that he or she is important, the object of God's special care (see paragraphs 48, 49). This story is retold especially for your younger boys and girls.

The Story Retold

Long ago, before God made the world, He* thought and thought. God wanted the world to be special, because He had an exciting plan. Do you know what that plan was? God planned to make people, like you and me, whom He could love. God wanted the world His people would live in to be just right.

Finally, when God was ready, He created the heavens and the earth. He began to shape them into a special home for us. Here's what the Bible tells us God did.

The very first thing, God spoke and said, "Let there be light!" And everywhere there was a warm, bright glow, shining in the air. But God knew that you and I would need darkness too. So God planned for times when the light would go away, and there would be night. God saw what He had done in making day and night, and He smiled. It was good.

What are some of the good things about day? What are some

---

* For clarity and impact, the author has chosen to capitalize personal pronouns referring to God in the Bible stories only. The rest of the content follows the style of the previous chapters.

of the things we like about night? How hard it would be for us to sleep if the sun was bright all the time. God made the night to help us rest.

At first the world was covered with thick, wet clouds. Then God spoke again. Most of the water settled down to cover the ground, and the deep blue sky appeared.

Then God gathered the water together into oceans and lakes and streams. And the dry land appeared. With another word, God covered the land with grass and flowers and trees. All the vegetables we like to eat, and all the fruits that grow on trees, were made for us by God. God looked around at what He had made and smiled. It was good.

How many different ways do we enjoy the plants and foods God made? (For instance, beauty, shade from trees, good taste, satisfying hunger, vitamins, etc.) What is your favorite fruit or vegetable? Do you think God knew that you would enjoy the (fill in favorite food) when he planned it?

When God spoke again it was to set lights in the sky. The two great lights that God made are the sun, for daytime, and the moon, for nighttime. God made the stars, too, and placed everything just right so we would have our seasons: our spring and summer, and fall and winter. God planned it all. We can count on God's sun coming up every morning. When winter is cold, we know spring and summer will come again.

What do you think night would be like without the moon or the stars? How would you feel at night without them? When we look out the window at night and see the moon or the stars, we know that God is there. What words tell how you feel when you see them, and know that God is near?

God made a beautiful world for men and women and boys and girls. But the world still seemed empty. So God spoke again. This time He filled the waters with fish, and created birds to fly in the sky and nest in the trees.

What's your favorite of the birds God made? Why does this bird seem special to you?

Then God spoke one more time. He filled the world with all kinds of animals. He looked carefully at all he had done, and God smiled, because it was good.

But God had one more thing to do. God had planned

the world as a place for people to live. God had filled the world with beautiful things. He had made fish and birds and animals for us to enjoy. Now God made the most special thing of all. Gently and lovingly, God shaped the first man and woman!

God made them very special. He made them in His own image and likeness. Only human beings are like God. Like God, we can think and understand. Like God we can feel, and love others. Like God, we can know what's right and wrong, and can choose to do what is right.

No animals are this special. Only people are made in God's image, to be like Him in these special ways.

When God had finished creating, He gave everything in the world to us to take care of for Him. God was very happy with what He had done, for it was very good.

How does it make you feel to know that you are special to God? What are special things about each member of our family that you think must please God? God loves each of us very much. Each of us is very special to God.

Action Idea

To strengthen the sense of specialness, try keeping a "special" diary for a week. Jot down unique things each child says or does. Afterward, read each the list of special things about him that you jotted down. Let each child know how pleased you are with him or her, and pray together. Thank God that your children are even more special to God than they are to you.

God Makes Us Special
Genesis 2

Background

Genesis 2 describes Eden, the garden God shaped for the first pair. The account is fascinating, for it shows how carefully God designed Eden to exercise every capacity of personhood. God himself enjoyed beauty, engaged in meaningful work, expressed creativity, sought fellowship, and exercised moral choice. Genesis 2 shows us that God carefully planned Eden to enable human beings, made in his image and likeness, to exercise these same capacities.

There is a unique joy to be found by young and old in a sense of personal achievement (see paragraph 48). There is also a joy found in the exercise of creativity: the joy of shaping something which is specially ours (see paragraph 50). If at some time your child is bored or seems discouraged, this Bible story is appropriate. It is also appropriate when you want to help your boy or girl experience affirmation and praise, or realize his or her own worth and value to God.

The story is retold for younger boys and girls. However, you can lead your nine- to eleven-year-olds directly into Genesis 2:4–23, to discover the things highlighted in the story. You can also use the talkables from this story with your older children, to help them sense their own special endowment with creativity by God.

The Story Retold

When God created Adam, God made him very special. The Bible says God created man in His own image. God made people to be like Him in very special ways.

For instance, God can think and understand. So can you and I. God can feel happy, or sad. So can you and I. God can love others, just as we can love.

When God created Adam, God wanted Adam to have the joy of using all the wonderful and special abilities Adam had been given. So God planned a special garden for Adam to live in. He called the garden Eden. God let Adam live in the garden, to discover just how special Adam was.

What do you suppose you would have seen or done in the Garden of Eden? What are some of the things you would have learned about yourself? Which things you did would have made you happiest? Why?

When God made the garden, he planted all kinds of trees in it. God chose trees that would look beautiful, because God enjoys beautiful things. And God chose trees for the garden that had delicious fruit on them: fruit God knew would taste good to Adam. So when Adam walked through the garden, he was thrilled with the beauty. And he enjoyed the taste of many different kinds of fruit.

You're special like Adam, because you can enjoy beautiful things. Let me tell you about the most beautiful thing I ever saw. Then you tell me about the most beautiful thing you ever saw.

What are some kinds of fruit that you've eaten? Which do you like best? Would you like to come to the store with me sometime and see if we can find fruit you've never tasted?

When God put Adam in the garden, he did a very wonderful thing. He told Adam that from now on Adam could take care of the garden. God had worked when He created the world, and knew how good it felt to do a job well. Do you remember? The Bible says God looked around at the things He had done, and saw that it was good. Well, God wanted Adam to have that same joy. So he let Adam work in the garden and take care of it. Maybe Adam decided to plant flowers in new patterns. Or Adam planned to put a hedge beside one of the rivers. Now Adam could do what he wished to make the garden look just the way he wanted. Then Adam could feel good about the work he had done.

What work do you do that you're proud of? Do you think doing your school work is like the work Adam had to do, or not like it? Why? (Share what makes work that you do satisfying.)

God had made all the animals and birds, but God did not name them. He left that for Adam to do. God knew how good it felt to create—to make something fresh and new and special. So He wanted Adam to have the fun of making up something fresh and new and special too. God let Adam make up the names.

Maybe Adam spent hours following the different animals, and watching the birds. He may have listened to the sounds they made, and watched them play. And then Adam named them. Whatever name Adam gave them was their name back then. Making up the names was making up something very new and special.

Can you think of anything special you have made up yourself? (Remind your child of a poem written, or a picture drawn, or an imaginative story told, etc.)

For a long time Adam may have lived in the garden that God made. He worked there and felt good about the things he did. He enjoyed the beauty of the garden and the taste of the fruits. Adam felt very satisfied when he saw animals sharing the garden, and called them by their names.

But something was still missing. You see, God made Adam so he would need another person to love. God wanted Adam to learn that having others to love is very important. Finally, when Adam knew that something was missing, God had Adam fall asleep. God took one of Adam's ribs and, just as God had shaped Adam, God made a woman, named Eve.

When God brought Eve to Adam, Adam knew immediately what she was. "Here is a person just like me!" Adam said, and called her "woman." Now Adam would have another person who could also love beauty and be proud of work and make up fresh, new things, to share with. Adam would never be alone again.

Later, when Adam and Eve had children, there were other persons to share the wonderful world God had made. And all the children, like Adam and Eve, could enjoy beauty, and feel proud of their work, and make up things fresh and new.

You see, you are special too.

And so am I.

God gave us many special abilities, and there are many wonderful things you and I can do.

Action Idea

Be alert for chances to praise your child for work done well. Also express appreciation for any creative efforts. You can also stimulate a number of shared projects. Use this story to launch a younger child on family chores. Let him or her choose from several possibilities, asking which would give the greatest satisfaction. You might also suggest that a seven- or eight-year-old create a poster for his or her room. Feature a poem he makes up and let him use construction paper to create his own design on a larger cardboard background.

Adam and Eve Are Tempted
Genesis 3

Background

The temptation theme occurs often in Scripture. While we are not to seek out such tests, it is wrong to view temptations as evils.

In fact, those moments of conflict between our desire to do what is right, and the pull toward a different choice, are moments which can actually strengthen our commitment to God. Every choice of God's way builds our moral character.

Genesis describes God placing the Tree of Knowledge of Good and Evil in the Garden of Eden. This is often misunderstood. The tree was no trap, meant to catch an unwary Adam and Eve. It was instead a wonderful affirmation by God of human specialness. God had made Adam and Eve in his image and likeness (Gen. 1:27). They, like God, could appreciate beauty, feel satisfaction in work, enjoy relationships with others and act creatively. But God is also a moral person. To truly be like God, man must also have moral capacity, and the opportunity to exercise moral choice. The tree, planted in Eden, and God's command not to eat its fruit, was actually a great gift. Because the tree was there, and Adam and Eve had a choice, they could live as responsible moral agents. Without the presence of that tree, and thus opportunity to choose, the first pair would have been puppets of flesh, not true human beings.

Our first parents made, at last, a tragic choice. We all share the burden that choice introduced into the perfect world God shaped. But the opportunity to choose was a good gift, even as the opportunities which you and I have to choose between right and wrong are good gifts from God. For God never tempts us to do evil (cf. James 1:13–18). Instead, with every temptation, He provides a way to escape that we might not fail (cf. 1 Cor. 10:13).

In this Bible story about the weeks, months, and perhaps years before the sin reported in Genesis 3, you can help your children explore some of the great truths which protect us when we are tempted and encourage us to choose God's way.

The story is suitable for children six to eleven. The older children are more likely to sense the deeper meaning of the truths it shares.

The Story Retold

Life was good for Adam and Eve in the Garden called Eden. God had made the garden, and He planned it to be very special. God planted the garden with beautiful trees, filled with tasty fruit. God let Adam and Eve take care of the garden. They probably planted special plots of flowers, and arranged the bushes just the way they wanted them.

Adam and Eve had friendly birds and animals for company. And they had each other to love.

There was one other very special thing about the garden. It was the most special thing of all. Evenings, God often came to be with Adam and Eve in the garden.

Adam and Eve knew that God loved them very much. He had made such a beautiful place for them to live. And God liked to be with them. In those days, they could actually talk out loud to God, and God talked out loud with them.

There was one other thing about the garden. God planted one special tree in the garden. And God gave Adam and Eve one command. "Don't eat any of the fruit from that one tree," God said.

God even explained. God told them that if they disobeyed Him, and ate, the fruit of that tree would make them die. Adam and Eve didn't understand what "die" means. But they knew that something very bad would happen if they disobeyed God.

We don't know how long Adam and Eve lived happily in the beautiful Garden of Eden. We don't know how many times they walked together, hand in hand, past the tree God warned them about. They must have looked at it many times. But they never touched it. Adam and Eve knew God loved them. They knew that doing what God told them not to do would hurt them. The tree looked beautiful. Its fruit looked tasty. The fruit even smelled very good. Adam and Eve may even have wanted to taste it. But they didn't. They turned away from it. And when they did, Adam and Eve must have felt very, very good.

How do you feel when you know you've done the right thing instead of something wrong or bad? How do you think Adam and Eve felt when they turned away from the tree?

When are you most likely to be tempted to do something you know isn't right? (Share a temptation from your own childhood.) What helps you to do the right thing when you feel tempted?

Why do you suppose Adam and Eve wanted to do the right thing, and to please God? Let me tell the story again. You listen for things that would help Adam and Eve to obey God. (Focus on evidence that God loved them, and wanted only the best for them.)

Action Idea

If your child has told about a personal temptation, there's a simple thing you can do to help him or her resist. In the process you'll strengthen your child's pre-conscience (see paragraph 65), and his or her motivation to do right.

For children from six to eleven you might cut out a construction paper tree, and a number of round, red "fruit." The tree can be taped to the wall of the child's room, or to a family bulletin board, or to the refrigerator door. Whenever your child resists the temptation he has told about, he can tape a fruit to the tree. Giving in to the temptation means a fruit should be taken off. At the end of a week, or after several days, talk about each fruit on the tree and your child's victories. Express your own pleasure and pride.

Older children, those nine to eleven, can be helped by *cuing*. If your boy or girl spoke of a temptation that occurs at a particular place, in the house, or at school, suggest that he or she cut out a small tree symbol, and place it in that location. Talk with older children about evidence that God loves them as he loved Adam and Eve. God shows us what is right because he knows that doing good is always best for us. When we turn away from a temptation—even though it's something we think we want—we know we are making a choice that is best for us as well as one which pleases God.

Adam and Eve Sin
Genesis 3

Background

The story of the Fall tells how sin entered our world and tainted the human race. Subsequent history demonstrates the tragic outcome . . . in injustice, war, and in the personal experience of every individual.

While the Genesis report traces the origin of our subjection to sin back to Adam and Eve, it never suggests that individuals today are not responsible for their actions. We each make choices, which mirror the choice of Eve and Adam. Like them, we too experience natural consequences of wrong doing, as suggested in this Genesis chapter. For this reason, the story of the Fall is especially helpful in reinforcing the use of natural consequences in discipline (see paragraph 63). This emphasis is particularly suitable for use with six- to eight-year-olds.

One other aspect of the story is particularly helpful. Genesis 3 thoroughly describes the process of Eve's temptation, and the avenues through which human beings still experience temptation. Satan's suggestion that wrong is not wrong, that whatever tastes or feels good is desirable, and that God cannot be trusted, remain factors in our own temptations. This story emphasis is more suitable for boys and girls nine to eleven, who are better able than young children to think in terms of "what if . . ." situations, which involve alternative actions and outcomes.

The story is retold here for the younger children, with the emphasis placed on consequences. However, a set of *talkable* questions, keyed to verses in Genesis 3, is included at the end of the story for use with older children. Read the story together directly from the Bible, using the *alternate talkables* at the appropriate times.

The Story Retold

Adam and Eve lived together in a beautiful place, planned just for them by God. Their days were busy and happy. God often came and talked out loud with them. Adam and Eve knew that God loved them very much. And they loved God too.

In the whole, big, beautiful garden where they lived there was only one thing Adam and Eve could not do. God had planted one tree in the garden whose fruit they were not to eat. God warned Adam and Eve. "If you eat that fruit, you will begin to die." Adam and Eve didn't know just what that meant. But they did know that something terrible would happen if they ate the fruit God warned them against.

Why do you suppose God warned them not to eat the fruit of that tree? Do you think eating it would be a good thing for them or a bad thing? What are some of the things you're not supposed to do because they would be bad for you?

For a long time Adam and Eve obeyed God. They didn't touch the fruit of that tree. But one day, when Eve was alone, Satan came in disguise and talked with her. Satan, who was God's enemy, tried to make Eve doubt God.

"Did God really say you're not to eat that fruit?" he asked. And then Satan lied to Eve. Satan tried to make her think God didn't love her and Adam. Satan said, "Terrible things won't really happen if you eat the fruit. God doesn't want you to have the fruit because it will be good for you."

Eve looked at the fruit and smelled it. It was beautiful, ripe fruit. It looked as if it would taste delicious. And Eve wanted to find out for herself what would happen if she ate it.

So she did!

Then she gave some to Adam. And Adam ate the fruit too.

How do you think Adam and Eve felt after they ate the fruit? How do you feel when you do something you know is wrong? Do you think Adam and Eve were really fooled by Satan, or did they know they were doing something wrong? How about us? Are we fooled, or do we usually know when we do something wrong? What do you think will happen to Adam and Eve now?

As soon as Adam and Eve ate the fruit, they knew they'd done wrong. They looked at each other and they felt ashamed.

Later, when God came to the garden to walk with them, Adam and Eve ran away and hid. They felt guilty and afraid.

Something happens inside us when we do wrong. We begin to feel bad about ourselves. What are some words that tell how you feel when you know you've done wrong? Can you think of a time when you felt ashamed and guilty and afraid? One good thing about doing what's right is that we don't have to have those bad feelings, or feel afraid.

When God found Adam and Eve they were trying to hide. God was very sad. "Have you eaten from the tree I told you not to eat from?" God asked. God knew the answer. But He wanted to give Adam a chance to admit what he had done. Instead Adam blamed Eve. "She gave me the fruit," Adam said. And Eve blamed Satan. "He tricked me," Eve said.

Do you think those were good excuses? Whose fault is it if we do something we know is wrong? Why? We can make excuses, but they don't help. We choose what we do ourselves.

God was sad. He told Adam and Eve what would happen now because they had disobeyed. Adam and Eve would have to leave the Garden of Eden. They would have to work hard, because weeds would come up now as well as vegetables and fruit. And that very day Adam and Eve began to grow old. One day they would die.

Adam and Eve hadn't known all the things that would happen if they disobeyed God. But God knew. God had told them what to do because He loved them. God didn't want the sad things to happen to them. How much better it would have been for Adam and Eve if they had chosen to do right instead of wrong.

Can you think of some wrong things that might hurt you if you did them (for instance, accept a ride from a stranger, run away instead of going to school, and so on)? We don't always know what will happen when we choose to do wrong. But we do know that it's always best for us to do what is good.

Alternate Talkables for nine- through eleven-year-olds

Genesis 3:6 *Satan did four things to get Eve to disobey. (1) He talked with Eve alone, instead of with Adam and Eve together. Why do you think he did this? (2) Satan tried to convince Eve that eating the fruit wasn't wrong. Do we usually know when a thing is right or wrong? How? (3) Satan tried to make Eve think that God is selfish, and told them not to eat for his own benefit. Why do you think God or parents tell children not to do certain things? (4) Eve wanted to try the fruit because it looked good and she wanted to try it for herself. Do your friends ever do something they've been told is wrong, because they want to find out for themselves? Have you ever felt like that yourself?*

Genesis 3:10 *How do you think Adam and Eve expected to feel when they ate the fruit? What three words here (3:7–10) tell how they did feel inside? Has anything like this ever happened to you? (Share experiences of doing wrong, and the feelings that result.)*

Genesis 3:23 *The story tells us some of the other consequences of Adam and Eve's sin. Usually doing wrong has consequences besides the feelings of guilt and shame and fear inside us. What do you think God wants us to learn from the story of Adam and Eve? What temptation that you experience might this story help you resist?*

Action Idea

This story, as told to children six to eight or studied with those nine to eleven, makes a good launch for family discussion of the reasons for family rules, and about consequences of disobedience.

Wise parents establish few rules, and those that are established are for the child's benefit. Coming home after school before going to another's house to play, doing homework before going to another's house to play, doing homework before bedtime, and picking up one's own clothes—these are simple regulations without great moral content. But they do have significant value to the child. The reasons for rules can be discussed, and natural consequences (see paragraph 63) can be established.

Also any moral issues, from stealing to lying to fighting, can be discussed. Children can be reassured that, even if they do not understand all the reasons behind our rules, obedience is best. The rules that God and parents make are established because of love.

God Calls Abraham
Genesis 12:1–9

Background

Abraham was a prosperous pagan merchant in the magnificent ancient city of Ur. Joshua identifies Abraham's time as a day when the forefathers "lived beyond the river and worshiped other gods" (24:2). Yet when God the Creator spoke to Abraham, the 75-year-old merchant responded to the Lord's voice. The Bible simply tells us that, when God told Abraham to leave his homeland and travel to a strange country, "Abram left, as the Lord had told him" (Gen. 12:4).

This first great act of faith helps to establish Abraham as the Old Testament's primary model of trust in God. Despite the limited nature of Abraham's knowledge of God, Abraham was ready to risk everything, convinced that the One who told him to move to a foreign land was trustworthy.

Today about one family in five in the United States moves each year. It's always hard for children to leave friends and familiar places for the unknown. Sharing the story of Abraham and discussing his move can stimulate your children to share their worries and concerns (see paragraph 87). And you can remind your children that God will be with your family wherever you go.

This Bible story is told in the form of a skit. You can read each part, or let older children in the family put it on for the rest of the family. You may want to use the name "Abraham," even though the Genesis 12 text calls him "Abram." Later on

"Abram" was extended to "Abraham," the name by which he is usually known.

The Story Retold

This story is about a 75-year-old man named Abram and his family. Instead of telling the story, we're going to pretend it. Listen as I (we) pretend to be Abram and Sarah and their nephew, Lot. See if you can tell how each one feels about moving.

(Door slams, run in place.)
Abram: (breathlessly) Sarah! Sarah! Lot!
 Sarah: My goodness, Abram. What's the matter?
Abram: Whew! . . . Just a minute. Let me catch my breath.
 Sarah: Here, sit down. Why, running like that at your age. You'll have a heart attack!
Abram: But Sarah, it's so exciting. Where's Lot?
   Lot: I'm here, Uncle Abram.
Abram: Listen, both of you. We're going to move!
(Sarah and Lot together:)
          Sarah: Move! *Lot:* What, leave Ur?
Abram: That's right. Sarah, it's the most exciting thing. God just spoke with me!
 Sarah: What, Nannar our moon god . . . ?
Abram: No. No, not Nannar. The true God. The God who made the whole world, and human beings too.
   Lot: But we don't know any God like that.
Abram: Well, I know Him now. The true God spoke to me, and told me to move. So we're moving.
 Sarah: Where are we going?
Abram: I don't know. But God will tell me when we get there.
   Lot: But . . .
Abram: And listen. God gave me wonderful promises. He promised to bless me, and make our family a great nation. God is going to protect us, and somehow all the peoples of the world will be blessed because I know God, and obey Him.

Sarah: (doubtfully) Well, if you're sure . . .

Abram: I'm sure. God spoke to me, and told me to move. And God is going to be with us, family. O there are such good things ahead for us!

Sarah: Well, I guess we'd better get ready to go.

Lot: Uncle Abram, what should we pack?

Abram: Bring everything. Our herds. Our money. All your dresses, Sarah. All our servants. And Lot . . .

Lot: Yes, Uncle Abram.

Abram: Lot, buy lots of tents.

Sarah: Tents!

Abram: That's right. We'll live in tents from now on. We can't bring our brick air-conditioned houses, you know.

Sarah: (unhappy) But I don't want to live in a tent.

Abram: Don't worry, Sarah. God is sending us. And God will be with us. O Sarah, I just know there are such good things ahead!

How did each person feel about moving? Why do you think each felt the way he or she did?

What's the hardest thing for you about moving?

Why do you think it was easier for Abram to plan to move than for Sarah or Lot?

Can you think of some hard things it's easier for us to do because we trust God, as Abram did? (Recall and share individual as well as family experiences.)

Thank God he cares for us today, just as he cared for Abraham.

Action Idea

Pretend with your children that God has spoken to you as he did to Abraham. You are going to move . . . in just one hour!

Have each family member take a paper grocery sack. Each of you has just five minutes to select things to bring along, and put them in the sack. Take what is important to you, but only what will fit in the sack. Everything else must be left behind. When time is up, show each other what you packed. Tell why each item is important to you. Then tell about anything that was especially hard to think of leaving behind.

There are two benefits to this activity. In sharing what is important to each as you unpack your sack, you communicate some of your values to your children. Boys and girls need to hear mom and dad talk about what is important to them, and why, during the formative years (see paragraph 3).

You can assure your children that everything important to them will be brought along when you do move.

Conclude this activity with prayer. Thank God that he is always faithful and will be with you wherever you go. You can trust God, just as Abraham trusted the Lord so long ago.

Abraham Fails to Trust God
Genesis 12:10–20; 20:1–18

Background

Abraham was a man of faith. But at times he too was fearful and failed to trust God. Like you and me, Abraham failed more than once. The Book of Genesis reports two incidents of fear that rulers would kill Abraham in order to marry his wife, Sarah. In each case, Abraham lied and said she was his sister. Each time God protected his faltering servant. And each time Abraham must have learned a little more of how good and trustworthy God really is. Abraham need not have been anxious about his imagined fears at all.

Children also are often gripped by fears of what might happen. They imagine monsters in their closets, ghosts outside their window, lions and tigers prowling the neighborhood. Some boys and girls just starting school are afraid of what they will find there. Older boys and girls may be beat them up. The teacher may not like them. They may find no friends. All these are natural anxieties (paragraphs 30 and 32). Such fears are very real to our boys and girls. Like Abraham, our children may need to be reminded many times that when we know God, we do not have to be terrified of things that "might" lie ahead.

Several of the Bible stories in this *Handbook* focus on common childhood fears. This story is told especially for boys and girls of eight or nine, though it can be told to younger and older children as well.

The Story Retold

Abraham had left his home in Ur when God told him to move. Even though he was seventy-five years old, Abraham gathered everything he owned—his herds, and his cattle, and the people who worked for him—and Abraham set out for a strange new country. But it must have been a hard thing for Abraham to do, leaving everything he knew to go to a place he had never been.

Do you think Abraham might have been worried or afraid when he started out? What are some of the things Abraham might have been afraid of?

Yes, Abraham probably was worried. But Abraham trusted God enough to obey Him. Finally Abraham did come to the land we call Israel. There were some cities in the land. But there were great empty fields and high, grassy hills too. Abraham traveled slowly across the new land and saw how beautiful it was. His flocks of sheep and herds of cattle grew. Abraham became even richer than he had been in Ur, his old home. God took good care of Abraham and everything Abraham owned.

But when Abraham pitched his tents in the southern part of Israel near a town called Gerar, Abraham began to worry. You see, Abraham's wife, Sarah, was very beautiful. Everyone thought she was the most beautiful woman they had ever seen. So Abraham began to imagine all sorts of terrible things that might happen. *Maybe,* Abraham thought, *the king of Gerar will want to marry Sarah!* And Abraham imagined what might happen then. Why, what if the king decided to kill Abraham so he could marry Sarah! What if the king's soldiers attacked him? The more Abraham thought about the terrible things that might happen, the more he was afraid. It got so bad for Abraham that he didn't even want to look toward Gerar, because he might see the king's soldiers coming!

What else do you suppose Abraham might have imagined that would frighten him? Do you think Abraham was wise to be so scared of something that might happen, but might never happen at all? If you were Abraham, what do you think you might have done?

What Abraham did was a terrible and foolish thing. He

forgot that it was God who had brought him to Israel. Abraham didn't stop to think that God would surely take care of him. Instead, what Abraham did was tell everyone at Gerar a lie, and make Sarah promise to lie too.

"This is my sister," Abraham said when he introduced Sarah. He was afraid to tell people Sarah was really his wife.

Well, the king of Gerar was very excited. He *did* want to marry Sarah, and had her come to his palace. Now Abraham and Sarah were really in trouble!

Have you ever been so afraid of something you told a lie instead of the truth? What happened then? (Share an experience of your own when you were afraid and acted unwisely.)

Abraham and Sarah were in deep trouble. Sarah was at the king's palace. And Abraham was even more afraid than ever. How could he go and tell the king he had lied?

Abraham had forgotten to trust God. But God still took care of Abraham. God spoke to the king of Gerar in a dream, and warned the king that Sarah was already married. God kept the king from actually marrying Sarah. And God told the king to send Sarah back to Abraham right away.

The very next morning the king called Abraham. The king was very upset. "Why have you done this to me and my kingdom?" the king asked. "Why, I almost married your wife. Why didn't you tell me the truth in the first place?"

How ashamed Abraham must have been. Embarrassed, he answered the king's question, and explained the reason.

What do you suppose Abraham said? Why do you think he was so afraid in the first place?

"Well," Abraham explained, "I said to myself, these people don't know God. Maybe they will kill me to get my wife."

What do you suppose was wrong with Abraham's reason? Was God there, even if the people of that land didn't believe in him? Can you think of anywhere at all where God isn't with us? God was with Abraham, so Abraham didn't have to be afraid.

Sometimes you and I forget God is with us, and imagine all sorts of things to be afraid of. But even when we forget God, He doesn't forget us. God is always with us, just as He was with Abraham even when Abraham was afraid.

Action Idea

Often children find it easier to talk about their own fears as if they were fears of someone else. Work together to make a list of things that the classmates of your child or children might be afraid of. Post the list on a family bulletin board. Include God's promise to Abraham, recorded in Genesis 15:1. "Do not be afraid, Abraham. I am your shield."

One of your artistic children might even draw a shield to decorate the list and remind him of God's promised presence.

Abraham and Lot
Genesis 13:1–10

Background

The Old Testament is honest in its portrayal of Bible characters. We see the same faults in them that we find in ourselves, and in our family. But we also discover God's redeeming work in Bible people, and discern relationships which help us deal with hurts.

Abraham and Lot were family: uncle and nephew. Yet tensions developed between them over their possessions. In a passage which begins and ends with a description of Abraham at worship (13:3, 4 and 13:18), we discover the godly way that Abraham dealt with a problem which is common in modern families.

While some quarreling is natural and even healthy between children (see paragraphs 7 and 72), children also need to explore their feelings and find better ways than angry bickering to resolve their disputes.

Undoubtedly Abraham's confidence in God's love for him was a freeing influence. When our children are reassured of our love, and of God's care, it is easier for them to surrender their "rights" for the sake of brothers and sisters, and of peace.

This story is retold especially for children six to eight years old.

The Story Retold

When God told Abraham to move, he left his home in Ur. Abraham gathered everything he owned—his herds, and his cattle, and the people who worked for him—and Abraham set out for a new country. Abraham's nephew, Lot, came along with him. Lot also brought all his own herds, and all the people who worked for him.

God blessed Abraham and his family in the new land. Their herds got bigger. There were more and more sheep to feed and water. Before long the people who worked for Abraham and the people who worked for Lot were quarreling with each other!

"Hey! We were here first," some of Lot's herdsmen probably yelled. "This is our grass!"

"You can't have it all," Abraham's herdsmen argued. "We want our share."

Pretty soon they were arguing about water too. "Wait till we're done watering our camels," Lot's herdsmen may have said, shoving some of Abraham's sheep away from a well. "It's our turn now!" Abraham's herders yelled back. "You're hogging it all!" Before long the men were quarreling all the time!

When are you most likely to feel like Abraham's and Lot's herdsmen? How do you think they felt about each other when they were quarreling?

Do you think the herdsmen were most upset when they thought they weren't getting their share, or when someone was taking something that was theirs, or when they thought it was their turn? What makes you most upset with your friends (or brother or sister)?

Abraham was unhappy about the quarreling. A little arguing might have been all right. But quarreling all the time wasn't a good thing at all!

Do you think quarreling made the men feel better or worse? Why? How do you usually feel when you've been quarreling with a friend (or brother or sister)? What do you think people can do to stop quarreling?

Well, what Abraham did was this. He came to his nephew Lot and said, "Let's not have any quarreling between you and me, or between your herdsmen and mine, for we're family." And Abraham had an idea. He suggested they each go off in a different direction for a time. "Let's part company," Abraham said. Abraham even let Lot have first choice of the land for his own herds.

Sometimes people need to part company for a while. Can you think of a time when deciding to play apart for a while would have helped you?

Abraham let Lot have first choice. And Lot was selfish. Lot chose the very best land, in the valley, and took his herds there. Abraham turned away into the hills, where there wasn't as much water, and where the grass wasn't as thick. But there was still plenty of grass and water for his herds.

God spoke to Abraham after Lot had left. He told Abraham not to be discouraged. "All the land that you see I will give to you and your children, forever."

Even though Lot took the best land, Abraham was satisfied. He knew he had done what was right. And Abraham knew that God was pleased with him. God would take care of him, and be with him forever.

If you gave a friend first choice of something you were quarreling about, and he took the thing you wanted, how would you feel? Would you rather have kept on quarreling? How would you feel about yourself if you did what Abraham did with Lot? Proud? Ashamed? Or how?

Action Idea

Three themes introduced in the talkables provide a basis for simple follow-up. First, there was exploration of the feelings for those who were quarreling. Except for normal bickering, these are uncomfortable feelings for children as well as adults. Then there were two possible solutions to a quarrel: separate for a time, or offer to let the other person have first choice of whatever you are quarreling over (which TV show to watch, a toy both want to play with, and so on). A simple way to help your children is to play a variation of "What If . . ." with them. Choose several common situations that stimulate quarreling around your house. Make the children a "panel of experts," and let the parents (or one parent and an older child) role play (spontaneously act out) one of these situations. Stop the role play, and let your children tell you how to solve the problem. Let them act out the solution they suggest, or tell you how to act it out.

And do take time together to thank God that he does take care of us and love us, so we can choose his ways without fear that we might lose out on something important.

God Makes a Promise
Genesis 15:1–21

Background

The covenant which God made with Abraham is the key to our adult understanding of the Old Testament. In Genesis 12, and again in Genesis 15 and 17, God promised Abraham's offspring the land of Palestine as their possession, and a special relationship with the Lord as their heritage. The books of history and the prophets return again and again to God's statement of his purpose in these key chapters, culminating in the birth of Jesus from Abraham's line to be the Savior not only of Israel, but of the world.

This great theological understanding of the covenant is beyond the understanding of children six to eight years old, to whom this retelling of the story is geared. Instead, the story is retold to pick up another emphasis given to the covenant in the New Testament book of Hebrews: an emphasis that tells us God made his promise, and confirmed the promise by an oath (covenant) "so that, by two unchangeable things in which it is impossible for God to lie, we who have fled to take hold on the hope offered to us [in Jesus] may be greatly encouraged" (6:18).

How good it is to know that you and I—and our children—have a God who cannot lie. His words to us are sure, and his promises will never fail. It is because of God's character as a completely trustworthy person that we can trust him so confidently.

Paragraphs 20 and 38 note that children will at times have trouble sticking to the truth. We can help our children realize the importance of telling the truth to us by helping them see how important it is that our God is a truthful and trustworthy Person.

The Story Retold

Abraham was about seventy-five years old when God told him to leave his home and move to a new country. Abraham did what God told him. He took his wife, Sarah, and his herds and his cattle and the people who worked for him, and they traveled for weeks and weeks. Finally they came to the land of Palestine. They had arrived in the special land God said He would give to Abraham and to his children!

Abraham traveled over the land and had many adventures. But one thing Abraham didn't have. Abraham didn't have any children! How could Abraham inherit the land for his family if he didn't *have* any family?

Do you know anyone who is seventy-five or eighty years old? They're too old to be mothers or fathers; they're old enough to be grandfathers and great-grandfathers. Do you think Abraham felt happy being so old and not having any children? How do you think Abraham felt when God talked about children Abraham didn't have? What do you suppose Abraham thought about that kind of talk?

We know that Abraham was very unhappy about not having children. Once when God promised to reward Abraham, Abraham complained to God. "O Lord," Abraham complained, "what can you give me, since I remain childless?" Nothing seemed as important to Abraham as the children he was too old to have.

But God spoke to Abraham and made a promise. "You will have a son of your own." God told Abraham to look up into the night sky. "See if you can count the stars."

Abraham looked up. The sky was filled with all the stars we can see today—far more than anyone could ever count.

And then God said something amazing to Abraham. "You will have a son, and he will have children. Your family will become so large that it will be impossible to count them!"

How do you think Abraham felt when he heard God say that? Abraham was very old. Do you think it was hard or easy for Abraham to believe what God said about him still having children? Why?

The Bible tells us, "Abraham did believe God."

Abraham was sure that God was powerful enough to make Abraham able to have a son. Most of all, Abraham was sure that God would never lie. Abraham trusted God, and God was pleased with Abraham.

How does it make you feel to know that God will never lie to you either? Can you think of someone who has told you a lie, and you found out about it later? How did that make you feel about that person? Will it be easy to trust him again, or not? Why?

Let's thank God that He is someone we can always trust. And let's ask God to help us be like Him, so others will be able to trust us, too.

Action Idea

To stress the trustworthiness of God, let your child do his own "promise search." Third-graders are old enough for a Bible of their own, and can find promises there, or in your Sunday school literature. Or suggest that your child select one of the following four verses: Hebrews 13:5; Zechariah 8:8; Jeremiah 33:11; Isaiah 41:10.

Your child can then make a promise poster for his or her room, or for the family.

Also, the next time your child strays seriously from the truth, talk about this Bible study. Remind your child how important it is to be the kind of person others can trust. As God's people, we want to be like him. We learn how to please God and to choose the right by remembering the kind of Person that God is.

Abraham Talks to God about Sodom
Genesis 18:16–33

Background

The Genesis report of Abraham's conversation with God over the destruction of Sodom is rich in insights for us. God shares with Abraham his intention to destroy the city. Abraham hesitantly questions the Lord. Would God not spare the city for the sake of 50 righteous persons? For 45? For 40? 30? 20? 10? God listens patiently to Abraham, and each time promises to spare the city for the sake of the diminishing number of righteous persons.

In the end, however, only one righteous person—Lot—is found in the city. So God rescues Lot and his family before the destruction comes.

What are the lessons here for us? For one thing, we cannot be more compassionate than God. Abraham's concern was commendable. But God showed himself more concerned than Abraham for the individual.

There is also an important lesson for parents and children in God's gracious response to Abraham. God overlooked what he might have taken as an affront. Why, Abraham dared to question him! Instead of being angry, God patiently listened and explained. God, the truly Good Parent, encouraged dialogue with this child of his.

For his part, Abraham was hesitant and respectful. He questioned, but did so politely. There was no rebelliousness or challenge in Abraham's attitude.

We want just this kind of communication in our families. We want our children to feel free to approach us, to question, and try to understand. We want to avoid the tragic mistake of lashing out as though they had no right to question us. When we are patient we help them avoid a rebellious, angry attitude. This simple Genesis story not only teaches us much about the compassion of God, but also provides a model which helps parents and children talk through family issues which may be in dispute.

One final thing. The passage gives us even more confidence in prayer. God is never angry when we come to him, to express our concerns as well as our needs, our doubts as well as our praise. Paragraph 55 especially deals with this subject.

The Story Retold

God had spoken to Abraham in his homeland, and told Abraham to move to a new land. Abraham listened to God, and traveled with his family to the land of Palestine, the country we call Israel today. In the years that Abraham lived in Palestine, God spoke to him several times. Abraham was just like God's own child, and God was like Abraham's Father.

Then one day the Lord told Abraham something He was about to do. One of the cities in Palestine, called Sodom, was a very wicked city. "Their sin is terrible," God told Abraham. And God told Abraham He was going to look over the city of Sodom one more time—and then destroy it.

Abraham stood there and thought about what God said. He thought very hard, and his brow wrinkled. He wanted to say something to God. But Abraham wasn't sure if he should. You see, Abraham didn't think what God was planning was fair. But how could Abraham say something like that to God?

Have you ever wanted to tell your parents or a teacher you think something they're going to do isn't fair? Can you tell us about it? (Share an experience from your own childhood, or a similar experience as an adult.) Is it easy or hard for you to tell an adult you don't think something they're doing is fair? Why? How do you think Abraham felt? Do you think he'll talk to God about it or not? Why?

Abraham felt worried. Would God be angry if Abraham spoke up? Well, Abraham knew that God loved him. So finally Abraham went up to the Lord and he blurted out what he was thinking.

"God, what if there are fifty good people in that wicked city? Lord, that wouldn't be fair! You wouldn't kill the good people with the sinners, would You? I think You ought to let everyone live if there are just fifty good people there."

How do you suppose God felt when Abraham said he wasn't being fair? What do you think God will probably do? Do you think maybe there was a better way for Abraham to tell God what was bothering him? Let's see if we can think of another way to say what Abraham felt. Let the children give suggestions. Add yours as well. Stress Abraham's freedom to express his feelings without accusing God of unfairness. For instance, Abraham might have said, "Lord, I know you are always fair. But I feel upset about destroying Sodom. There may be some good people there as well as sinners. What are you going to do about the good people?" It is not good to accuse.

Even though Abraham seemed to accuse God of being unfair, God didn't get angry. Instead He told Abraham, "If I find fifty good people there, I won't destroy the city."

But Abraham still wasn't happy. "Lord, please don't be angry with me now," Abraham said. "But what if there are only forty-five good people there? Will you destroy the whole city because there are five less than fifty?"

God was very patient. "If I find forty-five good people there," God promised, "I will not destroy the city."

Abraham still wasn't satisfied. He kept right on talking. Abraham asked what about forty people? And thirty? And twenty? And ten?

Do you think it's good if children keep on talking with their parents when they don't think something is fair? Why do you suppose God kept listening to Abraham? (You might note that Abraham was really worried and upset. Arguing just to argue is one thing. When a child, or person like Abraham really cares, then it's good for parents and others to be patient.)

God knew that Abraham was really worried about any good people in Sodom. God cared about any good people there too. So God was very patient. He didn't get angry at Abraham, but listened to Abraham carefully.

Finally Abraham was satisfied. God promised not to destroy the city if even ten good people lived there.

Talking it out with God made Abraham feel much better. And God had listened patiently, and had not been angry at all.

What are some of the things you like to talk out with mom or dad? Things that don't seem fair, or that you worry about? Is there anything mom or dad does that makes it hard for you to talk with us? Is there anything we can do to make it easier for you to talk with us? (Assure your child that you want to be like God, to listen and help. Explain too that it helps adults listen when children are respectful, as Abraham was with God.)

Moms and dads aren't always as wise as God, or as good. But Abraham could have known that God would do what is right. The Bible tells us that there was only one good man in Sodom, and his name was Lot. God wouldn't destroy even one good person with the sinners He had to punish. Instead God rescued Lot, and let Lot and his family escape from Sodom before the city was destroyed.

We can always trust God to do what is best.

Close in prayer, asking God to help you parents be as fair as he is, and to listen to your children when they want to talk about something important to them.

Action Idea

Make up several "listening" and "politeness" certificates. The "listening" certificates are for the children, and the "politeness" certificates for the parents. When a certificate is presented by either child or parents, the other is to make a commitment to honor it. Certificates might say something like the following:

Listening Certificate. "Good for ten minutes of careful listening. To be presented when I have a problem, or feelings that are important to me, that I want to talk about. To be honored by mom (or dad) as soon as possible."

Politeness Certificate. "Good for stopping and thinking, and then starting to talk again. To be presented when I feel I should be talked to with more respect. To be honored by (child's name) as soon as possible."

You may also want to talk over this story again when you pray together at bedtime, or as a family.

Ishmael Is Sent Away from Home
Genesis 16:1–10, 21:8–21

Background

The breakdown of a family always involves hurt and tragedy. Even when both parents are convinced a divorce is necessary, the children will suffer (see paragraphs 89 and 90). It is vital then that we be particularly sensitive to the children and to their feelings at this crucial, stressful juncture of their lives.

One difficulty many children have is that they feel guilty about the family breakup. They believe that somehow they are to blame. Or they feel neglected by the noncustodial parent. A child's contacts with one of his parents will be limited after a divorce. Most often the limited contact is with the father. Children of divorcing parents will know pain and grief, but grieving—and talking about their feelings—is the best way to recovery.

The story of Abraham and his son Ishmael has many parallels to the plight of divorcing parents today. Retelling this Bible story may help a child who has experienced the divorce of his parents. You can help him express and explore his feelings, and assure him that he is still important to God.

The Genesis account provides more information than is included in this purposeful retelling of the story. In Genesis we see the weakness of Abraham, who followed a cultural practice in having children by his wife's maid, Hagar. We also see the spitefulness and jealousy of Sarah, whose later antagonism toward Hagar and Ishmael created a bitter, acrimonious household climate. But these details, from which you and I can draw so many lessons, are not relevant to the stress felt by children of modern divorce. God's healing message to such children is a different one entirely. It is this healing message your children or stepchildren may desperately need to hear.

This Story Retold

When God spoke to Abraham and told Abraham to leave his homeland, Abraham obeyed. God was good to Abraham in the new land. And Abraham was thankful. Abraham trusted God, and usually Abraham tried to please God. But sometimes Abraham, like you and me, did wrong things. Abraham wasn't perfect, just as you and I aren't perfect.

In Abraham's day, people thought it was all right for a

man to have more than one wife. When Abraham's wife Sarah did not have any children, she wanted Abraham to have another wife* so Sarah could have children around her home.

But when Abraham did what Sarah wanted, Sarah wasn't happy. When a boy was born, and named Ishmael, Sarah was even angry. She didn't like Ishmael and she didn't like Ishmael's mother, either.

Do you think it's hard or easy for people to live together in the same home when they don't like each other? What are some of the things people might say or do then? How do you think people in that kind of family feel? How do you think the children feel?

Abraham's family lived together unhappily for many years. No one was very happy. But Abraham loved his son Ishmael very much. And Ishmael loved his father.

Then, when Ishmael was about twelve years old, Abraham's first wife Sarah had a baby boy too. She named him Isaac. Sarah loved Isaac, and she didn't like it when Abraham played with Ishmael. Sometimes Ishmael teased Isaac, and Sarah didn't like that either.

Finally Sarah said to Abraham, "You've got to get rid of Ishmael and his mother. Send them away."

How do you suppose Abraham felt? Since Abraham loved Ishmael very much, did he want to send Ishmael away from him? What do you suppose Abraham did? What do you suppose Ishmael felt and did?

Well, Abraham was very upset. How could he ever send Ishmael away! Why, Abraham loved Ishmael. Probably Abraham felt angry at Sarah for suggesting he send Ishmael away.

Then God spoke to Abraham. "Do what Sarah says this time. Send Ishmael away." It seemed hard.

God had made a promise. God promised to take care of Ishmael Himself. "I will make him a great people (nation)," God promised, "because he is your son." The next morning Abraham did what God told him. He sent Ishmael and his mother away.

---

* (Older boys and girls may understand that Hagar was a servant. For younger children, it's better to refer to her as another wife.)

How do you suppose Ishmael felt when he was sent away? Was he angry? Sad? Did he think it was his fault, or did Ishmael blame someone else? Do you suppose Ishmael liked his feelings? How long do you suppose he felt this way?

Abraham felt very sad. He loved his boy, and he didn't want him to be gone.

Do you think your father (mother) felt anything like Abraham did when the judge decided you couldn't live with him anymore? How do you think your father (mother) felt? How did you feel about being sent away? Do you suppose Ishmael understood he was loved, even when he couldn't live with his father any longer?

Sometimes hard things happen to people. The hard things don't mean that we're not loved. They don't mean that we're being punished, or that we've done anything wrong. Sometimes hard things just happen, like they did for Abraham and Ishmael. But Abraham felt good about one thing. God would take care of Ishmael, even if Abraham could not. God would always be with Ishmael, so then Ishmael would be all right, and grow up strong and well. When bad things happen we need to remember, like Abraham, that God still loves us. God will take care of us, whatever happens. God will never leave us alone.

Action Idea

If your child has shared thoughts and feelings through the telling of this story, help him express those same feelings to God in prayer. Be ready to talk when he or she brings the subject up again. It is important for a child to talk through his anxieties and other feelings, and the subject may come up again and again.

Jacob's Dream
Genesis 28:10–22

Background

Nighttime fears are common in younger children, as are frightening dreams (see paragraphs 27 and 30). They need reassurance that it's all right to be frightened. And they need reassurance that their fears are groundless. God, who is more real than any nightmare, is with us even in the dark.

In this retelling of the story of Jacob's dream, much of the background is left out. This is to help your child of six to eight (more likely to fear the dark and to have nightmares than are older children) focus on the specific issue of darkness and dreams.

The experience was an enriching one for Jacob. For the first time this grandson of Abraham had a direct experience with God. Despite his fear, Jacob would look back on this experience as a vital one for his own personal spiritual journey.

How good it is to know that even something as uncomfortable to our children as nighttime fears can be used by God to bring a sense of his own presence and his loving care.

The Story Retold

Jacob, one of God's Old Testament people, was on a journey. Jacob traveled all day, hurrying across an empty land. There were no towns or people where Jacob walked. How Jacob must have rushed, walking faster and faster, hoping to find someplace where he could stay at night.

Even though Jacob hurried, the sun seemed to hurry more. The sun kept on going down. It got lower and lower and lower. Finally Jacob knew. He was going to have to sleep out all night, in the dark, alone.

How do you suppose you'd feel if you had to sleep outside alone in the dark? Jacob was grown up. But do you think he felt a little afraid? (Tell of a time as an adult when you felt anxious or afraid.) There was nothing there in the dark to hurt Jacob. But even when we know we're safe, we can feel afraid.

We don't know just how Jacob felt there in the dark. But finally he used a stone for a pillow, and fell asleep. And when he was asleep, Jacob had a dream!

Do you remember any of your dreams? What's the best dream you ever had? What is the most frightening dream you ever had? (Share a nightmare of your own, and tell how you felt when you woke up.)

In Jacob's dream, he saw a great stairway. Its bottom rested on the earth, but its top seemed to reach all the way up to heaven. Looking carefully, Jacob saw God's angels going up and down the stairs.

And there, at the top, Jacob saw a figure he knew must be the Lord! The figure spoke to him. "I am the God of your grandfather Abraham and your father Isaac," God said. Then God made Jacob a promise. "I am with you and will watch over you wherever you go."

When Jacob woke up, he remembered his dream. Even though it was a good dream, Jacob felt afraid. Only later would Jacob remember God's promise to him.

What helps you most when you wake up from a dream and feel afraid? (Think of things like a parent sitting with him or her, a picture, a light in the room, remembering God is near, etc.) What do you think helped Jacob that night when he was alone?

When morning came, Jacob thought and thought about his dream. Then he remembered what God had said to him. He remembered God's promise. "Since God will be with me and watch over me," Jacob said, "the Lord will be my God forever."

Then Jacob gave the place where he had slept a special name. He called it "Bethel," which means "God's house." Jacob would always remember that night. From then on Jacob knew God was always with him, to watch over him.

How would you feel at night if God promised you what he promised Jacob: "I am with you and will watch over you wherever you go"? (Share a time when remembering God was with you helped you with your own fears.) It's not wrong to be afraid. But it helps us when we're afraid to remember that God is with us, and that God is watching over us. (You may want to show your child God's promise to all believers, recorded in Hebrews 13:5. This is the same promise of God's presence, especially for your child.)

After you've finished the story thank God that He does watch over us, and is with us even when we sometimes feel afraid.

Action Idea

It's important when we deal with children's fears not to add to their anxieties. What they need is reassurance and encouragement. And they need a basis on which to build a core of trust. We do not help them if we *insist* they trust, or make them feel guilty because they still fear.

The best way to help our children with nighttime fears or nightmares is to be there when they need us, and to share calmly our own assurance that God is with them. This reality is not likely to sink in immediately. But with calm and loving repetition, the message of God's presence *will* take root. Our children's fears will gradually be quieted by the Lord.

You may also want to suggest your child set up his or her own "Bethel" reminder. Let him select several stones and glue them together to make a pillar, or pyramid (cf. Gen. 28:18). The stone pillar can be glued to a construction paper base, and the verse "I am with you and will watch over you" (Gen. 28:15) printed on it.

It would not be out of line to have a small nightlight over the pillar, so that your child can see it when he goes to sleep, and if he wakes up at night.

Joseph and His Brothers
Genesis 37:1–38

Background

The stories of the Bible bluntly outline all our human weaknesses. It is against the background of our pettiness and foolishness that the goodness and the wisdom of God are most clearly seen.

One of the stories which mirrors human fallibility most clearly is the story of Joseph and his brothers. Reading it in Genesis 37 we see the folly of the favoritism Jacob showed his youngest son. We also see the insensitivity of Joseph. He apparently took no wrongful pride in his privilege, but he did not seem to realize how hurt and jealous his brothers were. Surely telling them of a dream in which he saw himself exalted over them and his parents was woefully insensitive. But the folly of Jacob, and the insensitivity of young Joseph, were no excuse for the brothers' behavior. They nursed their jealousy and anger, and finally plotted against their young brother. Their acts of sin were completely unjustified, no matter what their complaint.

Yet God used these human weaknesses. And God redeemed the situation. The brothers sold Joseph into exile in Egypt. There God finally brought him to a place of national influence. When famine swept the Middle East, God used Joseph to provide a place of safety for the family that had rejected him.

Today we are amazed at the wisdom of God and his goodness. How wonderful that God is able to take us as we are, and still work out his good purposes through us. How wonderful that in the process he forgives our sins, and in the end changes our attitudes and character, even as he finally changed Joseph's brothers.

It is also wonderful that these stories of the Bible serve as mirrors for us and our children. If your children quarrel and bicker, if they are troubled by jealousy, or if they need help learning how to relate to other boys and girls, the events reported here provide helpful insights.

This story is retold with *talkables* that are suitable for children between six and eleven, although older children will grasp more. For background on the themes touched on, see paragraphs 13, 36, 72, and 73.

The Story Retold

Families aren't always happy. Sometimes parents or children say things that hurt others. Or we do something that makes others upset. There's a story in the Bible about a family who did things that hurt each other too. While I tell the story, see if anything that happened in this Bible family has happened in our family.

The father of this family was named Jacob. He had many children, and eleven sons. His youngest son was named Joseph. Jacob loved Joseph very much. In fact, he did things that made Joseph's brothers think that Joseph was their father's favorite. So the brothers became very jealous. Then one day Jacob went out and bought a beautiful new set of clothes for Joseph. Jacob didn't get anything at all for his other sons!

Have you ever felt that someone else was mom's or dad's favorite? How did you feel inside then? (Share a time when you have felt left out in favor of someone else, and talk about your feelings then.) What did mom or dad do that made you feel that way? Sometimes parents don't really have favorites. Sometimes mom and dad just don't think how it might seem to you if someone else gets something special and you don't. (It's appropriate if your child has told about an incident to apologize and to reassure him or her that you really do love him.)

Joseph's brothers were hurt when their father showed that Joseph was his favorite. And they were angry at Joseph. It wasn't really Joseph's fault. But his brothers began to hate Joseph. They wouldn't even speak a kind word to him. They were very jealous of Joseph and felt angry at him all the time.

Why do you think the brothers were angry at Joseph? Have you ever felt angry at someone in the family because he or she seemed to be the favorite? Can you tell us about it? Joseph's brothers showed their anger by not speaking to Joseph, or by saying mean things to him. Do you suppose that helped them or Joseph? What might they have done? Do you think it would have helped if they talked with Jacob and told him how they felt? Why, or why not? If you ever feel jealous of or angry with one of your brothers or sisters because you think he or she is getting favorite treatment, you can tell us how you feel and we'll talk about it.

Joseph must have known how his brothers felt about him. He must have known too that he really was his father Jacob's favorite. But Joseph didn't seem to think about how his brothers felt. In fact, when Joseph had a dream, he did a very foolish thing. The dream was from God, and it promised that one day Joseph would be a great man. The dream promised that Joseph's whole family would bow down to him in respect. But instead of keeping the dream to himself, Joseph hurried right out and told the dream to his brothers. "Someday," he told them, "you and even my parents will bow to me in respect!"

How do you think his brothers felt when Joseph told them his dream? Were they happy for Joseph? How do you think you would have felt? Why? Do you think Joseph cared about his brothers' feelings? They had been mean to Joseph. Would telling about the dream help them stop being mean? What do you think Joseph could have done to help his brothers not be so upset and angry? Would it have helped if Joseph had said he was sorry they were upset, and offered to share what Jacob gave him?

There may not have been anything Joseph could do to help his brothers feel better. Really, they were upset because they thought their father didn't care about them. But Joseph didn't need to rub it in by telling his dream. That only made Joseph's brothers hate him more.

But then Joseph's brothers did a terrible thing. They didn't just say mean things to Joseph. The brothers were taking care of sheep in distant fields. When Joseph came from home with a message, they grabbed their brother. They took the special robe Jacob had given Joseph and dipped it in sheep's blood. Then they sold their brother Joseph to be a slave in Egypt. They told their father Joseph had been killed by wild animals.

It was one thing to be angry with Joseph, and to talk mean to him. That was bad enough. But to sell their brother to strangers was a very, very bad thing!

When we're angry or jealous of someone in the family, what might be the right way to show our feelings? What is the best thing to do when we're angry? What are some things we should never do, no matter how angry we are? (Talk about limits, making sure physical aggression is clearly off limits to your boys and girls as a way to express anger or jealousy.)

All the members of this family had been foolish and wrong. And now everyone was unhappy. Jacob, who had showed favoritism to Joseph, thought his son was dead. He wept and cried and no one could comfort him.

Joseph, who hadn't thought about how his brothers felt and had just made them more jealous, was a slave in Egypt. He was lonely, and positive he would never see his family again.

The brothers were sorry when they saw how unhappy Jacob was. And they must have felt guilty when they thought of the bad thing they had done to Joseph.

The way this family acted had now made them all feel miserable and sad.

But God loved Jacob and Joseph. And God loved the brothers too. In Egypt, Joseph became rich and famous. Years later when there was no rain, and food would not grow in Palestine where Jacob lived, the brothers came to Egypt looking for food. Joseph found them there, and Joseph was able to see to it that they had all the food they needed to eat. In fact, the whole family moved to Egypt, and Jacob saw his son Joseph again! Joseph forgave his brothers, and gave them all land to live on while they stayed in Egypt.

How much happier the family was then, when everyone forgave each other for their hurts. How good God was to help them love each other in the end.

When we're jealous or angry at members of our family, we want to remember this. God will help us forgive them.

When we do, everyone will be much happier, because God's ways are the best ways for us all.

Action Idea

Work with your children to develop "what to do" lists. The three lists you can develop are:

*What should I do if I feel hurt and jealous of my brother or sister?

*What should I do if I think my brother or sister is jealous or angry at me?

*What ways to show anger should never be allowed in our family? Supplement your children's ideas with suggestions found in paragraphs 13, 36, 72, 73, and 74. And encourage them. Just as God helped Joseph's family work out their problem in the end, God will help your family members learn to love each other too.

Joseph in Egypt
Genesis 39–41

Background

One source of a sense of self-confidence and achievement is the knowledge that we have made right choices, even when it was hard. This is a difficult lesson to learn. But it is an important one. As Jesus taught, faithfulness in small things prepares us for larger responsibilities (Matt. 25:23). Our boys and girls grow to healthy maturity by experiencing a series of situations in which they learn to make right choices—even when they are hard ones.

One of the most admirable characters in the Bible illustrates this principle clearly. Joseph was not without faults (see the previous story). But Joseph in Egypt did commit himself to do what was right. He did not become discouraged when things went wrong, and God was able to bless and to use Joseph later in a wonderful way. It is clear from the biblical record that the motivating force in Joseph's life was a desire to do what pleased God and what was fair to other people (Gen. 39:10).

In the telling of this story, boys and girls from six to eleven are helped to think about their choices and their motives. They are helped to see that it is always best to trust God and do the right thing, even when it's hard.

The Story Retold

Joseph was a stranger in the land of Egypt. He was a slave. Joseph's mother and father and all his family were thousands of miles away. And Joseph was only seventeen years old!

What do you think was hardest for Joseph in Egypt? How do you think Joseph probably felt when he remembered he was just a slave?

Joseph must have felt lonely and helpless at times. What could a slave do? What would become of him? But even when Joseph felt sad and unhappy, he tried to do his best.

Joseph worked for a man named Potiphar (pot-i-far). Joseph worked hard for his master, and soon Potiphar began to trust Joseph. God was with Joseph, too, and Joseph was successful in whatever he did. Soon Potiphar put Joseph in charge of everything he owned. Joseph must have felt good about that. He tried to do the right thing even when he didn't feel happy, and God had helped him do well.

What are some of the things you do well? What do you do that makes you feel good about yourself—things you're proud of? (Add several things your child is accomplishing that make you feel proud of him or her.)

Joseph must have felt as proud and satisfied as you do when you do something well. God had helped Joseph, even though he was still a slave.

But then a terrible thing happened. Potiphar's wife asked Joseph to do something he knew was wrong. Joseph refused. But his master's wife kept urging him. Again and again Joseph said no. "My master trusts me," Joseph said. "How could I do such a wicked thing and sin against God?"

No matter who asked Joseph to do something wrong, Joseph would not. He was determined to do the right thing. He would not disappoint his master, and he would not sin against God.

Are there times when you want to do something you know is wrong? (Tell about a temptation of your own when it's hard to do the right thing.) Who do you suppose is most disappointed if you do something you know is wrong? God knows how we feel, and he wants to help us choose what's right. And I trust you to do what's right, even when it's hard.

No matter how much Potiphar's wife urged Joseph to do the wrong thing, Joseph wouldn't do it. He would do what pleased God. He would not disappoint his master, who trusted him.

Usually when we do what is right, good things happen to us. But sometimes we do the right thing and something bad happens to us. Perhaps other people don't understand. Maybe our friends get angry at us. Or maybe we get blamed anyway.

Have you ever done something you know is right, and something bad happened to you anyway? Tell us about it. How did you feel when that happened? Were you still glad you had done the right thing? Why, or why not?

Well, Joseph did the right thing. But Potiphar's wife went to her husband and accused Joseph of doing something wrong! Potiphar was very angry. He didn't listen to Joseph. Instead he had Joseph thrown into prison for life!

But the Bible says that the Lord was still with Joseph, even in prison. God was pleased with Joseph. And Joseph was still glad he had done the right thing.

In the end, even though Joseph had felt hurt and upset to be in prison, God had a good reason for what happened. In prison Joseph met some officials of Egypt's king. Later, when the king of Egypt had a dream he couldn't understand, one official remembered that God had helped Joseph understand dreams. The king of Egypt called for Joseph, and Joseph explained the dream to the king. The king freed Joseph and made him a ruler of Egypt.

Joseph had kept on doing what is right, even when it was hard. And God rewarded Joseph in the end.

What do you suppose God has planned for you to do or be when you grow up? What would you like to be? When we choose to do what is right, even when it's hard, we're like Joseph. We are getting ready for the special future God has planned for us.

Thank God that he has a good future planned for your children, and that they can prepare for God's best right now, by choosing to do what is right.

Action Idea

The story of Joseph's experiences in Egypt is an exciting Bible narrative, covering chapters 39–41 in Genesis. Your children can be helped to know and identify with this great Old Testament saint, whose faith was so strong. Read one chapter together for three consecutive evenings or at meal times. Talk about Joseph's feelings at each stage of his adventure. And talk about how confidence in God helps us to choose right even if good things do not seem to result right away.

Moses Returns to Egypt
Exodus 4:1–17

Background

Most children are familiar with the story of Moses, as they are with the other Bible stories retold in this family handbook. They know about his birth, his discovery in a basketboat by the princess of Egypt, and about his experience with the burning bush. They know about his contest with Pharaoh and the plagues. They have seen pictures of Moses, beard rippling in the breeze, standing on Sinai with the Ten Commandments given Israel by God. Perhaps we're all used to seeing Moses as the great leader of God's people.

Moses *was* a great leader. But Moses was not a self-confident man. In fact, Moses had the fears of all timid people and seems to have been painfully shy at the thought of returning to Egypt, to appear before God's people there.

But God is used to working with weak people. It is often in our very weaknesses that his power and goodness are most perfectly displayed.

In God's dialogue with the hesitant Moses, recorded in Exodus 3 and 4, your shy child can find encouragement. God does understand and will help him or her.

The Story Retold

You remember the story of Moses and the burning bush, don't you? Yes, God spoke to Moses then. God told Moses to go back to Egypt, and free God's people from slavery. *How do you suppose Moses felt then? Would he be more frightened or excited? Why? How do you suppose you would have felt if that had happened to you?*

Moses didn't feel excited when he heard what God wanted him to do. Moses didn't even feel happy. Instead, Moses was worried and upset. He was afraid. What would the people there think if Moses tried to talk to them about God? How could Moses get up in front of them and tell about what happened?

So instead of saying, "Yes, Lord, I'm ready to go," Moses hesitated. "But God, what if they won't believe me?" Moses asked.

Have you ever felt like Moses . . . kind of afraid and worried and upset when you have to talk in front of others? (If you've had similar feelings, share them with your child.) Why do you think speaking up is so hard for Moses and other people? What do you suppose worried Moses most?

God knew that Moses was shy about going back to Egypt. But Moses was the best person for the job God wanted to be done. God could help Moses be successful, even though Moses felt shy.

Then Moses asked, "What if they won't listen to me?" God tried to help him. God gave Moses special powers to prove to the people back in Egypt that God had sent him. Moses' long shepherd's staff would turn into a snake when Moses threw it on the ground. And Moses could turn fresh water into blood. But Moses was still afraid. Sometimes even when we know we can do special things we still feel shy.

So Moses said to God, "O Lord, I've never been able to speak well. I talk slow, and sometimes I even stutter." Moses was so worried he'd seem foolish. Moses was worried that he wouldn't be able to speak up if he tried.

What do you suppose God will say to Moses now? Do you think there is anything that can help Moses feel better? What helps you most when you feel shy or timid?

God wasn't angry at Moses. Instead He reminded Moses of something important. "Who gave people mouths to speak with anyway?" (Of course, the Lord did!) And then God made Moses a promise. "Now go; I will help you speak and teach you what to say."

That was a very special promise. Do you think it made Moses feel better? Do you suppose he wasn't shy or timid any more? How do you think Moses felt now?

God gave Moses a wonderful promise. "I will be with you," God told him. "I will help you speak." But Moses still felt afraid. Moses was still shy, and he was still worried.

"O Lord," Moses said, "Please send someone else to do it." When a person is shy, sometimes it is hard even if he or she knows God is there to help.

God was not happy with Moses. But God still wanted Moses for this special job. So to help Moses even more, God said that Moses' brother, Aaron, could go with him to help.

It was hard for Moses. But he did go back to Egypt as God told him to do. There God did help Moses as He had promised. God helped Moses, a very shy man, become one of our greatest Bible heroes.

Action Idea

Shyness is very painful for children and for adults. And shyness doesn't just go away. There's no quick solution through advice ("Just speak up, dear") or urging ("Why not go next door and meet the new neighbors"). Only time, and a number of experiences with other children and adults (see paragraph 34), will help your child feel more comfortable.

What this Bible story is designed to do is to provide the transforming gift of hope. Children, like you and me, need to be sure that God and others will be patient. They need to feel we are not discouraged with them. Your shy child may want to hear this Bible story often. As you tell it, avoid giving advice and avoid urging special action. Instead, let the encouraging message of Moses—a timid man who becomes a great leader—create confidence that God will help your boy or girl, too.

God's People Rebel
Numbers 13:26–14:25

Background

The New Testament book of Hebrews returns to this incident, with warning. "Today, if you hear his voice, do not harden your hearts" (4:7). God had promised his Old Testament people a home-land in Palestine. God had freed them from slavery in Egypt and led them safely through the desert. He had given them his law, and showed his presence with them daily in unmistakable ways. These people ate the manna God supplied daily, and the Lord's fiery pillar stood over their camp. They had every reason to know and trust God. Yet, when God commanded them to go into the Promised Land and to take it from the strong nations that lived there, Israel refused. Fearful, unwilling to trust God, they rebelled against his command.

The story highlights the importance of obedience and the dangers of disobedience. God did know what was best for his people. He wanted to bless them. But they refused to obey and suffered the tragic consequences. See paragraph 66.

We and our children need to learn the lesson taught in this event. Obedience is important. God's way is best. We disobey at our risk, for there are always tragic consequences of disobedience to God.

The Story Retold

"Good news! Good news!" That was what Caleb and Joshua shouted when they came back to the Israelite camp.

The Israelites were camped outside the land God had promised to give them. For years they had been slaves in Egypt. But God had sent Moses to be their leader. And God had rescued them from Egypt! God brought them safely to the edge of the Promised Land. Every day God gave them special food to eat, called manna. Now God told them to go in and take the land the Lord was ready to give them.

No wonder Caleb and Joshua cried out, "Good news!" They had gone to scout the new land. Now they were so excited! It was a wonderful land. The fields were rich, and the crops that grew there were the best Caleb and Joshua had ever seen.

But when Caleb and Joshua got back, they found other scouts had returned with bad news! The crops were rich. But the people who lived in that country were very strong. They had powerful armies, and they looked as tall as giants.

Caleb and Joshua were surprised. Yes, the people of the

land were tall and strong. But God would certainly fight for His people. Caleb stood up and said to everyone, "We should go up and take possession of the land, for we can certainly do it!"

How do you suppose God's people felt when Caleb told them to go up to the land and take it? Why do you suppose Caleb was so sure they could do it?

God had told His people to take the land. God had promised He would be with them. But except for Moses and Aaron, and for Joshua and Caleb, everyone was afraid! "God just wants us to get killed in battle," some of the Israelites said. "Let's go back and be slaves in Egypt," others said. Before long, not one person there would obey God and go up to take the land.

Moses and Aaron were so upset they actually cried! Joshua and Caleb begged the people. "This is a wonderful land. God will give it to us if we only obey Him. Don't rebel against the Lord. Remember God is with us, and don't be afraid of their armies."

But the people of Israel wouldn't listen to them. They refused to obey God. They became so angry at Moses and Aaron and Joshua and Caleb, who did want to obey God, that they even talked about killing them.

Why do you suppose the Israelites wouldn't trust God and obey him? Can you think of times when it's hard for you to obey God? What do you usually do then? How do you think God felt about his disobedient people? What do you think God should do?

God was very angry. Even though He had done many wonderful things for His people, they refused to trust Him. But Moses prayed and asked God to forgive them.

God did forgive them. Still, these people who would not obey the Lord could never live in the Promised Land. Only when we trust God and obey Him can He give us the good things He wants us to have.

Instead, those people went back out into the desert. They traveled over the desert for thirty-eight years. Finally, when all the grown-ups who had rebelled against God died, their children went back to the Promised Land, just as God had promised.

When you and I obey God today, He is able to give us the good things He wants us to have. When we disobey, God will forgive us. But we may miss out on good things.

Action Idea

From a map in the back of a family Bible, trace or draw an outline of the Promised Land. Color in or cut out green construction paper to represent Palestine. Use yellow to represent desert all around its borders. Attach the map to a family bulletin board or corkboard.

With your six- to eight-year-olds, make up a list of ways they want to obey God. Use only the issues your children suggest. Then make up a small symbol for each issue, small enough to be glued to the head of a thumb tack.

Let your child place tacks either inside the green Promised Land area (which shows he is obeying God), or in the yellow wilderness area (which shows he needs to begin to obey God).

Praise your children for their acts of obedience. And be available to talk about things they find hard to do. Plan together to try to keep all the tacks in the green obedience area for a whole day or a week.

The Death of Moses
Deuteronomy 32:48–52; 34:1–11

Background

A death in the family brings grief to children. And it raises questions (see paragraph 88). When adults refuse to talk with boys and girls about the death of loved ones, children are left alone to deal with their grief, their doubts, and their fears.

Because the death of loved ones is a time of unique stress for children and for adults, several stories in this *Handbook* are related to dying. This Bible story is about the death of an older adult, who has lived a full life span. The story on page 340 focuses on unexpected death, and deals with a child's natural fears about his own dying. Stories on pages 320 and 326 explore what happens after death, and affirm our Christian hope.

Death brings stress to adults as well. Still, we need God's help to enable us to express our grief to our children, and to help them with theirs. Together we can find our Lord's healing touch in the memory of God's goodness to our loved one, and in the assurance that one day we will be together again in the Lord.

The Story Retold

Moses was very old now. His hair and his beard were white. He must have been tired. For many years Moses had worked hard, leading God's people, Israel. Moses had many hard times. He had good times too. And now, with Moses' work finished, everyone loved him. They all trusted Moses, and knew that Moses loved them.

God loved Moses too. Moses had been God's friend, and faithful to the Lord. But God knew it was time for Moses to die.

One day God told Moses that he was to die soon. We don't know how Moses felt. But Moses knew that God would be with him. So Moses wasn't afraid. I suppose Moses felt sad about leaving his people, because they were his family. In fact, Moses called everyone together to say good-by. Moses blessed them and promised them God's best.

And then it was time.

Alone, Moses began to climb up into the hills. He climbed on, up toward the top of Mount Nebo. But Moses was not really alone. God was with him.

God let Moses look out from the top of Mount Nebo. Across the river, in the valley, Moses could see the land God had promised to His people. Moses knew that soon the family he was leaving would be there, in the Promised Land.

Moses must have been happy then. Moses would miss his people. And they would miss Moses. But Moses knew that God would take care of the people he left behind.

Moses died then.

He was an old man.

Back in the camp all the people of Israel wept and cried. They had loved Moses very much. For thirty days they mourned Moses, and their hearts hurt with grief.*

But finally the time of grieving and weeping came to an

end. God helped to heal their hurt. Then they could remember Moses and talk about Moses without feeling quite so sad.**

God buried Moses' body there on the mountain. Moses was gone. But God would be with Moses' friends and loved ones always. One day, when Moses' friends grew old and they died too, they would be with Moses again. And with the Lord.

Action Ideas

This story is without *talkables,* for a reason. This may be a story you'll want to tell your children soon after the death of a beloved grandparent or other older family friend. At first children may grieve so much they will not want to talk. But they will sense God's healing touch in the story of Moses' death. It may not be wise to encourage children to talk at first. But your children do need to hear your voice speaking, reading with mixed sorrow and hope about dying.

You will probably find that your child will ask for the story of Moses' death often in the days and weeks following a grandparent's death. Soon your boy or girl may be ready to talk about grandpa or grandma. When they are ready, insert the following talkables when you tell the story, where indicated by asterisks (*).

*It's all right to be sad when someone we love dies. We know we'll miss that person and we hurt inside. How did you feel when grandpa (grandma) died? (Share your own feelings, and describe them as fully as you can.) It's all right to cry too. (Tell about your own tears if the child had no chance to observe you.) Even though we know God is with our grandpa (grandma), we miss him and are very sad.

**What happy things do you think Moses' people remembered about him? (Tell of some special time you remember with your own loved one, or of something special about him or her.) What happy things do you remember about grandpa (grandma)? Grandpa (grandma) was a very special person to us. Let's thank God for him and the good times we remember.

In time you may want to undertake a special project together which can be very healing. Make a "Happy Memories Book," using family pictures and your child's written accounts of good times with the loved one who has died.

Rahab's Choice
Joshua 2:1–24

Background

Rahab's story is one of the most fascinating in the Old Testament. She was a citizen of Jericho in the time of Israel's conquest. She, and all her people, had heard of Israel and feared Israel's God. No one in Jericho seems to have doubted the stories of God's power. Yet their reaction was one of antagonism and terror. They locked themselves inside their walled city, and waited, trembling.

But Rahab took a step no one else in Jericho was willing to take. When Israeli scouts entered the land, they came to Rahab's house. This pagan woman hid them, asking that when God gave Israel victory that she and her family be spared.

In this action Rahab's belief that God is real and powerful was translated into faith: she was willing to actually trust herself to the Lord.

Young children have difficulty understanding Bible terms like "faith" and "trust." Of course they "believe in God." So the story of Rahab will help them sense the underlying meaning of Christian, saving faith. Children will begin to see that faith in God means trusting oneself to him. See paragraph 122.

The Story Retold

"Israel is coming! Israel is coming!"

The soldiers of Jericho ran to close the great gates set in Jericho's giant stone wall.

Everyone else in the city ran to hide in their houses. They knew all about Israel. They had heard the stories of Israel's God. They knew the Lord had parted the waters of the Red Sea, and rescued Israel from slavery in Egypt. They knew God fought for His people, so Israel won its wars. Everyone in the city was terrified. They had no doubt at all that the Lord is God of heaven and earth.

But even though the people of Jericho knew how great God is, they decided to fight God's people.

Why do you suppose the people of Jericho wanted to fight? How do you think they felt? They knew that God is great and powerful.

They believed God is real. What do you think they might have done instead of fighting?

Everybody in Jericho was ready to fight God's people—everybody except one person. That person was a woman named Rahab. When the gates of the city were closed, two Israelites, who had come to see Jericho, were inside the city. Now the soldiers were looking for the two Israelites to kill them. But the two Israelites were inside Rahab's house, and Rahab was talking to them.

"We have all heard about the Lord," Rahab said. "The people of Jericho want to kill you. But I will hide you. Only promise me that when you take the city, I and my family can become one of you. I want to trust myself to you and your God."

Rahab's people were the enemy. Do you think God would accept Rahab? What do you think God would want the two scouts to do? God loves all people. But in the whole city, where everyone knew who God was, only Rahab was willing to trust herself to God. (You may want to share if you remember a special time when you trusted yourself to the Lord.) God will accept anyone who decides to trust him, and welcome that person into God's family.

So the men promised Rahab. When God's people took the city of Jericho, the enemy would be killed, but Rahab and her family would be safe. "Only hang a red ribbon outside your window," the scouts told her. "Then we'll know not to hurt you." Later that night Rahab helped the two Israelite scouts escape over the city wall.

Finally the Israelites attacked Jericho. God helped them, just as the people of Jericho feared. The city was destroyed and all the people in the city were killed.

All except Rahab and her family.

Rahab was safe. She became one of God's people. And Rahab trusted the Lord all her life.

Action Idea

Children in many Christian homes grow up knowing about Jesus, secure in his love as part of their first memories. They do trust themselves to the Lord, and not just know about him. But for many there is no memory of a conscious personal decision to trust.

Yet sometimes our children are troubled by a sense of sin and guilt. At such times, the story of Rahab can lend comfort, and even stimulate the decision which brings peace with God (Rom. 5:1).

Remind your child that Rahab was one of the enemies of God. But when Rahab was willing to trust herself to God, God accepted her and saved her.

Jesus came and died for us that we might be forgiven for our sins, and become members of God's family. No one who trusts himself to Jesus will ever be turned away. We have Jesus' own promise, in John 6:37: "Whoever comes to me, I will never drive away."

What a joy to be able to share this promise with our children. We can be confident that when a child is ready to respond, God will welcome him or her gladly. Trust in Jesus will never be disappointed.

Jericho Taken
Joshua 5:13–6:25

Background

Obedience flows from trust and love, not from fear. This is the basic teaching of Scripture—a teaching which is vital for us to understand as we nurture our children, and as we grow in our own relationship with God (see paragraph 66).

There is an important corollary. Obedience is necessary. The ones we trust—whether our parents when we are children, or God our whole lifetime—know far better than we what is best.

The story of Jericho illustrates this corollary truth. The familiar events there were intended by God as an object lesson for Israel. Israel must learn that obedience, even to instructions which must have seemed foolish, brings victory. Reading the story today as it is recorded in the Book of Joshua reminds us of this truth. God can be trusted to know and do what is best. Because he understands reality better than we, we are wise to obey.

The story of Jericho is one of the most familiar of Bible stories. To add interest to the familiar, and to help your children consider the lesson intended, the story is retold here in "correctable" form. That is, you will tell the story wrong, and let your boy or girl correct you when the story wanders from the well-known biblical text.

The Story Retold

"We've *got* to take the city of Jericho," Joshua was thinking. Joshua was the leader of God's people Israel. It was Joshua's job to plan the attack on the land God promised them. God would give Israel the land. But Israel would have to fight.

But how could Israel take Jericho? Jericho was a strong city, with great, high stone walls.

Joshua stood in the valley and looked up at the walled city. Well, there was only one thing the Israelite army could do. They would have to climb those walls, and fight the men who stood at the top to shoot at them with arrows and to throw down great stones.

Joshua went back to the Israelite camp and gave his orders. "Start making ladders, men," Joshua said.

What? That's not what happened. What do you remember? (Let your child tell of Joshua's meeting with the angel of the Lord, and recall God's instructions. For six days the people were to march silently around Jericho. The seventh day they were to march around it seven times, and then shout when trumpets were blown.) What do you think Joshua might have felt when God told him to do that? Had anyone ever heard of city walls falling down at a shout? Do you think it was easy for Joshua to give orders like that to the people of Israel? What would they think? Why do you suppose Joshua did what God told him to do?

No one had ever heard of attacking a city by just walking around it. But the people of Israel did what God had said to do. They must have wondered that first day as they walked silently around Jericho and returned to camp. The people of Israel probably felt foolish the second day. By the third day, they might have been embarrassed.

At first the people of Jericho had been frightened of Israel. They stood terrified on the walls, and watched Israel march up to their city. But all the Israelites did was walk around the city, and go back to their camp. The second day when the Israelites marched up again, the army of Jericho must have thought, *O my. This time they'll attack and we'll all be killed.* But Israel didn't attack. They just walked silently around the city again! The third day someone on the city wall probably jeered at them.

"Go on back home," one may have yelled. "Marching can't hurt us."

I suppose others started to ridicule the silent Israelites too. The people of Jericho weren't so afraid now. They laughed and yelled insults.

On the fourth day, all the people of Israel must have been really angry. They probably felt even more foolish, just marching around the city. Maybe that's why the people of Israel decided not to wait for seven days. They were so angry that on the fourth day they started to shout and yell without waiting for Joshua's command.

What? I've got that wrong? Well, what did happen then? (Let your child tell the story as it happened.) How do you suppose God's people felt when the people of Jericho jeered and laughed at them? Has anyone ever ridiculed you for doing something mom or dad have told you, or something you think pleases God? (Most children have been teased by others for wanting to go home when mom told them, or not cheating, or not throwing stones at passing cars, and so on.) How did you feel then? What did you do? Did you do what your friends wanted, or what you thought was right? Why? It's hard for us to be obedient sometimes. Especially when we want to do something else, or don't understand why what we've been told to do is right.

Well, you're right. The people of Israel didn't yell on the fourth day. Instead they did just what God told them to do. They marched in complete silence for six days. They probably didn't understand God. They knew if He told them something, it was best for them to do it. We don't always understand the reason for things parents and/or God tell us to do. But we know God loves us and wants the best for us. So we do what He says anyway.

Finally, on the seventh day, the people of Israel marched around the city seven times. Then the trumpets blew. Everyone shouted, and the walls of Jericho fell down!

The people of Israel didn't understand just why God wanted them to march around Jericho all those days. But they obeyed God, even when they didn't understand. God was able to help them win the battle, because they obeyed Him.

Do you think the walls would have fallen down if the people hadn't obeyed? What do you suppose God wants us to learn from this Bible story? God really does love us. We can trust him to know what is best for us. We want to obey him even when we don't understand all the reasons for his commands.

Action Idea

Both you and the Lord do want children to understand the reasons for the things you ask them to do. So make a list of family rules, and of Bible commands or moral precepts. Talk about the reasons for each as you understand them. You'll find that boys and girls will understand your words of explanation for some rules, but they will not really grasp the rationale. Explain that when children and adults don't really understand why God says "Yes" or "No" about such things, we have to be like the people of Israel at Jericho. We trust God to know what is best, so we obey him even when we don't understand.

Gideon Learns about Himself
Judges 6:1–40

Background

Gideon is another of the Bible's reluctant heroes. Gideon saw himself as the least important member of an insignificant family in Israel (6:15). Gideon was not even sure of God's ability to help his people. Despite the appearance of the Lord to Gideon, and several clear signs of God's presence, Gideon continued to hold back. Yet the timid young man did finally lead a liberation movement which drove foreign enemies out of the land of Israel. God graciously provided the needed reassurance, and helped the young Gideon gain confidence.

Many boys and girls have an image of themselves that matches Gideon's. They do not see themselves as able or as significant. Their doubts about themselves may be expressed as shyness or timidity, or as an unwillingness to try new experiences.

In time, with success experiences, hesitant and uncertain children can gain confidence and overcome their timidity. But in order to risk trying, children and adults need to have some basis for hope.

They need to believe that one day they will succeed. The story of Gideon, with the suggestions found in paragraphs 34, 48 and 49, will help shy children develop that hope.

Children of any age can be helped by the story of Gideon. But the themes developed are especially for your older boys and girls.

The Story Retold

Gideon looked around fearfully.

He looked to the left. He looked to the right. Gideon looked behind him too. Only then did he bend over to beat the grains of wheat out of the straw. Gideon was hiding as he worked because he was afraid the Midianites would see him and steal his family's food. When Gideon was alive, the Midianites had invaded Israel and conquered the country.

Gideon, like most Israelites then, felt weak and afraid. He wanted to hide, because he knew there was nothing he was able to do that could help.

Have you ever felt like Gideon: weak, and afraid, and helpless? Do you like those feelings? When are you most likely to feel that way? (At school, home, when asked to do something hard, when friends want to play a game, and so on?)

Gideon didn't think much of himself. He knew he wasn't as strong as some. Gideon wasn't popular like some others. Gideon's family wasn't rich or famous. So you can imagine how surprised Gideon was when an angel appeared to him as he was working, and said to him, "The Lord is with you, Mighty Warrior."

Mighty Warrior! Gideon almost laughed. But the angel said, "Go in the strength you have and save Israel from Midian."

"But Lord," Gideon said. "How can *I* save Israel? My clan is the weakest in our state, and I'm the least important in my family." Gideon didn't feel he had any strength. Gideon was sure that he was one of the least important people alive.

Suppose you were Gideon and the Lord called you a "mighty warrior." How would you have felt? Would you have been ready to "go in your strength" to try to save your people? Why, or why not? Do you ever feel like Gideon must have felt when you're asked to do things—like play games, or get ready for a test, or meet new people?

Gideon felt much too weak and helpless to be a leader. So Gideon hardly even heard the Lord's promise to be with him. Even when Gideon brought food, and the angel of God made fire flare out of a rock to burn it, Gideon still didn't feel strong enough to try.

But when the Lord told Gideon to tear down his family's altar, where the people of his town worshiped an idol instead of the Lord, Gideon did try. He was afraid to do it in the daytime. So Gideon snuck out at night to destroy the idol and its altar.

Why do you think Gideon did it at night? Do you suppose it was all right to obey God that way, instead of marching bravely out in the daytime? Gideon did try. It took a lot of courage to do even that much. We don't have to do something perfectly the first time. Being willing to try when we're afraid is very important, and pleases God.

After Gideon did break down the idol's altar, he ran and hid. He had tried hard and did obey God. But Gideon still felt timid and afraid. The men of the town were very angry, and wanted to kill Gideon for tearing down their altar. But Gideon's father protected him while he hid.

Do you think Gideon will ever get over being afraid and timid? Probably Gideon felt afraid and discouraged too. He was trying. But it was so hard. Gideon still didn't feel like a mighty warrior. Why do you suppose God had confidence in Gideon anyway? I know that I have confidence in you, even when you don't feel confident about yourself.

Later Gideon prayed to the Lord. "Lord," Gideon said, "please don't be angry. But if You really plan to use me to save my country, I'll put this sheepskin on the ground. Tomorrow if it is wet with dew and the ground is dry, I'll know You are with me."

The next morning, the sheepskin was wet and the ground was dry, just as Gideon had asked.

But Gideon still didn't feel confident. He still felt weak and afraid. So Gideon talked to God again. "Lord, please don't be angry. But if You plan to use me to save my country, tonight make the ground wet and the sheepskin dry."

The next morning, the sheepskin was dry and the ground was wet. God hadn't been upset with Gideon. God knew that Gideon needed encouragement to feel strong and able.

God wasn't in a hurry. God would help Gideon grow. The time would come when Gideon wouldn't be timid or afraid any more.

And you know, God was right about Gideon. God did help Gideon. And because Gideon kept on trying even when he was frightened, Gideon did become a great leader. The Midianite enemies were driven out. And all Gideon's life he was God's man to protect the people of Israel from their enemies.

Action Idea

You can read the whole story of Gideon in three installments at mealtimes or bedtimes (Judges 6, 7, and 8). Older children may enjoy making a large chart of Gideon's life. Use graph paper, and draw ups and downs. For instance, an "up" would be when Gideon tore down the altar, a "down" when he hid afterward.

This chart can be helpful in a number of ways. Talk about the length of time it took for Gideon to become confident. Talk about Gideon's feelings at each "up" and "down" point. Talk about the trust in God that enabled Gideon to keep on trying even when he didn't feel strong and confident. When we trust God and keep on trying, we grow too. We become the kind of person we want to be.

Ruth Leaves Home
Ruth

Background

Moving is a time of great stress for children from nine to eleven (see paragraph 87). It means leaving friends and the comfort of familiar sights, and the house in which they feel they belong. It's no wonder that getting ready to move may bring sadness and anxiety to boys and girls.

In another Bible story (that of Abraham's call by God, retold on pages 147–150), children were encouraged to think of moving as an adventure, and promised that God would be with them in their new home. In this story of Ruth, another emphasis is added:

an emphasis which grows out of one of the most beautiful of Old Testament stories.

Ruth, a girl from Moab, married into an Israeli family which had come to her country. After the death of Ruth's husband and of her father-in-law, Ruth chose to link her life with her mother-in-law, Naomi. When Naomi headed back to Israel, Ruth went with her. "Home" to Ruth was not to be found in a place, but in her relationship with this older woman she had grown to love.

One of the greatest comforts a child facing a move can experience is the assurance that, wherever the family moves, the family will still be together. We may leave familiar places behind us. But we will not leave the people we love most.

The Story Retold

"Ruth, I have something to tell you."

Ruth looked up. Her mother-in-law, Naomi, seemed so serious. Ruth knew that Naomi had been quiet the last few days, as if she were thinking hard.

Ruth sat down near Naomi.

"All right, mother-in-law. I'm listening."

Naomi looked uncomfortable and a little unhappy. But she began to talk. "Ruth," Naomi said, "you know how my husband and I moved here years ago from Bethlehem."

Ruth nodded.

"My husband and I and our sons settled down here. And you met and married my boy. Then both your husband and my husband died."

Ruth nodded again. How hard it had been when the men of the family died and left Naomi alone, with only daughters-in-law to be with her.

Naomi took a deep breath. "Ruth, I've decided to move back to Bethlehem, in the land of Israel. You have been very good to me. And I am going to miss you. But I feel I have to move."

How do you think Ruth felt when Naomi told her she planned to move? What do you think was hardest about the plan for Ruth? When we told you about our plans to move, what was hardest for you? (Share some of the things about the move that are hard for you too.) Moving away isn't ever easy for anyone.

Ruth thought a moment.

And then she said, "Naomi, I'm coming with you!"

Naomi hugged her. She loved Ruth very much. But she shook her head sadly. "You're still young, Ruth. You should stay here and get married again. Back in my country, Israel, you would be a foreigner, and it might be hard to find a husband."

But Ruth just shook her head. She loved her mother-in-law, Naomi. She didn't want to think of Naomi being alone. So Ruth gave Naomi a big hug back. "Don't ask me to leave you," Ruth said. "Where you go I will go, and where you stay, I will stay. Your people will be my people and your God, my God." When Naomi realized Ruth was determined to go with her, Naomi stopped urging Ruth to stay.

How do you suppose Naomi felt when she realized she wouldn't have to move alone? Why do you think that made moving easier? One of the things that helps me with moving is that our family will be together. When we get there we'll be together. Home isn't so much a place; it's us being together.

When the day came, Ruth and Naomi set out together for the land of Israel. They came there together. And they lived together. Ruth helped her mother-in-law Naomi, and her mother-in-law helped Ruth learn to live in this new country.

In time the people of Bethlehem noticed what a good person Ruth was. Finally, she married a man named Boaz, and had a baby. How happy Naomi was then. Ruth still loved her mother-in-law. And now at last Naomi was a grandmother.

The family was still together.

And the new land, Israel, was home for them all.

Action Idea

Plan ahead ways that you can help each other prepare for the move, and how you can help when you arrive (see paragraph 87). In the process talk about the things that concern or worry each of you. If the children worry about how to make new friends, plan how you will help them meet new boys and girls. Maybe you can promise a party for neighborhood children when you move in.

If you are worried about misplacing items, let your children work up a check-list and help you keep track of special treasures.

Whatever concerns are expressed by any family member, see if together you can work out ways to help each other meet the expressed need.

As you plan, speak now and then of how thankful you are that when you move you will be together. God has given you each other. "Home" is being family, not being in a particular place.

Samuel Listens to God
1 Samuel 3:1–10

Background

It's hard for children to listen to each other. And it's hard for us to listen to our boys and girls. By that I mean it's hard to really listen—to concentrate on what another person is saying, and to be sensitive to his or her feelings.

Listening is such a simple thing that it's difficult to realize how basic it is to communication (see paragraph 58). And how basic it is to our children's growth in their relationships with others (see paragraph 13).

The familiar Bible story of the boy Samuel, usually told to children of three and four, has very different implications when we look at it from the unique standpoint of its listening subtheme.

God, who had not spoken to Israel for generations, called to the boy Samuel. Perhaps this child was the first who was willing to hear what God had to say! Eli, the priest who oversaw Samuel's education, was also a sensitive listener when the boy came to him.

This Bible story teaches us the importance of being responsive to God. But in it we also see the importance of listening in every interpersonal relationship. As told here, for the six- to eight-year-old, this Bible story is helpful for training your children to listen to each other carefully and well.

The Story Retold

"Samuel! Samuel!" called Eli, the priest of Israel.

"Here I am," answered Samuel, running to Eli. "Samuel," said Eli, "it's getting late. Time to go to bed."

Samuel walked back to the tent-church where he lived and helped, and crawled into his bed. *I'm glad God chose me to live here with Eli,* Samuel thought.

Eli was getting very old, and a strong eight-year-old like Samuel was able to help in many ways. *Maybe,* Samuel may have thought as he drifted off to sleep, *maybe God will want me to be a priest and help people worship Him. I'll want to listen very carefully to all the things Eli teaches me.*

Soon Samuel lay down to sleep. Samuel's eyes were closed, and he had just drifted off when . . . suddenly . . . he heard a voice calling, "Samuel! Samuel!"

Samuel sat up straight. Then he jumped out of bed and ran to Eli. "Here I am, Eli. What do you want?"

Eli looked surprised. "I didn't call you, Samuel," he said. "Go back to bed."

Samuel was sure he'd been called. But he went back to bed. Samuel snuggled down and pulled up his blankets. And then he heard the same voice calling again. "Samuel! Samuel!"

This time Samuel was sure. So he jumped up and hurried to Eli's room. "Here I am, Eli," Samuel said. "What do you want?"

Eli looked a little upset. "Samuel, I didn't call you. You'd better go back to bed and go to sleep."

Samuel was really puzzled now. But he walked back to his bed and sat down on it. Sure enough, he heard the voice again. "Samuel!" the voice called.

So Samuel got up a third time and went to Eli. Eli started to send Samuel back to bed, but then Eli stopped. "I wonder," Eli said to himself. "I wonder if God . . ."

For many years God hadn't spoken to anyone in Israel. But Eli knew from the Bible that God had spoken in the past to special persons like Abraham and Moses and Joshua. In Eli's day people didn't even want to listen to God's voice. They were selfish and didn't care about the Lord or His ways. But maybe Samuel would be different! Maybe Samuel would listen carefully to God and care about Him.

So now Eli said to Samuel, "Boy, I think it was God's

voice you heard. Go back to bed and if you hear the voice again, say this: 'Speak, Lord, for your servant is listening.' "

From that day on God did talk with Samuel. Samuel grew up to become God's messenger to the people of Israel. He spent his whole life listening to God, and telling God's people what the Lord said.

How did each person in the story show he was a good listener? What do you suppose might have happened if Samuel hadn't been the kind of person who listened to Eli? What do you suppose might have happened if Eli wasn't the kind of person who listened to Samuel? Who are some people who listen to you? Listening to others is important for us too. No wonder God was pleased that Samuel was the kind of person who listened to the Lord.

Action Idea

If your children need help learning to relate to friends or to other members of the family, the Samuel story can initiate a helpful "listening" exercise.

You'll need to do this with your whole family, or when several of your child's neighborhood friends are at your home.

1. Divide family or friends into pairs. Take half the partners into another room. Instruct them to tell their partners about the best Christmas they ever had. Then return to the first room and instruct the partners to listen very carefully, because later each may have a chance to tell the partner's story to the others.

Bring the pairs together, and give them several minutes to talk and listen.

Then ask the storytellers to nominate a "best listener." As individuals are suggested, ask what makes that person a good listener. Have the storytellers see if they can list what a good listener does to show that he or she is listening carefully. Write down the "good listener" traits.

2. Then take the other partners into the adjoining room. Tell them to think of the most exciting (fun) thing that has ever happened to them, to tell to their partners. While they are thinking of what to talk about, instruct the partners in the first room *not* to listen. They are not to walk away, or make noises. But they are to act as though they don't care what their partners are saying. They are to pretend they aren't listening.

After a minute to two, stop.

Ask the storytellers how they feel. What happened to make them feel that way?

Tell what you asked their listeners to do, and explain why. One way that we help people feel loved and important is to listen carefully to them. If we don't listen, they feel hurt or angry or unimportant. We can let people know we want to be friends and that we care about them just by listening.

There is a spiritual lesson here too. Like Samuel, we want to listen to what God says to us in his Word, and to show that we are listening by obeying him.

Saul Is Chosen to Be King
1 Samuel 10:1–11:15

Background

Israel's desire for a king was rooted in warped values. Israel wanted to be like the nations around them, and have a king who would go out to fight their battles for them (8:5, 19–20). That desire was a rejection of what made Israel unique. Only in Israel was God king. And Israel's God was committed to fight for her. As the Lord told an angry and upset Samuel, "It is not you they have rejected as their king, but me" (1 Sam. 8:7).

The king chosen was acclaimed by the people of Israel. Saul fit their image of a monarch. He was taller than any other man in the nation, and he looked manly. When trouble came, Saul led a successful defense against Israel's enemies. What more could Israel want? Saul looked like a king. And he seemed successful.

Only later did the tragic flaws in Saul's character appear. Then the qualities God's people had valued were shown to be unimportant. Soon it became clear that the truly important qualities had been ignored.

Older children are beginning to make important choices. Our children six through eight play with boys and girls who live nearby. Anyone reasonably polite and cooperative is considered a friend. But those nine through eleven look more carefully at other children, and select as friends those with traits they value. A look together at the story of Saul's choice as king can help your older boys and girls examine the values that are important to them in the choice of their friends. Also see paragraph 10.

The Story Retold

"But you don't *need* a king!" Samuel said angrily. "Don't you understand? *God* is Israel's king."

But all the people of Israel muttered and complained. "We want a king," the people insisted. "We want a king to lead us, so we can be like all the countries around us. They have kings. So we want a king too."

"Yes," someone else added. "When enemies attack us, our king can go out and fight for us."

"That's right!" everyone said. "We want a king!"

Later God spoke to Samuel. "Don't be upset, Samuel," the Lord told His prophet. "It's not you they have rejected. It's Me. Do what they want, but warn them solemnly that having a king is not wise."

Why do you think the people of Israel wanted to be like everyone else? Have you ever wanted to do something or have something because everyone else has it? That isn't really wrong. We all want to fit in with our friends. But can you think of any times when it might not be a good idea?

The thing that was wrong in Israel was that Israel wanted to be like everyone else so badly the nation turned away from God. It's all right to want to be like others who are good persons. But the nations around Israel didn't believe in God. The people of these nations didn't do what was right. It's foolish to want to be like people who do wrong things—people who don't care about pleasing God.

So Samuel warned Israel.

But still the Israelites insisted that they wanted a king.

So God picked out just the kind of king the people of Israel would like. This man's name was Saul. He became Israel's first king. When Samuel pointed Saul out, and said that he should be king, almost everyone was pleased.

You see, Saul was very tall. He was good-looking too. He was a whole head taller than anyone else in Israel. *What a fine, big, good-looking fellow,* most people thought. *He'll make a fine king!*

Do you think the Israelites were wise to like Saul just because he was tall and handsome? What do you suppose would make a person a good king? Let's list some things that we would want if we were going to choose a king. (Make a list together.)

Sometimes people pick friends because of how they look, or because they're big and strong. Let's make a list of things most people look for in a friend. (Make as long a list as you can, including important and superficial traits. When the list is complete, go through it together and decide which are good reasons for choosing a friend, and bad reasons for choosing a friend.)

Later the people of Israel learned how foolish they were. Oh, Saul did help them some. He was a good fighter, and God helped Saul to win some battles.

But later Saul showed that he was a person who became jealous when others were praised. Saul was a person who didn't trust God enough to obey Him. He was a person who became angry at others, and he even killed some Israelites who made him angry. Saul was tall. And he was good-looking. But he wasn't really the kind of person Israel should have wanted for a king.

Do you suppose you'd want as a friend a jealous, angry person who didn't want to obey God? Why, or why not? Who is your best friend now, and what is he (or she) like? Why do you like him for a friend?

Are there some people whom you don't choose for friends? Who are some of them? Why don't you like to be with them as much as with others? Usually we like to choose our best friends from people we want to be like, and who are like us.

The next king of Israel was David. He wasn't as tall as Saul. He didn't look as impressive as Saul. But David was a man who loved God and wanted to obey Him. Under David the people of Israel returned to God, and they became great.

Action Idea

Our goal in exploring older children's friendships is not to suggest that our boys and girls should isolate themselves from immature or difficult children. You may even want to have difficult neighborhood children in your home often, as a ministry, even though they are more like Saul than like David! But it's important that older children develop their closest friendships with boys and girls whose basic values they share. It's good, when our boys and girls talk about new friends, that we encourage them to share things they like about the new acquaintance. In talking about things they like about their new friend, you can follow up on the themes introduced in this story, and focus your children's attention on deeper values rather than appearances.

King Saul Is Afraid
1 Samuel 13:1–15; 15:1–35

Background

Saul's inner weaknesses are illustrated in two early incidents from his reign. On each occasion Saul disobeyed God because of what he imagined might happen if he obeyed. Saul's fears of the unknown overwhelmed his trust in the Lord. As a result this man was rejected and not permitted to establish a dynasty. As God told Samuel, "Do not consider his appearance or his height, for I have rejected him. The Lord does not look at the things man looks at. Man looks at the outward appearance, but the Lord looks at the heart" (1 Sam. 16:7).

All of us are subject to fears of what we imagine might happen. Children, too, have many imaginary fears (see paragraph 32). Your goal in exploring the story of King Saul with your own boys and girls is not to make your children feel guilty about their fears, but rather to help them see that fears must not lead us to do wrong things.

This story is particularly relevant for older children who are susceptible to fears of what others might think, and who often worry about what might happen in neighborhood or school situations.

The Story Retold

Saul was king now, the leader of all Israel. It was exciting to be king. And Saul must have been proud. Saul was only thirty years old, but everyone was already telling him how great a man he was. Saul had led his people in one battle, and won it. Everything looked wonderful for this man who was not only king, but was the tallest and strongest man in all of Israel.

But then some new enemies attacked Israel. These were the Philistines, and the Philistine army marched out to do battle.

Saul sent messengers throughout Israel. "Come help Saul fight the enemy," the messengers said. And Samuel, God's prophet, made a special promise to Saul. "Wait for me at Gilgal. Within seven days I will come, and will pray to the Lord that you will win a great victory."

So Saul and the men of Israel gathered at Gilgal. From there, looking over a valley, they could see the army of the Philistines on a hill across from them. It was such a big army! Why, the Philistines had three thousand chariots, like our tanks. And Israel didn't have any! There were so many Philistine soldiers no one could count them! King Saul looked around at his men. There weren't nearly as many soldiers of Israel. And the Israeli weapons weren't as good as those of the Philistines. But, Saul may have thought, *Samuel is coming. Samuel will pray for the Lord to help us.*

Samuel didn't come the first day. Samuel didn't come the second day. And as the Israelites kept looking at the Philistine army, many Israelites were afraid. Saul was afraid, too. Saul began to imagine what would happen if Israel lost!

The third and fourth day passed. Samuel still didn't come. Saul saw that some of the men of his army were sneaking away. He was losing soldiers! And Israel was already out-numbered!

The fifth day passed. The sixth day came. More of Saul's army was sneaking away to go home. How anxious and worried Saul felt now. How could Saul fight the Philistines with so few men? When the seventh day finally came, Saul kept looking and looking for Samuel. But Samuel didn't come in the morning. Samuel wasn't there by noon. The whole army of Israel was terrified now. Saul was the king. What could he do? As more and more of his army left, Saul could imagine what would happen. If Samuel didn't get here, why, he'd be left alone! By the time there were only six hundred men left, Saul was so worried he decided to act.

What do you suppose Saul thought would happen? Do you think he really needed to be afraid? Why, or why not? (If your children know the story of Gideon, you might ask them how many men Gideon had when he defeated the Midianites. The answer is three hundred! Saul had twice that many, and should have trusted the God who helped Gideon to help him.)

It was all right for Saul to be afraid. But as king, Saul

was supposed to help his people trust God. Instead Saul imagined all sorts of terrible things that might happen—and Saul disobeyed God!

In Israel, only priests were allowed to present offerings to God. Saul was so afraid now that he decided not to wait for Samuel to come and make an offering. Saul started a fire on the altar, and made the offering himself. Just as Saul finished, Samuel came. Saul had been so afraid of what he imagined might happen. He had disobeyed God and done something he knew was wrong.

It's all right to be afraid. What's wrong is to let our fears of what might happen lead us to disobey. If you were to make up a story about a child your age who was like Saul, what would the story be about? What would the child be afraid of? What would he or she imagine might happen? What is the right thing he needs to do? What might he or she do instead, because of the fear? How do you suppose this story of Saul might help such a child?

That wasn't the only time Saul was afraid and disobeyed God. Later God sent Saul and Israel's army to fight a very wicked country. Saul was told by Samuel, "God wants you to destroy the whole country. Even their sheep and cattle are to be killed."

Saul attacked these enemies, and won a total victory. But then Saul took the king of that country captive. And Saul brought back all the healthy and strong sheep and cattle and calves and lambs that God had ordered killed.

God spoke to the prophet Samuel and told Samuel what had happened. "I am very upset that Saul is king," God said. "Saul has turned away from Me, and not carried out My instructions." Samuel too was upset, and all that night Samuel prayed about what to do.

The next morning Samuel went to meet Saul.

Saul was very excited about Israel's victory. When Saul saw Samuel, he laughed and shouted out a greeting: "God bless you!" And then Saul said, "I have carried out the Lord's instructions."

Samuel looked grim. "You did, did you? Then how come I can hear sheep bleating, and cattle lowing?"

Saul tried to make excuses. "I did what God said. I went

on God's mission and destroyed the wicked enemy. It's just that the people wanted to keep the sheep and cattle. We, ah, plan to use them as an offering to the Lord."

Samuel was furious. "Does God want offerings, or does He want obedience? Why didn't you do what you knew was right?"

Finally Saul broke down and told Samuel what really happened. "I knew I was doing wrong. But, Samuel, I was afraid of what the people might do if I said no to them."

How was this failure of Saul's like the first one? What was different? (In each case Saul imagined something that might happen. Instead of trusting God and obeying him, Saul did something he knew was wrong. In this case Saul wasn't even afraid of an enemy. He was afraid of what his people, his friends, would think!)

If you were to make up a story of a child your age who was like Saul, what are some of the things he would know he is supposed to do? What might he or she be afraid people would think or do? What would the others want him or her to do?

Have you ever been in a situation like this? What did you feel then? What do you usually do when you are afraid of what other people might think if you do what you believe is right?

Saul was very sorry afterward. But Samuel had a stern message for him from God. "Because you would not obey Me," the Lord told Samuel, "I will find someone else to be king."

God needed a person who would trust and love Him enough to obey, even when he was afraid. Only that kind of person could be king and lead God's people Israel.

Action Idea

Play "What If . . ." with your children using these two stories of Saul. Have your whole family participate.

Make up several possible terrible endings that might have happened to Saul if he had not made the offering. For instance, Saul might have been left alone, and been killed by a Philistine scouting party. Saul might have gotten into a fight with his own army, and had his tongue cut out, and so on.

Then make up as many possible good endings if Saul had obeyed. For instance, Saul was left with only 150 people, but God sent an earthquake and the whole Philistine army slid off the hill and crushed each other in the valley. Talk about which endings are most likely to happen, and why.

You can now use this approach to help your children analyze their own worries. First play "What If . . . ?" with situations your children may have described during story *talkables*. Then discuss other personal worries of theirs or your own in a "what if" way.

How good to know that with God committed to us, we can trust him and choose to do right, despite what we fear might happen if we do.

David's Youth
1 Samuel 17:34–37

Background

Younger children may have persistent fears of imaginary terrors: of monsters and ghosts and, for those six to eight, of wild animals. In fact, fear of wild animals is the most common of young children's fears, even when there are no lions or tigers or bears within hundreds of miles of a child's home.

Such fears are normal, and should not be belittled. Instead, we can work quietly to build the child's base of confidence, trust, and security (see paragraphs 30 and 32). This Bible story about the young David is told just for your six- through eight-year-olds.

Little is known of David's childhood. But we do know that David's youth, typical of so many in Israel, was spent in the fields caring for his family's sheep. David developed his skills in music then. David also developed a deep sense of awe for the God he saw revealed in nature as well as in his mighty acts in history. Confidence in God gave David the courage to confront wild animals that would prey on his sheep, and when necessary to battle them. This story, adapted from David's words recorded in 1 Samuel 17:34–37, is designed to help your children develop a sense of their own ability to cope with God's help, which will reduce their fear quotient.

The Story Retold

David settled down on the hide under a tree. From the cool, grassy spot where he sat, David could see his sheep grazing in the meadow.

David was a musician as well as a shepherd. He wasn't

a very tall boy. In fact, at sixteen David was smaller than most of his family. But David was strong. Living outdoors, and hiking over the fields with his sheep, had made David strong and healthy. His daily practice throwing stones with his sling had made David's arm strong, too.

But now David was sitting down, resting. David was playing songs on a harp, an instrument like a small guitar, and singing songs he made up himself. Many of David's songs were about God. Some songs were about the storms David saw in the mountains. Others told about the brooks and rivers and the animals he saw.

Maybe David even made up songs about the bears and lions in the outdoors where he lived.

It was because of the bears and lions that David had to stay awake in the afternoon, and watch. Those wild animals were dangerous. And wild animals liked to eat sheep! David had to stay awake to protect his sheep. Usually, if David saw a bear or a lion, he'd pick up a stone, put it in his sling, and throw the hard stone at the wild animal. The stone hurt, and usually the lion or bear ran away. It must have felt good to David to have that sling in his hand, and some hard stones ready to throw to drive the wild animals away.

Most of all, though, David knew that God loved him. The wild animals were dangerous. But God would help David and protect him.

Then one day something terrible happened. A big brown bear crept up on David's sheep. David threw stones with his sling. But the bear grabbed one of the sheep in his mouth and started to drag it away!

I've got to save my sheep, David thought. He probably felt afraid then. But David believed that God was able to save him from the claws of the bear. David jumped up and ran after the bear.

David carried a wooden staff, like other shepherds. When David got to the bear he beat it over the head with the staff. That hurt! The bear let loose of the sheep. David dragged the sheep right out of the bear's mouth, and started to carry it back to the flock.

My, that bear was angry! The sheep was to be its dinner! The bear growled and roared, and turned on David. But David had a knife too. When the bear attacked, David jumped on the bear's back, grabbed its hair, and held on. The bear couldn't reach David to bite or claw him. But David could reach the bear. Holding onto the hair tightly with one hand, David stabbed the bear with his knife, again and again. He stabbed the bear until the bear died!

Then David realized what he had done, and he thanked God. "Lord," David said, "You have saved me from the bear. Thank You." David had been very brave! With God's help, David had been able to kill a dangerous wild animal.

What part of the story do you like best? What do you think was David's best weapon against the bear? The sling? The staff? The knife? How did knowing God was with David help him, out there in the country, where wild animals live? Let's thank God that he takes care of the people who trust him, just as he took care of David.

Action Idea

It's usually best not to confront children with their fears, although it is good if our boys and girls feel free to talk about them. This true story of David's victory over dangerous wild animals may stimulate your child to share his fears and feelings. If not, don't press him.

Instead, make a model with your child of David's "best weapon against the bear." A sling can be made with a piece of leather as a pocket, and two longer strings, one attached to each side. This biblical sling was swung around the head, one thong released, and the stone which fit into the pocket thus flung at the target. A staff can be formed from a tree branch in your back yard, or drawn on construction paper. The staff was a long stick with a hook at one end, used to lift sheep out of mountain crevasses into which they had fallen. A knife can also be outlined and cut from cardboard.

You may want to add a Bible verse to the chosen reminder: "The Lord who delivered . . . will deliver me" (1 Sam. 17:37). Let your child take his symbolic weapon into his bedroom, to remind him that with God's help even the young need not be afraid.

David and Goliath
1 Samuel 17:1–58

Background

It's hard to think of a more familiar Bible story. Yet the tale of David and the giant Goliath remains a favorite of boys and girls. Probably it is so well liked because this story carries a clear message to children who live in small bodies in an oversized world: even when life's problems seem too big to battle, with God's help everything will be all right.

This favorite Sunday school story, a feature of every curriculum, often asks children to identify the "giants" in their life (their fears) and then remember that God can help us win if we confront our fears. Rather than take this approach, we want to return to the root cause of children's fears (see paragraph 30). We want to help boys and girls sense that, because we can trust God, many of the things which seem to be dangers are not dangers at all.

This story is retold especially for younger children.

The Story Retold

King Saul sat slumped inside his tent. "Close that tent door," Saul yelled angrily at one of his soldiers.

The soldier jumped to obey. No one liked to be around King Saul when he was grumpy.

Of course, everyone knew why Saul was grumpy just now. It was ten in the morning, and that awful giant, Goliath, was going to march out and insult the army of Israel again.

It happened every morning. The two armies—the army of Israel and the army of the Philistines—were camped across from each other. But the Philistines had a soldier named Goliath who was nine feet tall! And he was strong. Why, his metal shirt alone weighed 125 pounds! His weapons were giant, too. And every day Goliath marched out into the valley between the two armies and yelled insults at the Israelites. Goliath dared the Israelites to send somebody out to fight him. Goliath called all of God's people cowards. But no matter how loudly he yelled, or what terrible insults he shouted, no one dared come out to fight. Goliath was just too big!

The biggest man in Israel, King Saul himself, sat inside

his tent with the door closed so he couldn't see Goliath. You see, King Saul was afraid, too!

After days and days, a young shepherd boy visited the army to bring some food to his brothers, who were soldiers. You know the shepherd's name, don't you? Yes, it was David. Well, that morning David saw Goliath march down into the valley. David heard him insult God's people and challenge the Israeli army.

David looked around, expecting to see some soldier jump up and run out to fight Goliath.

But no one moved. Instead, everybody muttered and looked around, or looked at the ground. Everyone seemed to be afraid! David was really surprised. He asked some nearby soldiers, "Who is this Philistine, to defy the armies of the living God?" Goliath was big, yes. But God surely is bigger. With God on Israel's side, David knew the giant didn't have a chance.

But David's oldest brother heard him and was angry. "Who are you to talk?" he said. "I know how conceited you are. You're just talking, David."

Actually, David's oldest brother was just as afraid as all the army. He was angry because he was afraid. David had reminded them that with God on their side, they really didn't have to be afraid.

Well, someone told King Saul what David was saying. David was brought to the king. "I'll go fight Goliath," David volunteered. "I've fought lions and bears to protect my sheep, and God has always protected me. God will protect me now from the giant."

Saul tried to give David Saul's own armor. But David was much smaller than Saul. The armor just wouldn't fit. So David went down into the valley, without any armor at all, to fight the nine-foot-tall Goliath.

How angry Goliath was when he saw David coming! Why, it was an insult! This wasn't a fighting man. It was only a boy! And instead of a sword, David carried only his wooden shepherd's staff! How Goliath howled!

But David called out to Goliath. "You come against me with your sword and spear and javelin, but I come against

you in the name of the Lord, the God of Israel, whom
you insulted. Today God will give me the victory, and I'll
cut off your head. The whole world will know how great
God is!"

David took a smooth stone he had picked up and put it
in his sling. He ran toward the giant, swinging the sling
around his head. David let the stone fly. Straight and hard,
that stone flew right at Goliath and hit the giant in the
forehead. Knocked out cold, Goliath fell flat. David ran
to him, took Goliath's own sword, and cut off the giant's
head!

David was right!

God's people don't have to be afraid of giants. God loves
and helps His people. God's people don't have to be afraid
at all.

Action Idea

Children identify so naturally with David that it seems best
not to draw out additional implications, or to underline a message
so easily understood.

As paragraph 30 explains, when boys and girls see something
they fear in the perspective provided by knowledge of God's loving
presence, the paralyzing sense of overwhelming danger recedes.

It's enough for you and me, when we sense our children are
afraid, to remark, "It's a good thing God is with you as he was
with David when David fought Goliath." God made the difference
then. He makes the same difference today.

Saul's Jealousy
1 Samuel 18:1–16

Background

Jealousy is natural among children in any family. Children compete for their parents' attention and, in a sense, compete for love.
You and I can't make jealousy go away by saying it is wrong.
But by following some of the suggestions given in paragraph 73
we can reduce incidents which stimulate jealousy, or which might
be misunderstood by children as parental favoritism.

We can also explore with older boys and girls something of

the nature and the destructive impact of jealousy. In few biblical passages is the tragic impact of jealousy so clearly seen as in those which describe the declining years of King Saul.

Saul's weak character was seen early in his reign (see pages 198ff.). When young David appeared and defeated Goliath, the contrast between David's fresh faith in God and Saul's own failures were glaringly clear. Rather than admit his own failures, Saul became more and more bitter in his hatred of David. Saul's fear of this young man, who was all Saul was not, finally led him to attempt murder.

Jealousy that is caused by insensitivity to others is explored in Bible stories retold on pages 167–171. In this story we invite our children to look within themselves for roots of bitterness which may be the cause of their jealous feelings.

The Story Retold

After David killed Goliath, King Saul made David an officer in Israel's army. This pleased everyone. David was a hero, and naturally everyone cheered when David came along.

In fact, people even made up a song about David. It was a joyful song—one meant to be danced to. When the army came marching home after defeating the Philistines, the soldiers were met in every town by happy, dancing people, singing:

> "Saul has slain his thousands,
> and David his tens of thousands!"

How do you think Saul felt when he heard this song? Why would he feel like this? Can you tell about a time you felt as Saul probably did? (Share a time when you felt jealous.) Sometimes we have a good reason to feel jealous. Do you think Saul had a good reason? Why, or why not? Saul was the tallest man in Israel. He should have fought Goliath himself, but Saul was afraid to. How do you think Saul felt about himself when he looked at David?

Saul was very angry about the song. *I'm the king,* Saul thought. *And yet David gets more credit than I do.* From that moment Saul began to be jealous of David.

What are some of the things people say or do that make others jealous? What are things mom or dad do that make you feel jealous of your brother (sister)? Sometimes people, even moms and dads, do thoughtless things that make others jealous. How do you think Saul's jealousy was different from this?

Saul was jealous because Saul saw how successful David was. Everything the king asked David to do, David did well. When David led the troops, the army of Israel always won. It was clear that God was helping David, and Saul became more and more afraid of David. Perhaps Saul remembered all the times that he had disobeyed the Lord. Saul knew inside that he wasn't as good as David. It was this that made Saul afraid and jealous.

What can a person do when he's angry and jealous because of something he knows is really his fault? What do you think would have happened if Saul went to God, confessed how he felt, and admitted the things he did wrong? Saul didn't do that. Instead, he continued to be angry and jealous and afraid all the time. Do you think you'd like that? Why, or why not? If those feelings are so bad, why do you suppose Saul didn't confess to God and let God change his feelings?

Poor Saul. He knew deep down that he was wrong. And David was always so helpful and loyal to him. But Saul just couldn't admit his own faults. Since Saul would not admit his failures or confess his sins to God, even God couldn't help the king.

Saul became more and more miserable. He had times when he felt terribly depressed. Other times Saul flared up in anger. Saul even threw a spear at David while David was playing a harp to soothe his unhappy feelings. Jealousy is such a miserable thing. The person who is jealous will hurt others, and he is never happy himself.

For the rest of his life Saul was an angry, jealous, unhappy man.

What lessons do you think God wants us to learn from Saul's unhappiness? Do you think God would have helped Saul if Saul had asked for help, even though Saul's jealousy was his own fault? Why, or why not? If you ever feel angry and jealous and it's because of something you've done wrong, what will you do?

Action Idea

Tell this Bible story when you sense jealousy in one of your older boys or girls. Don't accuse them of Saul's kind of jealousy.

It may be that something you have said or done unwisely made your child feel momentarily unloved. Some of the *talkables* in this story are designed to help you find out if this is what has happened.

But it may be that some sense of personal guilt or failure is at the root of your child's feelings. If so, this story may encourage them to admit the problem and seek the healing, cleansing gift that is ours when we confess our sins to the Lord (see page 218).

Abigail Helps to Calm David's Anger
1 Samuel 25:1–44

Background

What do children do with their anger? They're likely to feel angry often, particularly when something happens to them they don't feel is fair. But there are very few ways we let children express anger. Yelling and shouting aren't popular with parents. Surely we can't let them express anger physically, by striking out or hitting others. And we do want to help them control their anger, learning to master it rather than having anger master them.

As we saw in paragraph 36, God encourages us to face the reality of our anger. The feelings are there: we can't deny them. But God also wants us to know that those angry feelings will change. God wants us to be able to work through our anger and find alternatives to the sins to which anger moves some.

The story of David and Abigail is a story about David's anger. He was treated unfairly by a foolish rancher. But that anger almost moved David to do something very wrong. When Abigail confronted David, she did more than try to make amends. She pointed out that David had almost let his anger move him to sin. David recognized his fault, and appreciated this woman who was willing to risk David's fury to help him find a better way.

This, too, is a story for older children. But mature sevens and eights can profit by talking through this Bible story with you.

The Story Retold

King Saul had finally driven David away from his capital. In fact, Saul was determined to kill David. So David hid in the wildest part of Israel. David was joined there by other men who were loyal to him. But it was a hard life. David and his men were often hungry and cold.

Near where David and his men were hiding lived a rich man named Nabal, who owned thousands of goats and sheep. Those sheep grazed on the side of the mountain where David was in hiding. All the weeks that Nabal's shepherds had his flocks on the mountain, David and his men didn't take even one. In fact, David's men protected the shepherds and Nabal's sheep from any thieves and from wild animals.

So when it came time for the sheep to be sheared, and for Nabal's crops to be harvested, David thought it would be fair if the rich farmer gave some of the harvest to his men. David sent messengers to Nabal, and asked very politely.

Do you think it was fair for David's hungry men to be given some of Nabal's harvest? Why, or why not? What would you do if someone had helped you, and when he was hungry asked only for some of your extra food? What do you suppose Nabal will do?

Nabal listened to the messengers. But Nabal didn't even ask his shepherds if what the messengers said was true. Instead Nabal insulted David. "Who is this David, anyway? Why should I take my bread and meat and share it with some lazy scoundrel?" And Nabal sent David's men away without any food.

How do you think David will feel when he hears? What do you think David should do? Should he just forget it? Should David go down and take his fair share? Or what? What would you advise David to do if he asked you?

When David heard, he was furious. David's face turned red, and his blood pounded inside. In a terrible, angry voice, David shouted at his men.

"Put on your swords!" David shouted. And David started to rush down the mountain with about four hundred of his men. David wasn't just going to get his fair share of the food. The angry David was going to kill Nabal and every man that worked for him! "It isn't fair," David muttered as he marched. "I took care of this fellow's property, and he's paid me back evil for good. I'm going to get him!"

Do you think David had good reason for being angry? What about David's plan to kill Nabal and his men? Why do you think David is doing it? Why do you suppose people want to hurt others when they are angry? Have you ever felt about anyone like David felt about Nabal? (Share times when you have felt angry too.)

It was all right for David to feel angry. David hadn't been treated fairly. But what David planned wasn't right.

Back at Nabal's house, some of the shepherds David had helped came to Nabal's wife, Abigail. They told Abigail how David had helped. And they told her all the terrible things Nabal had said about David. "You'd better do something," they told Abigail. "That wicked master of ours has insulted David, and something terrible will happen."

Quickly Abigail gathered bread and meat and grain, and collected pressed cakes and raisins and figs. She loaded all the food on donkeys, and she headed toward the mountain where David was. On the way she met the angry David, marching at the head of his men coming down to kill Nabal.

When Abigail saw David, she got off her donkey and bowed low. She apologized to David, and begged him to pay no attention to the wicked things Nabal had said. "His name means fool," Abigail said, "and he is a fool."

And then Abigail was very brave. She spoke up to David. She said, "It's not right to take revenge by hurting and killing your enemy. God has sent me to keep you from sinning. God punishes His people who sin. You should fight God's battles, and not let your anger lead you into a sin that would always be on your conscience."

How do you think David liked to have Abigail tell him what he planned to do was a sin? Do you think she was right or wrong? What's the difference between feeling angry with someone and planning to do something to hurt them?

God knows that everyone feels angry sometimes. But God doesn't want us to be so angry that we do something we know is wrong. If David had killed Nabal for insulting him, that would have been a sin. David felt angry because Nabal wasn't being fair. But that didn't make it right for David to hurt Nabal.

When David heard Abigail tell him he was planning to do wrong, David thanked her. "Praise the Lord for sending you to me today," David said. "May you be blessed for your good judgment, and for keeping me from bloodshed today. If you hadn't found me, I would have done wrong and killed Nabal."

So David took the food Abigail brought for his men, and went back to the mountain. There David learned the end of the story.

You see, the next morning Nabal heard what his wife had done. Nabal was so upset he had a heart attack, and died! God did punish David's enemy. David didn't have to take revenge at all.

So David learned an important lesson.

What lesson do you think David learned? How would you explain that lesson to someone else? When do you think you need to remember the lesson yourself?

Let's thank God that we don't have to take revenge either. We may get angry sometimes. But we don't have to let anger make us sin, and try to hurt the person who has hurt us.

Action Idea

With your children make up a list of things to do when they feel angry—and things not to do. The list might include:

* Don't try to hurt the other person back.
* Don't plan revenge.
* Tell God how you feel about the unfair situation.
* Tell your feelings to a parent or friend who can help you as Abigail helped David.
* Be ready to accept an apology.
* If the other person really sinned, let God pay them back instead of you. Remember, no one really gets away with sin.

One important thing. You might plan how to help each other when you feel angry. Promise that if one of you feels angry, he or she will talk about it with one of the family. It's all right to express feelings verbally. And talking does help our feelings change. It is not all right to do wrong or to take revenge.

David Spares King Saul
1 Samuel 24:1–22; 26:1–25

Background

It's hard enough to do the right thing. It's even harder when friends are urging us, telling us it's all right to do something that we are sure isn't right.

All of us understand the power of peer pressure. It's difficult enough for adults. It's sometimes worse for boys and girls, who want to please friends who are *there* more than they want to please parents who aren't there!

People of the Bible experienced the same kinds of pressures. At times the pressures to do wrong were even greater on them than on us and our children. Certainly when David's men urged David to kill his mortal enemy, King Saul, David had many reasons to do so. Samuel had anointed David to be king after Saul. Saul and his army were trying to kill David. No one knew how long David could avoid death or capture. Yet, on two occasions when Saul was within striking distance, David resisted the temptation to kill Saul—a temptation heightened by the pressure of his friends.

David was not always perfect. But in this case, David stands as an example of a man who was aware of the presence and power of God, and who thus was able to resist temptations to do wrong. Older boys and girls are most likely to feel peer pressures, and to grasp the truths unveiled in this story. But children of all ages can profit from its telling. See paragraph 17.

The Story Retold

Jealous King Saul finally decided he must kill David. David had been a faithful officer in Saul's army, and a good friend to Saul's son, Jonathan. David was even married to Saul's daughter. But that didn't make any difference to Saul. Saul was so jealous of David that he was determined to kill him.

David ran and hid in the wilds of Israel, and was joined by friends who were loyal to him. But Saul called out his army and marched to find and kill this man he hated so much.

David had always been loyal to King Saul. But that didn't make any difference to Saul. All Saul wanted to do was to kill David.

One time when Saul was chasing David with three thousand soldiers, David hid from Saul in the back of a deep cave. David and his men huddled in the darkness, waiting for Saul and his soldiers to go away. They must have been frightened back there. There was no other way out. If Saul discovered David's men, they would all be killed.

And then King Saul himself came into the cave!

"Quick!" one of David's friends whispered. "This is your chance! Kill King Saul and all your troubles will be over!"

"Yes," another one urged. "God said you were to be king someday. This is your chance! God has given your enemy into your hand!"

All around David his friends whispered. "Kill Saul. Kill your enemy now!"

What do you suppose David will do? How would you feel if all your friends urged you to do something, and said it was all right to do? Has that ever happened to you? Tell about that time and what happened.

David crept up in the darkness. He was so close he could reach out and touch King Saul! But Saul didn't even know David was there. In his mind David could hear all his friends, urging him to kill this king who was trying to kill him.

David pulled out his knife.

And he hesitated.

It didn't matter that his friends said it was all right. David knew he would have to decide for himself what was right. David knew that God was watching, and David wanted to please God far more than he wanted to please his friends. David would have to do what was right.

What do you suppose David will do? What would David do if he wanted to please his friends? What do you think God would want David to do? Why?

David reached out with his sharp knife. But he didn't plunge the knife into Saul. Oh no. All David did was cut off a piece of Saul's clothing. Saul never even felt him do it.

Saul left the cave, called his soldiers, and marched on down into the valley.

When Saul was gone, David's friends were upset. "You could have killed him, David! Why didn't you listen to us!"

David told his friends they were wrong. "Saul was anointed king in God's name. Even if he is a bad king, and is trying to kill me, I don't have the right to fight back against him." David knew that God would protect David if he did what was right. So David was determined to please God first.

When Saul and his soldiers were down in the valley, David came out of the cave and called to Saul. David showed Saul the piece cut from his coat. He said to Saul, "Some of my friends urged me to kill you just now. But I spared you. Please, see that I am not guilty of rebellion or wrongdoing. I haven't harmed you, but you are trying to kill me."

David told Saul one more thing. "God will punish you for what you do wrong. But I will not touch you or harm you."

How do you suppose Saul felt when he heard David? Do you think David felt good about what he had done, or bad? Why? How do you suppose your friends feel if you decide to do what you believe is right instead of what they want you to do?

Can you think of things that helped David make the decision he did, when all his friends wanted him to do something else? (Focus on doing the right thing, trusting God, knowing God was watching, knowing that God would punish Saul so David did not have to, and so on.)

Saul felt ashamed when David spoke to him. He stopped chasing David that time. But later the jealous Saul tried to kill David again and again. Finally Saul was killed in a battle with the Philistines.

David's men stayed loyal to David. When David became king later, everyone was glad they had a king whom they could trust to do the right thing.

Action Idea

Make a list of things friends sometimes urge your children to do which your boys and girls do not think are right, or are not sure about. When the list is made, talk over those situations which recur most often. It may be helpful to your children to role play situations together, and practice different ways of saying no to peer pressure.

Whenever one of your children does tell of successfully resisting peer pressure, express your own appreciation. Also express your assurance that God, who watched over and approved of David, is watching and is pleased with them.

David Confesses His Sin
2 Samuel 11:1–12:23; Psalms 32, 51

Background

Conscience has two dimensions, each of which is explored in paragraph 65. One aspect of conscience moves us toward what is right. The other aspect condemns us for what we do wrong. But even the sense of guilt is a gift of God. That inner ache is implanted by God and tells us we have done wrong. Guilt is not intended to bind us, powerless, to our past. Guilt feelings are intended to point us to God, to seek forgiveness (see paragraph 69).

The story of David and Bathsheba is an adult story, in our modern X-rated sense. It is certainly not necessary to try to explain all the details to our children. But this incident did stimulate David to write one of the Bible's most powerful psalms—a psalm of deeply felt guilt, and great relief in forgiveness.

David's story, and his psalms of guilt and forgiveness, bring the Bible's powerful message of hope to us and to our children. Each of us, like sheep, has gone astray (Isa. 53:6). For straying children, this story of David is intended to bring understanding of forgiveness and hope.

The Story Retold

David was a good person, who trusted God. Usually David tried to please the Lord. But David was like everyone else. There were times when David did wrong.

One of those times happened after David became king. David was standing on the roof of his palace. Looking out at the rooftops below him, he saw a beautiful woman. David watched her, wishing that she was his wife.

She wasn't his wife, of course. She was married to one of David's army captains. But this time David didn't stop to think about pleasing God. David wanted her as a wife, anyway.

Have you ever wanted something, or wanted to do something, that you knew was wrong? (Share a time you felt a strong desire to do something you knew was wrong.) Sometimes everyone wants to do something and doesn't stop to think about pleasing God or doing what is right.

David didn't stop at all. He just sent for the woman to come to his house, and be just like his wife.

How do you think David felt after he did this? Do you think he was happy, or unhappy? Why? How have you felt after you did something you knew was wrong?

After David did this wrong thing, he didn't say anything to anyone. David even pretended that everything was all right. But deep inside David felt very guilty. Later David wrote poems that we have in the Bible book of Psalms. These psalms tell how he felt inside, even when he was trying to pretend to everyone else that everything was all right. One poem says,

> "When I kept silent,
> my bones wasted away
> through my groaning all day long.
> For day and night
> your hand was heavy upon me;
> my strength was sapped
> as in the heat of summer" (Psalm 32:3, 4).

Inside David felt weak and miserable. He may have looked happy outside, but he was groaning deep inside.

Do you suppose you've ever felt guilty? When? What had you done to make you feel that way?

David didn't realize it, but those unhappy feelings were God's messengers. In fact, when we feel guilty today, those feelings are one way the Lord talks to us. The feelings tell us that we have done wrong and need to be forgiven.

But David didn't listen to those feelings inside. He tried to pretend to himself that he hadn't done wrong. So God sent a prophet named Nathan to David. Nathan came to the palace of King David. Nathan came right up to the king's throne. And Nathan bravely told King David that David had sinned and deserved to be punished.

Finally David was ready to admit he had sinned. Humbly David prayed to God.

"Have mercy on me, O God,
    according to your unfailing love;
According to your great compassion . . .
    cleanse me from my sin" (Psalm 51:1, 2).

Do you think David deserved to be forgiven? He had done wrong and refused to admit it. What do you suppose God will do? What do you suppose God does when you and I sin? Does he forgive us when we admit our sin and ask him?

When David asked for forgiveness, he didn't ask God to forgive because David deserved it. When we do something wrong, we deserve to be punished. But David asked God for mercy "according to your unfailing love," and "according to your great compassion." God forgives us because He loves us in spite of our sin.

Like David, you and I will do what pleases God most of the time. But sometimes we'll forget to think about God, or to do what is right. Sometimes we'll do something wrong. How good it is to know that we can come to God then and confess our sin, knowing God will forgive us. Then our guilt and our miserable feelings will go away.

Action Idea

The concept of restitution, and of asking others for forgiveness, is developed in other Bible stories. This story focuses on the guilt feelings which come when we act against conscience. This story highlights the forgiveness God offers us then.

It will probably be helpful to your children if you memorize together the verses from Psalm 51 quoted in this story. Repeat them together several times in subsequent days and weeks. When you do, link the verses with guilt feelings. You want any violation of your children's conscience, and consequent guilt feelings, to trigger recall of this vital Bible passage, which turns thoughts to the lovingkindness of God, and to the forgiveness we receive from him.

David Sleeps
2 Samuel 15:1–16:14; Psalm 3

Background

Bedtime fears, and fear of the dark, are common for children six to eight. Because such fears are so common, several stories in this *Handbook* deal with fears, in a variety of ways. This particular Bible story tells of the time David was forced to leave Jerusalem because of the rebellion of his son, Absalom. Rushing out of the city, heartbroken at the faithlessness of his people as well as his son, David is traveling in the open when night falls. Pursued by enemies, almost alone, David peers into the gathering dark. Surely no one could have criticized David if his thoughts were filled with dark foreboding and fears.

Instead, we are given a unique insight into David's feelings in Psalm 3. David is heartbroken and discouraged at the rebellion. But his thoughts turn to God. He sees God surrounding him as a shield, he senses God strengthening him. He remembers that God answers prayer (3:3, 4). Sustained by God, David says, "I lie down and sleep . . . I will not fear" (3:5, 6).

God gives each of us a gift when we turn our thoughts to the Lord. It is the gift of inner peace. How wonderful that this gift is offered to our fearful boys and girls as well as to you and me. See paragraphs 27 and 33.

The Story Retold

"David!"

King David turned slowly and looked at the excited messenger.

"King David!" the man shouted, breathing hard as if he had been running. "You've got to run! Your son Absalom has led a rebellion! All your people are following him!"

David knew that Absalom wanted to be king. But a rebellion? Why, Absalom would have to kill David before Absalom could become king.

David didn't hesitate. "Hurry," David said. "We've got to flee. If we don't leave right away, Absalom will be here and kill us all."

Without even waiting to pack, David rushed out of his

palace. But most of his officials and friends didn't want to
go with David. Many deserted David, and followed Absalom.

Hurrying, David and his few friends left the palace. They
rushed out of the city of Jerusalem. Maybe they could go
south and find faithful people who still wanted David as
king.

David traveled as fast as he could. The few people who
were with David kept looking back. Was that Absalom's
army back there? No, it was just the dust raised by a herd
of cattle. But as they hurried most of them were afraid.
Absalom's army might be right behind them! The army
might catch up with them that night, when it was dark,
and kill them all.

Then it began to get dark. The sun got lower and lower.
There were no buildings or hotels where David could stay.
David was out in the country and would have to sleep out
in the dark.

Soon it was too dark for David's party to travel any more.
Even the moon didn't seem to want to come out. Only a
few stars were there in the sky. Down below, David and
his few friends sat in the dark, pulling blankets around their
shoulders. As they sat there, they must have worried that
their enemies were creeping up on them even then.

*What else do you suppose they might have been afraid of, there
in the dark?* (*If you remember your childhood fears of the dark,
tell something about them.*) *Do you ever feel scared in the dark?
What do you worry about at night?*

David was very sad that night, as well as afraid. The
people David had led as king didn't want him any more.
They were even trying to kill him. David may have looked
around at the dark fearfully, too. But then David began
to think about God.

All his life, God had been David's friend. David had tried
to please the Lord, and David knew God had helped him.
So David talked to God.

"You are a shield around me," David said (Psalm 3:3).
Thinking about God, David began to lose his fear. Later
David wrote another poem about that night.

"I lie down and sleep;
     I wake again, because the Lord sustains me.
  I will not fear the tens of thousands
        drawn up against me on every side" (Psalm 3:5, 6).
Because God was a shield for David, protecting him from
every danger, David could go to sleep, even there in the
dark.

Action Idea

Don't follow up this story with conversation designed to apply
it. Instead let the clear message of the story sink into the awareness
of your child six to eight. It's likely if your child is afraid of the
dark he or she will want to hear this story often.

You may also want to work together with your child to make
a shield-shaped poster for his or her bedroom. "You are a shield
around me, O Lord" or "I lie down and sleep . . . the Lord sustains
me" are appropriate verses that might be printed on it.

Elijah Runs Away
1 Kings 19:1–18

Background

To many children, there's something almost shameful about
fears. This reaction is intensified if adults ridicule, or dismiss, or
seem angry when boys and girls feel that touch of terror which
comes to everyone now and then.

Some stories in this *Handbook* focus on specific kinds of fears,
and suggest truths that will help boys and girls meet them successfully. This story builds on a question raised in paragraph 30: how
should you and I react when our children are afraid? And on
the corollary of that question: How does God react when his children fear?

This Bible story demonstrates God's wonderful gentleness with
us. He is not angry when we're afraid. He does not shame or
ridicule us. Instead, the Lord is very gentle, supporting us when
we need support, and speaking in quiet, loving tones to reassure
us that we are safe.

This Bible story will not only encourage your children. It is a
story which provides an example for you and me of how good
parents respond to children who are afraid.

The Story Retold

"God," the prophet Elijah cried out, "show Your people who is really God, so they will trust You once again!"

Elijah was standing on Mount Carmel, with his arms lifted up in prayer. Thousands of the people of Israel were watching. In front of Elijah was a stone altar. The wood and a sacrifice on it were soaking with water.

For years an evil king and queen had led God's people to worship idols. Now Elijah was ready to prove to Israel that the Lord is the only true God.

"God," Elijah cried out. And as soon as Elijah prayed, fire came down from heaven. The fire from God burned up the water. It burned up the sacrifice and the wood. The fire even burned up the stones and the ground around the altar. God had performed a great miracle. When God's people saw it, they fell on the ground and cried out, "The Lord, He is God! The Lord really *is* God!"

How strong and powerful Elijah must have felt then. God had answered Elijah's prayer. God's people knew again that the Lord is the only true God.

But the evil king and queen weren't happy at all. They hated God. So the queen sent Elijah a message. "I am going to have you killed by this time tomorrow!"

What do you suppose Elijah will do now? Why? How do you think Elijah will feel? Do you think you'd be afraid of a queen after God had just answered your prayer with a miracle? How would you feel?

Elijah might have laughed at the queen. Elijah knew God was powerful. Elijah knew God answered his prayers. But for some reason that Elijah himself couldn't understand, all Elijah felt was fear!

In fact, Elijah was so afraid that he just wanted to run away. He didn't think about God. He didn't think about anything. He just felt afraid—and he ran.

Sometimes everyone feels afraid, even when there isn't a good reason. When is the last time you felt afraid? (Share a recent fear of your own.) Did you really need to be afraid, or did it just happen? How did you feel about yourself when you were afraid? How do you think other people would feel about you if they knew you were afraid?

Elijah ran and ran, because he was afraid. Elijah ran past the last town on the edge of a desert, and traveled out further into the desert. Finally Elijah was so exhausted he couldn't run any more. He just slumped down on the ground, all worn out, and wished he could die.

I'm no good at all, Elijah thought. Elijah was so ashamed of himself that he asked God to let him die.

You might think that God would be angry with His prophet. Or that God would be ashamed of Elijah. But God sent an angel to bring Elijah food and water. God didn't say an angry word to Elijah. God comforted Elijah, and told him to rest.

Elijah did rest. After Elijah had slept a while, God's angel touched him gently. "You're all worn out," the angel said comfortingly. "Here, eat and drink some more."

The next morning Elijah felt better. Elijah traveled for many days, till he finally came to the mountain where God had spoken years ago to Moses. Then Elijah was tired again, and lay down to sleep.

How did God react when Elijah was afraid and ran away? How do you know from the story that God wasn't angry with Elijah? Why do you suppose God was so gentle? How does God feel about Elijah now?

We all have times when we are afraid. Sometimes we even run away. We forget that God is taking care of us, and that makes our fear even stronger. But God still loves us, even when we forget. God still loves us when we're afraid. God will never be so angry with us that He won't help us feel better, and become stronger too. God will always love us, and He will help us get over our fear.

Action Idea

Work together on a "family agreement." You might want to agree together that when one of the children feels afraid of anything, he will come and tell a parent about it. Often talking about what we're afraid of can help. You will also want to agree that anyone who feels afraid will not be ridiculed or made fun of, and that parents won't be angry. Instead, like God, mom and dad will try to comfort and to help. You might add a third clause to the agreement. Together you and the child will tell God about the fear, and ask God to help your child even as he helped Elijah. Elijah overcame his fear in the end. Your child needs to know that he too will one day be freed from his fears.

It's best to work out your own language for the agreement, planning together how to express it in words most meaningful to your boys and girls.

Naboth's Vineyard
1 Kings 21:1–29

Background

Children want things. This is understandable in children. They're so oriented to touch and feel and do. And, of course, TV constantly bombards them with the same message it carries to adults: have this toy, use this product, and you'll be happy. It's hard enough for adults to see through our attractive but superficial materialism. We shouldn't be surprised if our children are tempted to think that happiness for them is wrapped up in having something their friends have. We shouldn't be too surprised if, at some time or another, one of our children simply takes something he feels he must have.

It is important for us to focus on the values and motivations expressed by any stealing incidents (see paragraph 37). In this retelling of Ahab's longing for what belonged to Naboth, you'll help your boys and girls think about what is important in their own lives. By using the follow up *Action Idea*, you'll be able to establish well-understood consequences should a child give in again to the impulse to steal.

The Story Retold

Sitting in the palace, King Ahab could see the field of grapevines that belonged to Naboth.

"I want it," Ahab said to himself. "I like that field. It would make a good garden." So Ahab went to see Naboth.

"Let me have your vineyard," King Ahab said. "I'll trade you another vineyard for it, or give you money."

But Naboth was shocked. "Why, Your Majesty," Naboth said, "this field has been in my family since God gave us this land. I can't give you what I inherited from my fathers."

King Ahab was upset and angry. Ahab was king. He should be able to have whatever he wanted! At least, that's what Ahab thought. So Ahab sulked. He lay down on his bed, stuck out his lower lip, and wouldn't talk to anyone. Ahab wouldn't even eat. If he couldn't have that field where Naboth's grapevines grew, he just didn't want *anything*.

Have you ever known anyone who acted that way when he didn't get what he wanted? What words do you suppose tell how Ahab felt? Do you think King Ahab was right to feel sorry for himself, just because he couldn't have something he wanted? Why, or why not?

Ahab's wife, Queen Jezebel, heard that her husband was sulking. She came in to see him. "Why are you so sullen?" Jezebel asked. "Why won't you eat?"

In a whining tone of voice Ahab told her. "Naboth won't give me his vineyard."

What do you think Ahab's wife should say to him? What would you say to a person who was unhappy because he or she couldn't have something he wanted? Have you ever seen things you wanted and couldn't get them? How did you feel? What did you do?

How about things you wanted, and did get? (Give an illustration ". . . like that truck you asked for Christmas.") How long did it make you happy? Do you think you could be happy now if you didn't have it? What are some of the things people really need to make them happy and well? (Develop a list with your children.)

Queen Jezebel didn't try to help Ahab see that he was being foolish. Jezebel didn't try to help Ahab be thankful for the things he did have. What Jezebel did was a terrible thing. "You're king," she told Ahab. "You can have what you want. Get up. I'll get that vineyard for you."

Queen Jezebel made up a plan to steal the vineyard. She knew that she couldn't steal it while Naboth was there to watch out for his property. So she plotted to accuse Naboth of a crime, and have him killed.

And she did just that!

Just because King Ahab wanted something he couldn't have, the evil queen plotted to steal it. And even to kill for it. Nothing is important enough to steal for. Nothing is important enough to hurt other people for. And later God punished both King Ahab and Queen Jezebel for the terrible things they did.

Do you suppose it's wrong for us to want something we don't have? When do you think it becomes wrong? When we sulk about it? When we just take it, or steal money to get it? It may be foolish for us to think that some of the things we want will make us happy. But wanting things is only wrong when we do something wrong, like stealing, to get the things we want.

Action Idea

Exodus 22:7–9 sets out a simple principle for dealing with stealing. The thief is to pay back double for what he or she has taken. Restitution is not enough, for it only means return of what was taken. Restitution doubled provides a consequence which is likely to deter future thefts, and repay the person for any mental anguish during the period of loss.

It is always helpful to establish beforehand with children the consequences of wrong actions, and then to follow through faithfully in seeing that the consequences are paid. You may want to use this biblical principle in setting out understood ways you will deal with any future incidents of stealing.

Elisha Is Protected by Angels
2 Kings 6:8–23

Background

It's easy not to be afraid when mom and dad are near. Somehow, most children feel that their parents will be able to cope. All too often, children feel they are *not* able to cope in situations which hold some real or imagined terror.

Because fears are so common with young children, and with older boys and girls as well (see paragraph 30, 31), several *Handbook* Bible stories deal with fear. Each story approaches fear from a slightly different perspective. Some try to help a child reevaluate what he fears. Others try to help him feel more able to cope. Some, like this Bible story, seek to help your child feel protected.

Of course, for you and me, the sense of protection is far more than a feeling. We have a quiet assurance, based on great realities. God *does* guard his children. Because God is real, and because he does watch over us, there is a solid basis for the confidence we want to help our boys and girls develop in the Lord.

The Story Retold

The King of Aram was angry. His army had been trying to trap the King of Israel. The king set up his army camp in what he thought was the best place. But every time the Israeli army avoided the trap.

"Who is the spy?" the king of Aram shouted one day. "The king of Israel knows everything we plan."

His generals looked very serious. No one wanted to be called a spy for the enemy. Then one of the officers explained to the king.

"Your majesty, there is a prophet of God in Israel, named Elisha. It's his fault. God tells the prophet what we plan, and then Elisha warns the king of Israel."

The king of Aram rubbed his hands thoughtfully. "Then, all we have to do is kill Elisha!"

So the king of Aram shouted out his order. "Go, find out where Elisha is. Then send out some soldiers and capture him." The king of Aram let his generals leave. Then the king smiled. As soon as he killed or captured God's prophet Elisha, the king of Aram was sure he would be able to defeat Israel.

When spies found out where Elisha was, a large army of chariots and soldiers marched all night. They came to the little town of Dothan, where Elisha was spending the night, and they surrounded the town. Now Elisha was trapped! No one could get in the city. And no one could get out.

When the sun started to come up, very early in the morning, Elisha's servant went outside for some fresh air. Suddenly he gasped, and ran inside. "Elisha! Elisha!" he called. "There's an enemy army all around the city! Oh, Elisha, what will we ever do!"

How do you think Elisha's servant felt when he saw the enemy army? What do you think he was afraid might happen? Can you think of reasons why Elisha's servant should have been afraid (for instance, Elisha couldn't fight an army alone, and so on)?

Elisha's servant grabbed the prophet by his sleeve, and pulled Elisha outside. Surely when Elisha saw the enemy army out there Elisha would be afraid too.

But Elisha didn't seem afraid at all.

Elisha looked at the enemy soldiers.

Elisha saw their chariots, and their spears. Elisha saw they were all around the little town.

And then Elisha said something very strange to his servant. "Don't be afraid. There are a lot more than they have on our side."

On our side?

The servant's mouth hung open. He looked all around. There wasn't a single soldier of Israel anywhere in sight. The servant and Elisha were all alone.

Before the servant could say anything more, Elisha prayed. "God," he said, "please let my servant see what is really here."

And suddenly Elisha's servant could see!

There, between Elisha and the enemy army, was a great army of angels. They were bright and shining and glowed like flames of fire. God was protecting His people. Even when Elisha and his servant seemed to be alone, God's angels were there to take care of them.

How do you think the servant felt when he saw the angels? Have you ever felt afraid because it looked like you were alone? Can you tell me about that time? Would it have helped you if you knew angels were there, taking care of you, too? How would it have helped?

The Bible says that angels serve and take care of God's children (cf. Heb. 1:14). So angels are here, to take care of you and of me too. We may not be able to see angels. But we know God is caring for us, even when we feel afraid and alone.

God did take care of Elisha and his servant. God did not let the enemy soldiers recognize Elisha. Elisha led the enemy army right to the king of Israel, where they were captured. We don't always know how God will help us.

But we can know that God is here, and His angels are watching over you and me.

Action Idea

Why not help your children make—or give each of them—small angel symbols to tape on school books or possessions. Or if you're good at sewing, sew angels on shirts and dresses and jeans where other children have foxes and alligators. Simple reminders that God's unseen angels are with our children can comfort them and help them cope.

Hezekiah Is Healed
2 Kings 20:1–21

Background

Sickness is common in childhood. Measles and colds and tummy aches all come, and afterward are soon forgotten. Boys and girls live much in the here and now. They don't think back about sicknesses, or ahead.

It's when a child is sick, or an older family member is sick, that children are likely to be concerned. This is especially true if they sense the anxiety of older members of the family.

There are many things that parents can do to reduce the fears of boys and girls, and to deal wisely with serious illnesses (see paragraph 45). In addition, there is the path taken by godly King Hezekiah when he was terminally ill. We can turn to God in prayer (see paragraph 46). God will not always answer our prayer for healing as we wish. But we and our children can be sure that God does hear. And that God cares.

This Bible story, retold for children of all ages, focused our attention on the great truth that God does hear our prayers and that he does care. We cannot promise our children that loved ones will always be made well. But we can promise that God will never abandon their loved ones or them.

The Story Retold

King Hezekiah was a good man. He loved God, and all the years that Hezekiah was king over God's people, he tried to rule them wisely. Hezekiah also encouraged his peo-

ple to worship God. Hezekiah was one of the best kings
God's Old Testament people ever had.

You'd think maybe that such a good king would live
for a long, long time. But one day when Hezekiah wasn't
old at all he became very sick. The days passed, and Hezekiah
didn't get better. Hezekiah grew worse. Finally Hezekiah
was so sick that everyone was sure he was about to die.

God hadn't forgotten Hezekiah though. God didn't want
this good king to think the Lord had forgotten him. So
God sent the prophet Isaiah to speak to Hezekiah.

Isaiah didn't have good news. "Hezekiah," Isaiah said,
"God has told me that you will not recover from this sickness." God knew what was happening. God wanted Hezekiah to know that the Lord cared, even if Hezekiah wasn't
going to get well.

*Even people God loves don't always get well when they are sick.
Do you think Hezekiah was glad to know that God still loved him
anyway? What do you suppose Hezekiah wanted most?*

Hezekiah must have been glad to know God still loved
him. Sometimes sick people forget that God loves them and
feel that they are being punished. But what Hezekiah now
wanted most of all was to get well. Hezekiah knew that
someday he would die. But he didn't want to die now.

So Hezekiah prayed to the Lord.

"O Lord," Hezekiah prayed, "remember how I have tried
as hard as I could to do what pleases You." Hezekiah cried
too, asking the Lord to please make him well.

*Do you think God will answer Hezekiah's prayer? God hears all
our prayers, and he answers them all. But sometimes God says
"No" to what we ask. Do you suppose God doesn't love us when
he says "No"? Why do you think God might say "No" sometimes
to what we pray for? (Point out that just as sometimes mom and
dad say "No" because something is best for children, God sometimes
says "No" because it is best for us.)*

Hezekiah prayed very hard that God would make him
well. God heard that prayer, and God had a very special
answer. Before Isaiah the prophet got outside the king's
palace, God spoke to Isaiah. "Go back to Hezekiah," the
Lord told Isaiah. "Tell Hezekiah that the Lord has heard
your prayer, and said 'Yes.' I will let you live for fifteen
more years. You will not die from this sickness."

Then Isaiah told the doctors the medicine to use for Hezekiah. And King Hezekiah began to get well.

God had heard the prayer of good King Hezekiah when he was sick. God had said "Yes" when Hezekiah prayed that he might get well.

How do you know what to pray for (the sick person)? What shall we say to God? Let's pray for him (her) now.

Action Idea

One of the most meaningful things we can do to build our own children's confidence in prayer is to make a "we asked"—"God answered" record book. The book should not only contain a list of requests for friends or family who are sick. It can contain a list of all the daily concerns of adults and children that are brought to the Lord.

It's exciting to realize that talking with God is talking with our loving Father. God cares about everything that concerns us. And the Lord also wants to share our joys. When children learn that there is nothing too small or too big to share with the Lord, they have taken a great step in their spiritual life.

Cultivating the practice of prayer is something we adults need to do as well. Making up an answer book to keep a record of family prayers will be as enriching to us as it is to our boys and girls.

One more thing. Why not let one of the children take the responsibility of being the recorder of prayers and answers? This will be a way to provide meaningful responsibility for an older child, and will let that child have a meaningful ministry to the rest of the family.

Esther Does What Is Right
Esther

Background

The Book of Esther is fascinating for several reasons. Theologically, it is the book of Providence: a book which never mentions God by name, but which shows in the arrangement of circumstances that God remains in control. God does not need to use miracles to deliver his people. God can work through natural cause and effect.

The Book of Esther tells the true story of a young Jewish woman, chosen to be queen of a vast pagan empire nearly 500 years before Christ. When Esther's people are threatened in an empire-wide plot, the young queen must decide whether to risk her life and try to help, or to keep silent and perhaps be safe.

The Book of Esther is another of the great books of our Old Testament which reads like a story. Your family will enjoy reading the whole tale as a continued story, one which can extend for nine exciting mealtime or bedtime adventures.

This retelling focuses on the choice which Esther had to make. Like Esther we and our children often find ourselves facing similar decisions. Will we speak up for what is right, or keep silent? Will we be God's agents for good, or hold back?

It's difficult for adults, much less children, always to make right choices. Yet the story of Esther can help each of us realize that God is at work even when his hand is unseen. The story of Esther can help strengthen our resolve to choose to do good (see paragraph 65).

While this story can be told to children of all ages, the talkables are geared to older boys and girls.

The Story Retold

Haman smiled cruelly as he left the king of the great Persian Empire. Haman had the king's permission! Now he would have revenge on his enemy!

Of course, Mordecai [Mor-dek-i] the Jew wasn't much of an enemy. Mordecai was just a minor official at the palace, a clerk in one of the courtyards of the palace. But whenever Haman walked through the palace, everyone else bowed down. They even kneeled on the ground when Haman came by. That is, everyone kneeled down but Mordecai. Mordecai didn't seem to know how important Haman, the king's favorite friend, was!

And that made Haman angry.

Haman was very, very proud. And Haman decided to get revenge on Mordecai.

But the cruel Haman was so proud that it wasn't enough for him to hurt just Mordecai. Haman decided that he would have all of Mordecai's people killed too. Mordecai was a Jew.

That's why Haman was smiling as he left the king.

He'd asked the king for a favor.

Haman had told the king of Persia there was a troublesome race of people in the empire. It would be better, Haman told the king, if those nasty Jews were all killed.

The king had nodded.

"Do what you please with them."

So Haman left the king with permission to kill all the Jews in the world.

Haman hurried and wrote orders to be sent throughout the empire. On a certain day, people were allowed to kill Jews and to take their property. On that day, Haman thought gleefully, the people of his enemy Mordecai, who wouldn't kneel when Haman came by, would all die.

Mordecai did not kneel down before Haman because Mordecai worshiped God, not powerful men in the Persian Empire. When Mordecai heard of the decree that Haman had sent throughout the world, he knew that somehow God would protect His own people, the Jews. But how? Once an order was sent out in the king of Persia's name, no one could change it, not even the king. That was the law in Persia. Even the king couldn't change his own orders.

But there was one thing that the king of Persia didn't know. There was one thing that the wicked Haman didn't know. That thing was that the new young queen of Persia, Esther, was a Jew too! Esther was a cousin of Mordecai's. Mordecai had brought her up as if she were his own daughter. So Mordecai went to see Esther.

Mordecai sent Esther a copy of the king's order, and begged Esther to go to the king and beg for mercy for her people.

Esther was afraid.

"Don't you know," she sent a message back to Mordecai, "if anyone goes to see the king without being sent for, that person will be put to death? Only if the king raises his golden scepter will the guards spare that person's life."

No wonder Esther was afraid! If she went to the king and spoke up for her people, Esther might be killed!

How do you suppose Esther felt about speaking up? What do

you think she thought about? Would it be a hard decision for her to make? Do you ever have times when you see others doing something wrong, and wonder if you ought to speak up? Can you tell about a time when that's happened to you? How did you feel? What did you think about? What did you do?

Sometimes it's very hard for us to speak up when others are doing something wrong. Esther thought she might be safe if she kept quiet. After all, Esther was the queen, and no one knew she was a Jew. Besides, Esther knew that if she went to the king without being called, Esther herself might be killed.

So Esther sent a message back to Mordecai and told him she was afraid.

What do you suppose Mordecai said? What would you tell Esther if you were there? What would you tell friends who are afraid to speak up when they see other people doing things that are wrong?

Mordecai sent a message back to Esther. First he warned Esther that it wasn't safe for her to just keep quiet. Then he told her two things. "If you don't speak up, God will find another way to save our people. But have you thought? Maybe you have become queen just so you will be able to speak up at this time!"

Esther was still afraid.

But the more she thought, the more she realized Mordecai was right. She was Queen. She could try to go to the king. So Esther should be the one to ask for the life of her people.

Esther sent another message to Mordecai. "Please, ask everyone not even to eat, but to pray for the next three days. After three days, I will go and speak to the king, even though it is against Persian law. And if I am killed, well, I will be killed."

Do you suppose Esther felt better when she decided to do the right thing and speak up? Was she still afraid? Why do you think she decided to go to the king? What helps you decide to do the right thing, even when you are afraid of what others might think or do?

Three days later, Esther did go to the king. The king didn't have her killed. In fact, because Esther was brave and did the right thing even when she was afraid, the Jewish people were saved.

God didn't do a miracle to save them.

But God used Esther and Mordecai and other things that happened to ruin Haman's evil plan. In the end the king of Persia had Haman hung, and God's people were saved!

If you'd like to find out how, we can read the whole story at mealtimes (bedtimes) from the Bible.

Action Idea

The retelling here focuses on Esther's difficult decision. The *talkables* are designed to help children think about their own choices in situations where speaking up is threatening. The wonderful lesson of the Book of Esther is that we can trust God to be at work through circumstances, and thus are free to do what is right.

As you read the story together, keep a record of the circumstances which play such a key part in this true Bible story. After reading each chapter, talk about how God seems to have arranged the circumstances to save his people. Talk too about the fact that God doesn't need to use miracles to help us today. God takes care of us without our even knowing it. Because God is in control, we can be like Esther. We can choose to do the right thing even when it seems dangerous or hard to do.

Daniel in the King's School
Daniel 1:1–17

Background

Daniel was probably in his early teens when he was brought with a group of Judean captives to Babylon. It was the policy of King Nebuchadnezzar to train promising upper-class youths from subject nations as administrators for his kingdom. Daniel and three other Jewish youths were placed in this "king's school." The four were given Babylonian names, clothing, and food. If they passed their examinations, their destiny was to live in the capital of that alien land.

Daniel's long life spanned three succeeding world empires. Daniel lived in their capitals, and rose to prominence in their administrations. Through it all, Daniel remained faithful to God. He was more than the avenue for notable Old Testament prophecies. In Daniel's own time he must have been able to intercede often for the well-being of God's people. Daniel's life of usefulness began when he passed his first test of faithfulness to God, as a teen in the king's school.

One of the most significant facts of life for our boys and girls is that they are influenced by each other and not just by adults. Daniel's firm decision to follow the Lord helped his friends stand firm. Daniel's respectful attitude toward those who unwittingly wanted him to do wrong won the day. Our boys and girls can learn much about how to take a stand for what is right, and how to be sensitive to others, from this familiar Bible story. Also see paragraphs 17 and 67.

The Story Retold

"All right," said Ashpenaz, looking over the teen-aged boys lined up in front of him. "We'll take him . . . and him . . . and him. And oh yes, be sure to take that one. The one they call Daniel."

For two days Ashpenaz, an official of the Babylonians who had taken thousands of God's people captive, questioned and tested the sons of the Israelite nobility. Ashpenaz was looking for the smartest boys, who were also handsome and athletic. King Nebuchadnezzar had given him strict orders. "Take the best of them," the king said. "Teach them the Babylonian language, and teach them our ways." The teens selected were to be trained in the king's school for three years, and then would serve the king as officials in Babylon.

The soldiers motioned the four boys whom Ashpenaz chose. "You four!" one said harshly. "Come this way."

So Daniel, Shadrach, Meshach and Abednego marched away from their friends, and were taken to the king's school.

At the school the boys were treated well. They were given a place to sleep and to study. The boys were even given the kind of food and wine that the king himself ate and drank.

But that was the problem! In the Bible God told the Jewish people they were to eat only certain kinds of food. The people of Babylon didn't follow God's rules for the Jews. So the food that was brought to Daniel and his friends was food Jewish people were not allowed to eat!

Daniel made up his mind.

Daniel determined he would obey God and not eat the forbidden Babylonian food. Daniel boldly told his three friends what he planned.

How do you think Daniel's friends felt about being given food they knew they shouldn't eat? Do you suppose they would have decided not to eat it if Daniel hadn't spoken up? Why is it easier for us to do the right thing if we have friends who do what's right too? It's hard to do right if we think we're the only one who will.

Sometimes we help other people choose what's right by speaking up for it. Can you think of a time some friend helped you do what you knew was right, by saying he or she would do it? Have you ever been the leader for your friends, spoken up for doing right?

It was hard for Daniel and his three friends, in the king's school, to decide to keep God's rules for the Jews. But when Daniel took the lead, his friends followed. It was easier now. Each one knew he would not be alone. Each would help the others do what is right.

Who is the friend who most helps you do what is right? Do you like being with this friend? Why, or why not?

Daniel knew that he would have to obey God. But he also knew he should be polite to the Babylonian officials. So very politely Daniel asked the officer in charge for permission not to eat the king's food.

The Lord had helped Daniel already, by making the officer like Daniel and his friends. But the officer shook his head when Daniel asked him for a special diet.

"The king himself ordered your food and drink. What if I let you eat your special diet, and you don't look as healthy as the other young men in the school? Why, the king would have me killed for something like that!"

Daniel understood why the officer was afraid. He wasn't upset or angry. He could see the officer was worried and not just being mean.

So very politely Daniel said to the officer, "Please let us try our diet for ten days. Just give us vegetables and water, and see how we look after that."

The officer agreed to this test. And at the end of the ten days, Daniel and his friends looked healthier and stronger than those who ate the royal food. So the officer took away the rich food and drink of the king, and let Daniel and his friends eat only food allowed the Jews in God's law.

For three years Daniel and his friends helped each other follow God's rules for them. And they studied hard. Then, when the three years were past, King Nebuchadnezzar himself tested them. Daniel and his friends showed more wisdom and understanding than all the others, and the king gave them important jobs in his kingdom.

God does help us when we do right. And it's good to have friends who also want to obey God, who will do what is right too.

Action Idea

Make a list of friends. Talk about three different traits. Which are friends who will choose what is right and do it—if someone else does right first? Which are friends who will take the lead and do what is right, no matter what others do? Which are friends who will do right or wrong, depending on what other children they are with do?

Explore with your children their relationship with each of these clusters, talking about how they might help others do right and how others help them. The kinds of friends we want to have as "best friends" are boys and girls whom we can help to please God, and who will help *us* to please him.

Daniel in the Lions' Den
Daniel 6:1–28

Background

Why are fears of wild animals so prominent among young children? It's hard to tell. Perhaps to children they represent everything that is strange and different and, thus, beyond their control. Whatever the reason, such fears are extremely common. Wild animals are real, even though they may not be near. The uncontrollable real does seem terrifying.

But while situations may be out of your control or out of mine, they are never out of God's control. This is the comforting message communicated so powerfully in the familiar story of Daniel in the lions' den. Daniel is in danger, but nevertheless is protected by God. This story helps children sense, without our preaching, the freedom found in knowing and obeying God. When we trust ourselves to follow the Lord, God guards us, and remains in control of our life's circumstances.

This story is best told to six- to eight-year-olds. It will be of value to older children, of course. But our boys and girls need to be introduced to this story while they are still young. Through it they will sense the loving touch of God, and find their own fears quieted by him. See also paragraphs 27, 29–32.

The Story Retold

Slowly Daniel kneeled down beside his open window.

He turned to face the far-off city of Jerusalem, where the temple of God once stood, and he began to pray.

"See!" came an excited whisper.

Several men were hiding in bushes outside Daniel's window. Now they pointed at the praying Daniel and smiled wickedly at each other. "I told you so," said the leader of Daniel's enemies. "I told you he'd never stop praying to his God. We've got old Daniel at last!"

Then the men hurried away to tell the king about Daniel.

You see, Daniel was a high official in the Persian kingdom. Daniel was in charge of other officials. And Daniel was very honest. So as long as Daniel was in charge, watching them, the other officials couldn't do anything dishonest.

Finally the Persian officials decided that they would have to get rid of Daniel. The officials watched Daniel carefully, looking for something to accuse Daniel of. But Daniel was trustworthy and hard-working. His enemies could never find anything bad to accuse Daniel about.

Finally one of them had an idea. Everyone knew that Daniel loved the Lord and prayed to God at least three times a day. Maybe the evil officials could find some way to use that against Daniel.

Finally the evil officials went to King Darius.

"You're such a great king, O Darius," they said, flattering him. "All your royal advisors and governors have agreed there's only one way to let everyone know how wonderful you are. You should write an order that, for thirty days, no one can ask anyone except you for anything. And, O yes. You're so great that no one should even pray to any god for thirty days."

Darius was flattered.

Yes, Darius thought, *I am great.* Without even wondering why Daniel wasn't there with the other officials, Darius wrote out the order.

The very first day the order was given, Daniel got up and left his office at noon, as he always did. Daniel walked to his home. Daniel went up to his room and opened the window, as he always did. And Daniel prayed to the Lord.

Outside, Daniel's enemies watched and pointed and laughed. At last they had trapped Daniel! Daniel had disobeyed King Darius' order. And the penalty for disobeying the King? To be thrown into a den full of starving, hungry lions!

Why do you suppose Daniel disobeyed the king and prayed anyway? Do you suppose Daniel felt afraid when he prayed? Why, or why not? Who do you think Daniel thought was more powerful, King Darius, or the Lord? How would that help Daniel decide whether or not to pray?

While Daniel prayed, his enemies rushed to see King Darius. "King Darius!" their leader said. "You made a decree that anyone praying to any man or god but you would be thrown to the lions. Well, Daniel paid no attention to your orders. We all saw Daniel, and he still prays three times a day to his God."

Then King Darius was very upset. King Darius was a good man. Darius never thought about Daniel when the others tricked him. But there was a law in Persia. No decree published by the king could be changed. Even Darius himself couldn't change what he had written. Darius tried. But King Darius couldn't figure out any way at all to rescue Daniel.

Almost in tears, the king gave the order.

"Go get Daniel."

Daniel was brought to the king, and Darius sadly gave the command to throw him to the lions. "I hope," Darius said to Daniel as the soldiers took him out, "I hope your God, whom you worship so faithfully, will rescue you."

The soldiers pushed Daniel inside the den full of fierce

lions. The king himself sealed the door. Then Darius went back to his palace. But Darius couldn't sleep or even eat. All Darius did was walk back and forth, waiting to see what would happen to Daniel.

When dawn came, and the first light showed in the west, Darius hurried to the den of hungry lions. "Daniel," Darius called. "Daniel, servant of the living God. Has your God whom you worship so faithfully been able to rescue you from the lions?"

The king was quiet then.

He listened.

And Darius heard Daniel answer! "O King," Daniel's voice came from inside the lion's den. "God sent His angel, and the angel shut the mouths of the lions. The lions have not hurt me, because I've done nothing wrong."

How excited King Darius was! And how happy. His friend Daniel was all right! God had taken care of Daniel after all.

And then King Darius remembered the men who had tricked him and tried to get Daniel killed. "Bring them here," the angry king said. And when the frightened enemies of Daniel were dragged in, Darius said, "Throw *them* to the lions!"

Those men didn't have an angel to protect them.

Those men didn't even believe in God.

And the lions leaped on them, and killed them immediately.

Later, Darius sent a letter all through the Persian kingdom. "No one must ever say anything bad about Daniel's God, because He is the real and living God. Daniel's God is able to rescue the people who trust Him, and save them. He is a wonderful God, who rescued Daniel from the lions."

How good it is for us to know that Daniel's God is our God. God is real and living. And God can rescue you and me when we're in danger, just as He rescued Daniel.

When are you most happy that God takes care of you, as he took care of Daniel? When is it hardest to remember God is with you to protect you? God does love you and me, and he is always with us to care for us.

Action Idea

To visualize the teaching of this story make a "circle of God's love" tableau. From construction paper, cut a large circle. Then draw or purchase a figure of a man. Stand the man outside the circle. Outside, place several lion figures, obtained from a hobby shop or drawn and cut out. Also cut out a picture of your child, and place it inside the circle with Daniel.

Place the tableau as a centerpiece on your table, or in your child's room. Remind your child that God who protected Daniel from the lions protects us as well. We are safe inside the circle of God's love.

Jonah
Jonah 1–4

Background

Why do we discipline children? Our goal is not really to punish. Our goal is to help our children learn to make right choices. Good discipline is corrective—not punitive.

Few stories in the Bible illustrate this so clearly as the story of the reluctant prophet, Jonah. Commanded to go north to Nineveh, Jonah disobeyed God and headed south! But God worked on in Jonah's life. God brought Jonah to the place where he would choose obedience.

The story of Jonah illustrates many principles of the spiritual life. It illustrates the reality of the second chance: God doesn't give up on us when we fail! It illustrates the purpose of good discipline. It illustrates the wonder of forgiveness. And it helps us to believe in ourselves. God will not give up on us, so we need never give up on ourselves.

The introduction to Jonah provided in the story retold here focuses on these themes, discussed in paragraphs 49, 63, and 69. The story is suitable for use with children of every age.

The Story Retold

"How much money will it cost me to travel with you to Tarshish?" the little man asked the sea captain. The captain thought a minute and named a price. The little man looked around, as if he were afraid someone was watching. Then he took out his purse, paid the captain, and hurried on board the sailing ship.

Mmmmm, thought the captain. *That man acts like he's running away.* But the captain didn't think about the little man for long. The captain had cargo to load. His ship was getting ready to sail.

Inside the ship, the little man, whose name was Jonah, found a quiet corner and went to sleep. He was so tired. Jonah had hurried all the way from his home city, rushing to the sea. Jonah was one of God's prophets. And God had sent Jonah on a mission.

There was only one thing.

God said, "Go north to Nineveh."

Jonah was going south. Jonah was disobeying God!

How do you suppose God felt about Jonah disobeying him? How do you suppose Jonah felt? What do you think God should do to Jonah? Why? What happens to you when you disobey on purpose? Why do you suppose mom or dad do that to you?

Jonah was so tired that he didn't even wake up when the ship put out to sea. Jonah didn't wake up when the wind filled the sails, and the ship moved out over the waves. In fact, Jonah didn't even wake up when it began to storm. The wind blew harder and harder. The waves got higher and higher. Everyone else on the ship was awake, all right. They were all terrified! The crew even threw the cargo overboard to make the ship lighter.

It was then they found Jonah, still asleep.

The captain woke up Jonah.

"How can you sleep like that?" the captain shouted. "Get up and pray! Maybe your God will notice us and we won't all drown."

When Jonah saw the storm, he felt terrible.

But Jonah didn't say anything. And Jonah didn't pray.

As the storm grew worse, the men drew lots to find out if someone had done something wrong and if that was why the storm came.

Jonah drew the short straw!

"Tell us," all the sailors said. "Who are you? Where are you from?"

Then Jonah confessed. "I am a Hebrew (Jew) and I worship the living God, who created the sea and the land."

Terrified, they asked Jonah, "What have you done?"

"Men," Jonah said, "this storm has come because of me. The only thing you can do is throw me overboard. Then the ship will be safe."

Do you think God is trying to kill Jonah? Does God hurt or kill us when we disobey him? God loves us too much to want to hurt us. God wants what is best for us. Disobeying God isn't just wrong or bad. Disobeying God is foolish. God wants us to have what is best, and so God would not let Jonah get away with his sin of disobeying.

The sailors didn't want to throw Jonah overboard. They were sure Jonah would drown. So they tried to row to shore. But the waves were too big.

Finally the sailors asked God to forgive them and did what Jonah said. They picked Jonah up and threw him into the stormy sea. As soon as they did, the waters began to get calm again. The sailors knew now that God had sent the storm. And that God had made the storm stop. But when the sailors looked around the ocean, they couldn't see Jonah anywhere. The disobedient prophet was gone!

But Jonah wasn't dead.

When Jonah hit the water and began to sink, Jonah was sure he would drown. But before Jonah could drown, a great fish, specially prepared by God and sent to just that spot in the ocean, swallowed Jonah whole. Inside the great fish, Jonah finally began to pray!

Do you think God will listen to Jonah's prayers? Does God listen to our prayers when we have done wrong? What do you think Jonah will say to God? What do you say to God when you've done something wrong?

The first thing Jonah prayed was "Help!"

And then Jonah prayed something else. Jonah promised God that he would go back home and do what God told him to do. You and I can always ask God for help. We can tell God we will obey the Lord again, even after we've done wrong.

Three days later the great fish threw Jonah up on a beach back in Israel. Then God told Jonah again. "Go north, to the city of Nineveh, and take them My message."

So Jonah went north.

God gave Jonah another chance to obey Him. Jonah was ready at last to do what God said.

Action Idea

Talk about your family discipline practices. Explain that, like God, you discipline because you want your children to do the right thing. You do not want just to punish them. You want to help them do what is right.

Talk about incidents of discipline in the past few weeks or months. Have your punishments helped your children choose what is right? Would other discipline practices be of more help?

Assure your boys and girls that you believe in them. Like Jonah, they will learn to do what is right. And you will keep on giving them another chance.

The Birth of Jesus Is Promised
Isaiah 7:1–14

Background

Paragraphs 20 and 38 describe problems some boys and girls have with telling the truth. They suggest ways we can help our children realize that truth-telling is vital if they are to be trusted by others. The Bible lays a similar stress on God's Word to us. Scripture is Truth, the Bible says. Because the Word is truth, we can totally rely on what God tells us. In a very real sense, God himself is the model for us and for our children when it comes to truthfulness.

Prophecy is one great biblical theme which demonstrates God's truthfulness. God announces beforehand what will happen. God makes promises and keeps them. God's people can rely on what the Lord says will happen. Old Testament prophecy touches on many topics. One of the most common is that of the coming of a promised Savior. God has kept these Old Testament promises about Jesus. Because God has always kept his word, we can trust him to keep his word in all things.

As parents we need to be truthful with our children. We need to help them see the importance of truthfulness in every interpersonal relationship. This Bible story will help your boys and girls think about the importance of being trustworthy, and help them explore their relationship with others.

The Story Retold

King Ahaz was afraid.

Two nearby countries had agreed to attack Israel.

Ahaz's heart pounded. What could he do? The two countries were much stronger than his own land!

That's when God sent the prophet Isaiah to Ahaz with a promise. Isaiah, carrying his baby in his arms, met Ahaz and delivered God's message. "Don't worry," God told Ahaz. "They will not invade your country."

How do you suppose Ahaz felt when God made that promise to him? How would you feel if you were afraid, and God told you not to worry, that your enemies would not hurt you?

King Ahaz didn't feel happy about that promise. The king didn't feel relieved. Ahaz didn't even feel thankful. You see, Ahaz didn't really believe what God said.

God spoke again to Ahaz then. Isaiah the prophet told the king, "Ask God for some miracle as proof."

But Ahaz only shook his head. Ahaz wouldn't do what God said. "I will not ask," Ahaz said.

How do you suppose God felt when Ahaz wouldn't believe God was telling the truth? Do you think God was telling the truth? Why? When we always do tell the truth, as God does, then people can trust us. We can always trust God, because he always tells us the truth.

God was upset with Ahaz. God always tells the truth. There was no reason Ahaz shouldn't believe what God said.

Do you think we should trust people who don't always tell the truth? How do you feel when someone whom you know tells you made-up stories about something that happened? How do you feel when someone who doesn't keep promises makes you a promise? No, we can't trust people who don't tell us the truth. That's one reason it's important for you and me to tell the truth to others. We want to be the kind of person others can trust.

God was upset that Ahaz wouldn't believe Him. God always tells the truth. Just to prove to everyone, everywhere, that we can always trust God, God made a special promise.

"One day," God had the prophet Isaiah say, "a young woman will have a child all by herself, without a man as the father. That special child will be a boy, and he will be God, come to be with us."*

What a wonderful promise. God promised that His Son would come to earth and be born as a baby! What an impossible thing, some people might think. But it did happen, just as God promised. And you know who that special child was. Yes, it was Jesus. Hundreds and hundreds of years before Jesus was born, God told us He was coming. And it happened, just as God said.

God wants us to know we can always trust him. So God always tells us the truth in the Bible. How do you suppose you'd feel if you tried to tell someone something important, and they didn't believe you? Has that ever happened to you? Tell us about it. How did you feel when they wouldn't believe you?

When other people learn that we tell them the truth all the time, they learn to trust us. They won't be able to trust us if we don't tell them the truth.

Most important, God wants us to learn to be like him. Because God is the kind of Person everyone can trust, God wants you and me to be trustworthy persons too.

Let's thank God now that we can always trust him, because he never lies to us or breaks his promises.

Action Idea

Together look up other promises in the Old Testament about Jesus' coming. See how each one was fulfilled. You can do this as a pre-Christmas activity, as well as an activity linked with encouraging truthfulness.

Important Old Testament promise passages, are found in: Isaiah 9:1–2, 6–7, 11:1, 53:9, 12; Micah 5:2; Zechariah 9:9, 11:12–13; Psalms 22:18, 69:21, 22:1, 31:5, 34:20.

Mary Is Told of Jesus' Birth
Matthew 1, Luke 1

Background

Christmas is one of the two focal events of the Christian year. During this season we remember the Incarnation: the birth of Jesus as truly Man and fully God, to become our Savior. The meaning

---

* The name Imanuel means "God with us."

of Christmas can be clouded by the excitement of giving and receiving gifts. Its meaning can be distorted, as Santa replaces the Christ child as central figure in winter's culminating drama. It is important that in our homes a special place for Jesus be retained.

This is the first of a series of three Christmas stories, retold in this *Handbook,* with suggestions for family activities which can enrich your Christmas season, and keep Christ at the center of your family life. See paragraph 94.

The Story Retold

Mary was sewing.

My goodness, she thought. *I'll never get this dress done in time. Now, where did I put that white thread?*

It was exciting to be sewing on these particular clothes. You see, Mary was engaged to be married. She was preparing the clothes she would bring to her new home when the marriage took place. Why, she and Joseph would be married in just ten more months. There was so much more to do!

We don't know just what Mary was doing one special night. But we do know something wonderful that happened to her. As Mary was working around her home, an angel came to her.

"Greetings, Mary," the angel said. "You are highly favored by God. The Lord is with you."

Mary was upset at first. After all, angels don't come and speak to people very often! Besides, Mary didn't know what the angel's words of greeting might mean.

The angel explained. "Don't be afraid, Mary. God plans something wonderful for you. You are going to have a baby boy, and you are to name Him Jesus. This child will be very great. He will be the Son of God, and will be King over an endless kingdom."

Mary was shocked. "But," she said to the angel, "how can I have a baby? I'm not even married!"

The angel answered Mary's question. "Your baby, Jesus, won't have a human father. God Himself will make the baby grow, so the holy child that you have will be the Son of God."

Mary didn't even wait to think about it. "I am the Lord's

servant," she said. "Whatever God wants, I want it to happen too."

Then the angel left Mary to think about the wonderful and amazing promise God had made. Every other baby born into our world would have a human father and a human mother. But this baby, Jesus, would only have a human mother. God would be the Father of Jesus. Jesus would be the Son of God.

Later Mary made up a song to celebrate. She was so happy about Jesus being born, that she wanted to sing for joy. Here is part of her song:

"I praise the Lord,
  I am full of joy in God my savior.
God has remembered even me,
  and everyone will think of me as
  blessed to be Jesus' mother.
The Mighty God has done such great things for me—
  He is holy,
  He is full of mercy for everyone
    who worships Him."

Mary must have sung her song of joy many times as Jesus' birth drew near. Now we all celebrate the birth of Jesus together. Sending Jesus to be our Savior is one of the most wonderful things God has ever done.

Action Idea

Use the story to launch preparations for your own family celebration of this season. Let your children take part in all your preparations. What are some of the things you might do together? One fun family project is to make up your own joy songs of celebration, like Mary's. Pick a theme for your songs, such as "Jesus loves me" or "How Jesus helps me." When everyone has written their own poem (joy song), read them to each other. You may want to print them on large sheets of construction paper with a felt-tipped pen, and attach them to your walls. Of course, it's also traditional to decorate the house during the Christmas season. In keeping with the celebration theme, plan with your boys and girls how to make your home look joyful. Plan for the inside and, if you wish, the outside also. You'll also find it's fun for your children to visit a Christian bookstore and pick out tapes or records that can fill your home with joyful Christmas music.

Keeping the family focus during the Christmas season on celebration and joy, you will help your boys and girls grasp the true meaning of Christmas.

Jesus Is Born
Matthew 1, Luke 2

Background

This is the second in a sequence of three stories which focus on Christmas. This season we remember the incarnation of Jesus: the great miracle which God performed when the eternal Son of God became a human being. The meaning of the Christmas season is not summed up in gifts or vacation or TV advertisements for expensive toys. The central figure at Christmas is not Santa, but Christ. Yet our goal at Christmas time is not to completely shut out the secular world, for this would be impossible. Our goal is simply, through family times together, and by the atmosphere of our home, to affirm the fact that Jesus is the One in whom we rejoice at this special time of year. See paragraph 94.

This particular Christmas story is one I read with my family on Christmas Eve, though you may use it at any time during the season.

The Story Retold

Mary swayed back and forth on the back of the little donkey.

Mary was tired. And the baby inside her seemed heavier than ever.

"How much further?" Mary asked Joseph.

"Not far now," Joseph said, as he walked along beside Mary and the donkey. "We're almost to Bethlehem."

Mary and Joseph were going to Bethlehem because Joseph's family came from Bethlehem, where his ancestor King David had been born. Mary and Joseph had to go to Bethlehem. The people of Israel were being counted, and everyone had to return to his hometown for the census. Even though Mary's baby was almost ready to be born, Mary had to go to Bethlehem.

Mary may not have known it. But many, many years

ago God promised that the Savior would be born in Bethlehem. Because of the census, Mary would be in Bethlehem when Jesus was born.

How Joseph must have worried as the two of them came near the little town. Where would Mary stay? Bethlehem was a small town. There weren't hotels and motels. There was just a small inn where travelers could stay. But now many, many people would be coming back to Bethlehem to be counted. The inn might be full.

It was nearly night when Mary and Joseph came to Bethlehem. Mary's back ached from the baby and the long ride. Joseph was tired and dusty. Both of them were cold, because a chill wind blew. And just as Joseph had feared, the inn was full!

"But what can we do?" Joseph asked the innkeeper. "Where can we stay?"

The innkeeper shrugged. "I'm sorry," he said. "The town is just full. And my inn is full, too."

"It wouldn't be so bad," Joseph explained, "but my wife is just about to have her baby."

The innkeeper looked at Mary. Yes, there was no doubt. She was going to have a baby. And soon!

"I'll tell you what," the innkeeper said. "I could let you stay in my stable. It's nice and warm, and there is soft straw to rest on. It's probably the best place you'll find here these days."

"That will be fine," Joseph said gratefully.

So the innkeeper led Mary's donkey out behind the inn. There, not far along a stony trail, was a deep cave in the rocky hill. The innkeeper had put a wooden wall in front of the cave, and built stables inside for some of his animals.

As soon as Mary went into the cave-stable, she felt better. Friendly cows looked at her with warm, brown eyes. Young sheep moved close, to nuzzle her ankles curiously. Their bodies had warmed the air in the cave-stable, and for the first time that day Mary began to feel warm herself. Gratefully she lay down to rest on a pile of straw. The straw felt so much softer than the back of that donkey! Before Mary knew it she had fallen asleep.

Joseph moved quietly, unloading his donkey and finding

a place where he could rest too. Like Mary, Joseph was thankful. God had provided a place for Mary to rest, warm and safe, even though the inn was full.

It was later that evening when Mary suddenly woke up. She could feel the baby moving inside. She could feel her own body squeeze together, pushing the baby down further and further in her body. "Joseph," Mary whispered, "the baby! The baby is going to be born tonight."

That same night shepherds, living in nearby fields so they could take care of their flocks of sheep, saw something wonderful. An angel suddenly appeared, and they were surrounded by a bright, glowing light. The men were terrified. But the angel spoke to them. "Don't be afraid," the angel said. "I have good news . . . news of great joy for you and for everyone everywhere. Today, in David's town of Bethlehem, the Savior has been born. He is the Christ, the Lord. And you will find the child lying in a manger, wrapped in strips of cloth."

Then many, many angels appeared. They sang and celebrated, and praised God for the wonderful birth of Jesus. "Glory to God in the highest," they sang, "and peace on earth to men on whom God's favor rests."

The angels sang and praised God while the amazed shepherds watched. When the angels left and returned to heaven, the shepherds talked excitedly to each other. "Let's go!" they said. "Yes. Let's go the Bethlehem. We want to see this wonderful thing the Lord has told us about."

The shepherds hurried toward Bethlehem, Mary, and her baby. Just as God had told Mary, the baby was a boy. Just as God had told her, Mary named the baby Jesus. They didn't have diapers or "Pampers" in those days. So Mary carefully washed her new Son and wrapped His body in strips of cloth. Mary laid the baby beside her in the manger. Looking down at her very first child, the very special child who would grow up to be our Savior, Mary was very happy.

Then the shepherds came. The shepherds pounded on the door of the inn. They told the innkeeper and all the guests about the wonderful things they had seen in the field. The shepherds told of the angels' songs of celebration, and the message from God that the promised Savior was born that night. And then everyone hurried to the cave-stable, to see the baby.

The manger didn't seem a special place. But as everyone peered at Mary and her baby, and as the quiet animals watched, they all knew that this was the most special place of all. And this was the most special night of all. Jesus was born! God had kept His promises. The Son of God was here to be our Savior.

Action Idea

Reconstruct the manger scene in your home. Plaster of Paris sets for molding Mary, Joseph, the baby, shepherds, and several animals are available during the Christmas season at hobby shops. Make casting and painting these figures—and setting up your own manger scene—a family project.

The Wise Men Visit
Matthew 2

Background

This is the third in a sequence of three stories for the Christmas season. With their *Action Ideas* these stories are designed to help you keep your family's focus on celebration of Jesus' birth. Our world promotes many competing emphases. There is the emphasis on giving and receiving gifts. There is the emphasis on Santa, with secular carols like "Rudolph, the Red-Nosed Reindeer." So it's particularly important to keep the emphasis in our homes on the real meaning of Christmas. We celebrate the coming of God's own Son, and his incarnation as a human being to be our Savior. By filling our homes with a sense of celebration (page 100) and maintaining our sense of wonder at Jesus' birth (pages 100–101), we can keep Christ in our Christmases.

This particular Christmas story can stimulate the practice followed in our home all during the children's growing-up years, of having a special family "birthday gift" for Jesus. Christmas day was not only a day we showed love to each other by giving gifts. It was a day during which we remembered God's gift of his Son, during which we gave to God our own special "thank you" gift.

The Story Retold

Far away from Bethlehem where Jesus was born, wise men called Magi studied. They studied ancient books. They studied mathematics. They studied the stars. For hundreds of years Magi studied and learned many things. Each generation wrote down what it learned—and taught others. Studying wasn't very exciting. But learning was important. And so the Magi spent all their time trying to learn more.

Then one night something very exciting happened.

A special, bright star began to shine.

The Magi were very excited. What could that star mean? They studied all their old books. They studied the books of foreign countries, like the Old Testament books of the Jews. And finally they found out what that special, bright star meant!

"I've found it," one of them told the others. "The promised King of the Jews has been born. That's what the star means! God's Son has come to earth at last!"

"Oh," another shouted. "How wonderful! We've got to go and see Him." "Yes," a third agreed, "we have to go and worship Him. Let's hurry and get ready."

They were so excited. It was a long journey, and it would take them many months to get to Palestine. But right away they started to get ready.

The Magi had servants pack up special tents, for they would camp out while on the journey. They carefully selected the food they would take along. They didn't want to be hungry on the journey. The wise men took soft bedding too. It wouldn't do to sleep on the ground. They picked out the camels they would ride. And they thought a long time about how much money to bring. The Magi knew they would need money as they traveled. These wise men planned very carefully, and finally they knew they had everything they needed.

"Now wait," one of the wise men said. "We have everything we need to live comfortably on our journey. God has taken good care of us. But God has done even more. God has given us His Son, as the star told us. What are we going to bring on our journey as a gift for the Baby King, to say 'thank you' to God?"

The wise men thought very hard.

What gifts would be good enough for God's Son? How would they say "thank you" for giving Jesus to the world?

After thinking very hard, and planning very carefully, each wise man picked out his own special gift to give to Jesus. The gifts were packed, and the wise men started on their long journey.

Months later, the Magi came to Jerusalem. There they began to ask, "Where is the One who is born to be King of the Jews?" No one knew what they were talking about. The king then was Herod, and Herod hadn't had any children recently. "Well," the wise men said, "we saw His star in the East, and have come to worship Him."

When King Herod heard about the wise men and their question, he was upset. *He* was king, and Herod didn't want any other king around. So Herod called all the teachers of the Bible together and asked them an important question. "Where does the Bible say the Christ, the Son of God, will be born?" The wise men opened their Bibles. They knew the answer to that question! "King Herod, the prophet Micah has written that the great ruler of God's people will be born in Bethlehem" (cf. Micah 5:2).

So King Herod called the Magi to a secret conference. Herod asked them when the star first appeared. "Almost two years ago," the Magi told Herod. Then the king sent them to Bethlehem, to look for the child. "If you find the child," Herod said, "come back and report to me."

The happy Magi hurried off toward Bethlehem, just a few miles away. They had traveled so far, for so many months. As the Magi went, the star they had seen in the East shone brightly. "There it is!" they said. And the star's light glowed especially bright on one particular house.

The wise men stopped and got down off their camels. One of them knocked on the door.

Mary opened the door.

Inside the Magi saw a little boy, just able to stand beside his mother. Then the Magi got down on their knees and bowed down to Him. Jesus looked like other boys. But the wise men knew. Jesus was the Son of God.

Now the wise men got out the gifts they had selected so carefully. They hoped their gifts would show how thankful they were to God for the gift of His Son, Jesus.

One wise man opened his treasure box and gave Jesus a gift of gold.

One wise man opened his treasure box, and gave Jesus a gift of very expensive perfume, called incense.

One wise man opened his treasure box, and gave Jesus a gift of expensive spice, called myrrh.

How thrilled and happy the Magi were to be able to give gifts to Jesus, to show their thanks to God.

The wise men didn't go back and report to Herod. God warned them in a dream to go back to their homes a different way. When the angry Herod heard, he sent soldiers to Bethlehem to search for and kill the baby Jesus.

But before the soldiers got there, an angel came and told Joseph in a dream to hurry to Egypt. Joseph and Mary had been very poor. They had not had enough money for a long trip like that. But with the rich gifts that the Magi gave Mary and Joseph there would be plenty of money now. They used it to hurry with Jesus to safety. God used the Magi's "thank you" Christmas gifts in a very special way.

Action Idea

This Christmas make your own treasure chests, in which to save loose coins or other money for a special "thank you" gift for Jesus next Christmas (see paragraph 94).

Jesus Sees Nathanael
John 1:29–49

Background

Most younger children have a strong desire to please adults. But it's often hard for children when only friends are near. Then they want to please their friends, even though the things they do may not be right (see paragraph 17). Children will sometimes do things then that they would never do if an adult, whose approval they valued, were present.

One of the wonderful realities taught in Scripture is that God is omnipresent. God is able to be in all places at the same time, totally aware of each of us as individuals. God's promise, "I am with you always," is one of the great heritages you and I are able to pass on to our boys and girls.

Perhaps most exciting is the realization that God does not stand over us as a Cosmic Policeman or Universal Nag. God's purpose in being close to us is to support and encourage us, not to catch us out in a fault. Through awareness of God's presence with us at all times, God intends us to have a growing sense of his approval as we make choices to please him.

This Bible story, told for six- to eight-year-olds, is designed to help you build into your youngster's awareness a warm sense of God's approving promise. That sense of God's presence can help your child make right choices when you and other adults are not there (see paragraph 65).

The Story Retold

Jesus grew up in the little town of Nazareth. For many years Jesus worked there with Joseph. Jesus and Joseph were carpenters. But when Jesus was about thirty years old, He knew it was time. From now on, Jesus would travel around Israel and teach God's Word to His people. Finally Jesus would die on the cross, to pay for our sins.

But when Jesus began, He needed helpers. The helpers would be called Jesus' disciples. They would travel with Him, and learn to know and to obey God's Word. Then, when Jesus went back to heaven, the disciples would teach others to love God and obey His Word.

What do you suppose was the best thing about being a disciple? Do you think you would have wanted to be one of Jesus' disciples if you lived then? Why, or why not?

One of the men who preached God's Word in those days was named John the Baptist. John knew that soon God's own Son would come. So John went all around the country telling people to get ready. John didn't know who God's Son was. But John knew that He was coming.

One day John saw Jesus, and God told John, "Jesus is

the One!" John was so excited, he couldn't keep the news to himself. "Look," John said to some friends, "this is the One I was talking about. Jesus is the Son of God."

The next day John told others. Some of the men whom John told ran and asked Jesus if they could spend the day with Him. As Jesus talked to them, these men also knew who Jesus was.

One of the men who spent the day with Jesus was named Philip. Philip was so excited. Like John, Philip wanted to tell someone who Jesus was. So Philip went to look for his brother Nathanael.

But where could Nathanael be? Philip looked everywhere. He looked around the town. He looked in the valley. He climbed the hills. Finally Philip found Nathanael, resting under a tree, over a hill and out of sight.

"Nathanael!" Philip called excitedly. "Nathanael! We've found Him. The One the Bible promises. Our Savior is Jesus, a man from Nazareth."

Nathanael wasn't excited at all. "Nazareth," Nathanael said. "Why, no one special could come from that little town."

But Philip was sure. "Come and see for yourself," Philip urged his brother. So Nathanael got up and came with Philip. As they came up to Jesus, Jesus looked at Nathanael and smiled. "Here is a good man," Jesus said. "Here is an honest and faithful person." Nathanael was shocked. How did Jesus know him?

How do you suppose Jesus knew the kind of person Nathanael was? Do you think Nathanael liked being called a good person? How do you feel when mom or dad or someone else praises you? It's good to know that people like you and approve of what you do.

But Nathanael couldn't understand how Jesus could know him, to say nice things about him. Nathanael didn't know that Jesus was the Son of God. And God can see everyone, all the time.

"Nathanael," Jesus answered, "I saw you while you were still sitting under the fig tree, before Philip called you."

And then Nathanael knew.

Jesus had seen him.

Jesus knew what Nathanael was doing, even when Nathanael was out of sight. Only God can see us always. So Nathanael knew Jesus must be God.

So Nathanael said, "Teacher, You are the Son of God. You are the King of Israel."

How do you suppose it made Nathanael feel to know that Jesus always saw him? How do you feel when you think about Jesus seeing you always? (Share how the sense of God's presence makes you feel.)

God didn't watch Nathanael to catch him doing something wrong. God watched Nathanael to see all the good choices Nathanael made. And Jesus was pleased with Nathanael. Jesus called Nathanael a truly good person.

Jesus sees you and me, and is very pleased with us when we make right choices as Nathanael did. When we have a hard decision to make, it helps to remember Jesus is watching. We can please Jesus by choosing the right thing.

What are some times when it's hard for you to choose to do right—times when mom and dad aren't there to see you? Let's thank God that he is there to watch you. Jesus is always happy with you when you do the right thing to please him.

Action Idea

It may be fun and helpful to your children if your whole family joins "Club Nathanael." There is only one rule for club members. When they are away from each other, they will remember to do what will please Jesus, who is always with them.

You may find it helpful to your boys and girls to have one or two club meetings a week for a month or two. Let your children make up a club motto, choose a club password in the John 1 passage, and work up a meeting agenda. One feature of the club meeting should be a report of times when remembering that Jesus sees us helped a member make a choice he believes pleased God.

Jesus Heals an Official's Son
John 4:43–54

Background

Going to the hospital is difficult enough for many adults. It's especially hard for children, who may be even more anxious if they have to be separated from their parents. There are a number of things moms and dads can do to help. Along with following the suggestions given in paragraph 44, telling and talking about this Bible story may minister God's comfort to your children.

The Gospels report many miracles of healing performed by Jesus during his time on earth. Often Jesus' acts of compassion and love carry distinctive touches. The story told of the healing of a royal official's son in John 4 is such an incident. The distinctive here is one of distance. The father of the sick child traveled from his home in Capernaum to Cana to seek Jesus' help. Although the father begged Jesus to come with him, the Lord refused. Instead, Jesus simply promised the boy would be well. The man trusted Jesus' word and turned back toward home. On the way he was met with good news. At the very moment Jesus spoke with him, the child began to recover. Distance and separation were unable to limit the loving, healing touch of God.

Children today will find comfort in the realization that even when parents are not there, God is with them. And God is able to make them well.

The Story Retold

The worried father walked back and forth. His forehead was wrinkled, and he rubbed his hands together nervously. His son was very sick. But the father wasn't there with him. Even worse, the father knew if he were there, he wouldn't be able to help. What could he do to help his sick boy?

As the father walked back and forth, he noticed excited people outside. They were talking loudly and waving their hands. He could hear them shout joyfully to their friends. It sounded like . . . yes, it was! They were saying that Jesus was coming into town!

The father knew about Jesus. Everyone had heard about Jesus! Why, Jesus went from town to town and taught people about God. And the father knew something else, too. Jesus had made sick people well!

How excited the father felt then. Here was something he could do for his son. The father could ask Jesus to come to his home in Capernaum! Quickly the father hurried out the door and followed the crowds. The father would talk to Jesus, and get Jesus to help!

When the father found Jesus, he rushed up to him. "Jesus," the father begged. "Please come and heal my son. I'm afraid he will die if You don't help!"

Jesus shook His head. "Can't you trust Me unless you see Me perform a miracle?" Jesus asked.

But the father only cared about one thing. "Sir," he said to Jesus, "please come down to my home before my child dies."

Jesus smiled at the man. "It's all right. You can go home now. Your son will live."

The father believed Jesus.

Jesus wasn't there in the room with the sick son. But the father believed that Jesus could make his child well wherever Jesus might be. Relieved and happy, the father started back toward Capernaum. While he was still on the way, some servants met him with the good news. His boy was alive and getting well! When the father asked when the boy got better, the servants told him. It was just the time that Jesus had said, "Your son will live."

How glad the father was that he had talked with Jesus about his son. How glad the father was that Jesus could heal his son, even when the father wasn't there and when Jesus was in Cana too. Jesus is with us *wherever* we are. And Jesus will help us as He helped the father of the sick boy.

Action Idea

Rather than talk with your child to help him develop his own insights from this story, use it as a basis to explain your relationship with him or her while in the hospital. You may not be able to be there, just as the father in the story couldn't be with his sick child. But like the father, you will be thinking about your child.

Like the father in the story, you will talk with Jesus to ask his help. You will pray for your child while he's in the hospital. You will visit when you can. But you know that Jesus will be with your child whenever you can't be there. You also trust Jesus to take care of your child and work through the doctors to make him or her well.

Your expression of trust in Jesus will help your boy or girl trust, too, when he or she is most likely to need comfort and reassurance.

Jesus Touches a Leper
Mark 1:40–45

Background

One of the most basic skills children need to develop is the ability to sense what others feel. We need insight into the point of view of others, and the ability to do something social scientists call "social role-taking." This is difficult for younger boys and girls. Many up to ages eight and nine simply haven't developed to the place where this is possible for them. Such children simply cannot divorce themselves from their own viewpoint, to see things from the perspective of another. This capacity will develop as our children grow. It's just that we can't tell the age when the ability for such sensitivity will develop in a given individual.

What can we do then? One thing parents can do is to encourage social role-taking. Then, as children do develop the cognitive capacities needed, they will begin to sense the importance of sensitivity in personal relationships.

The sensitivity of Jesus to the inner needs of individuals, as well as to their more obvious problems, is one of the most attractive features of this Gospel's portrait of our Lord. As you share the story of Jesus healing the leper, as reported in the first chapter of Mark, you can help your boys and girls sense the importance of sensitivity. Putting into practice the suggestions provided in paragraph 13, and the *Action Idea* following this story, will assist you in helping your boys and girls develop this vital relational skill.

The Story Retold

Jesus got up very early one morning. He left the house where He was staying and found a place where He could be alone. There Jesus prayed, talking with God the Father.

When Jesus' disciples found Him, they were upset. "Everyone is looking for You, Jesus!" they said.

But Jesus shook His head.

"It's time to go on," Jesus said. "I must go to other towns

where people need me. I have to teach them about God. And there are people who hurt, whom I want to help."

What do you suppose were some of the hurts Jesus wanted to help people with? Can you think of ways you have hurt this last week? Do you have any friends who have been hurting this week?

As Jesus traveled from town to town, He helped many people who were hurting. One of them was very special. He was a man with the disease of leprosy.

Leprosy was a terrible disease in Bible times. We don't have much leprosy in our country. But people who had leprosy then suffered very much. Their bodies had great sores on them. Some lepers found their fingers and toes and even ears became very dry and hard. Then the ends of the fingers and toes wore away.

Everyone was afraid of leprosy in Bible days. No one would come near a leper. Everyone was terrified he might get the sickness too.

When the leper came to Jesus, he didn't get close to Him. Instead the leper crawled up and begged Jesus on his knees. "Please," the leper sobbed, "if You are willing, You can make me whole and well again."

What do you suppose Jesus will do? How do you think Jesus felt about the leper? How are Jesus' feelings different from the feelings of people who are afraid of the leper? Do you think the leper is one of the hurting people Jesus wanted to help? Where do you think the leper hurt most?

Jesus looked at the leper. He knew how much the leper's body hurt. But Jesus knew the leper was hurting inside too. For years no one had loved the leper. No one had touched him. No one had hugged the leper, or told the leper that he was loved. The leper was so lonely, without a single friend, that he hurt deeply inside.

Jesus knew how much the leper hurt inside, and Jesus was filled with compassion. Jesus cared very much for the leper, because He understood how he felt.

Do you ever hurt inside? What happened to make you feel hurt inside? Did anyone help you then? How did someone help you feel better? Can you name some of the feelings that you had when you hurt inside?

Jesus knew how much the leper hurt inside. Jesus knew how alone and friendless the leper felt. The leper needed to have his disease healed. But Jesus knew the leper also needed to be loved. "I am willing," Jesus told him. "Be well." And Jesus did something else. He reached out and touched the lonely leper, to heal the hurt inside.

When Jesus touched the leper, and his sickness was healed, the man knew that someone loved him. The leper would not have to be lonely any more.

How do you think Jesus knew the leper hurt inside? How can we tell when someone is lonely, or hurts inside in some other way? (Talk about how people might look, and try to imitate their faces. Talk about what they might say, or do. Talk about how members of your family act when they feel badly, and want someone to care.) What can we do to help someone who may hurt inside? What helps you when you hurt inside?

One thing that makes Jesus so special is that He cares when we hurt inside as well as when our bodies hurt. Caring how people feel inside, and wanting to help, is called "compassion." How glad Jesus must be when you and I have compassion for our friends, and try to help them when they hurt.

Action Idea

Make a list of all the words your children can think of that describe unhappy or hurting feelings. Write each feeling on a 3 x 5 card. You might want to make this a family project, to last a week. Have each family member keep looking for new feeling words to add to your cards. Words may show up in reading, or older boys and girls may look in a dictionary.

When you have a complete list, you can use the cards in a number of ways. You may make a game for the family to play. Each person draws a card at random. Then he or she tries to act out the feelings, so others will guess how he feels inside. The acting can be pantomime. Or you may use words. When the family has guessed the inside feeling, each can (a) tell of a time he or she felt that way and what happened to bring on the feeling, or (b) suggest ways to help a person with those feelings.

The goal of this family game is to help your children recognize clues to others' feelings by their behavior. Practice can help them become more sensitive to others, learn how to put themselves in others' places and respond with Christlike compassion to others' needs.

Jesus Calms the Storm
Matthew 8:23–27, Mark 4:35–41

Background

The children in my Sunday school class were drawing pictures to show what they liked best about this Bible story. Most of them picked dramatic themes. They drew great waves and a tossing boat. Or they drew Jesus standing in the boat, with his arms raised to calm the storm. But one nine-year-old drew a very different picture. She drew a picture of a room, with a bed and window, and in the window she showed a quarter moon. When I asked her to tell me about the picture, she explained.

"What I like best is that at night, when I'm afraid of the dark, I remember that Jesus is with me like he was with his disciples in the boat."

My young friend captured and beautifully applied the wonderful message of this story for boys and girls—and for adults. The disciples were frightened on that storm-tossed sea, because they had forgotten that Jesus was present. Yes, there was danger. But Jesus was there, and Jesus is able to overcome any danger that threatens those he loves.

Children's fears are discussed in paragraphs 30 through 33. Fears are very real to boys and girls. But the sense of Jesus' presence can bring an inner calm into their lives. When Jesus is present, life is not out of control. Jesus is able to calm our storms as well.

The Story Retold

Jesus was very tired, there on the lakeshore. Jesus had been teaching the people of Israel about God for hours and hours. And still more people came, wanting to hear Jesus, and hoping Jesus would help the sick get well.

Finally Jesus had to leave the crowd that pressed around Him to go to another place. He got into a boat with His disciples, and they pushed the boat out into the big lake.

Jesus was so tired He fell asleep right away.

The disciples put up the sail. Probably the disciples tried to be very quiet. They didn't want to wake Jesus up.

But as the boat got out into the middle of the lake, a terrible wind began to blow. Suddenly, without any warning at all, giant waves began to toss the little boat.

Jesus' disciples were fishermen. They had spent most of their lives working in boats on this lake. But this storm was the worst one they had ever seen. Before long the disciples were sure the boat was going to sink. Water from the high waves was splashing in, and the boat was about to fill with water.

Jesus was still asleep!

Finally the disciples cried out in terror. Shaking Jesus to wake Him up, they said, "Lord, save us! We're about to drown!"

(Give each family member a sheet of paper and crayons. Have each person draw a picture of the disciples' faces when they saw how terrible the storm was.) Let's talk about our pictures. How do you think the disciples felt in that boat? How did you show that feeling in your picture? Do you remember ever feeling the way the disciples felt? Tell us about when you felt afraid.

The disciples were very afraid.

But when Jesus woke up, He was surprised.

"Why are you so afraid?" Jesus asked them. "Don't you trust Me?" The disciples should have known that nothing could hurt them, because Jesus was with them.

Jesus stood up in the tossing boat.

Jesus looked at the waves and felt the howling winds. He looked at the wild waters. Then Jesus said, "Stop!" Immediately the wind was still. Immediately the waves stopped tossing. Immediately the lake was completely calm.

How do you think the men with Jesus felt then? Why would they have those feelings?

The disciples were amazed. They had never dreamed that Jesus could even make the storm, the winds, and the waves obey Him.

The disciples were learning just how wonderful Jesus is. When Jesus was with them, the disciples would never need to be afraid.

Draw a picture of what you like best about this story. Tell us about your picture, and why you drew what you did.

Action Idea

Continue to use drawings to help your children apply this story to their own fears. Have each family member draw a picture of a time when he or she is glad that Jesus is with him, as Jesus was with the men in the boat. If your children need help, remind them of times they mentioned when you did the first *talkable* together.

Let each family member tell about the picture he or she has drawn, and tell why fears come at that time. Assure your children that Jesus is with them at the times they feel most afraid. Jesus is able to protect them, just as he protected his disciples in the boat.

You may want to let each child hang his or her picture in the place where the fears come, as a reminder. You may also find it helpful to pick up from your local Christian bookstore a packet of stamps showing Jesus. Place one sticker on each picture, to remind your children that the Lord really is with them when they feel afraid. Jesus loves them, just as he loved the disciples. Jesus always watches over those he loves.

Jesus' Friends Reject Him
Matthew 13:53–58; Luke 4:13–30

Background

Children are often unthinkingly cruel to one another. One day girls are best friends. The next day one won't play with or even talk with another. Or the neighborhood boys run off to play, leaving your son out. "You can't come. It's just for our club!" is a phrase which makes club membership seem special to those who are in— but can deeply hurt those left out.

Normally all children experience some rejection from friends. The rejection hurts. But hurt is a normal part of life, and children, too, must learn to cope. At times, though, the rejection pattern becomes more serious. If the girls aren't back to being friends in a day or so, and our son isn't out playing with the other neighborhood boys later in the afternoon, we may need to do more than to sympathize. Paragraph 12 contains some suggestions. And this Bible story is designed to help.

You can use this Bible story of Jesus' rejection by his neighbors in his home town to help your children explore their feelings when rejected. The *talkables* are designed on the assumption that talking about what has happened will help your boy or girl to be better able to handle rejection experiences. Also, talking about what has happened will give you clues as to whether this is a normal childhood experience, or may be part of a more serious rejection pattern with which you'll want to deal.

The Story Retold

Jesus was famous now.

All over the land of Israel, people talked about Jesus. People were amazed at what Jesus taught them about God. People were amazed at the miracles Jesus did to help others. Everyone was sure that Jesus was very special.

Can you name some people who think you are special? (Be sure to share ways in which your child is special to you. Also encourage your child to name friends who may think he or she is special too.) How does it make you feel to know that others like you and think you are special?

Of course, Jesus was more special than anyone who ever lived. Jesus was God's own Son. And Jesus came to show the people of the world how much God loves them. People who were sure that Jesus is special were right.

And then Jesus came to His hometown.

Jesus was born in Bethlehem, but His family moved and settled in Nazareth. Jesus lived in Nazareth for years and years, and worked there as a carpenter. Nazareth was a small town, so Jesus knew almost everyone. And everyone knew Jesus.

All Jesus' neighbors had heard about the wonderful things Jesus was doing in Israel. That weekend, everyone was in the synagogue-church when Jesus came.

How curious they were.

What would Jesus do?

Well, that morning Jesus got up and read from the Bible. He read a part of the Bible that told about His own coming to be our Savior. Jesus' neighbors listened. But they weren't happy about what Jesus said. Instead they resented Jesus.

"Who does Jesus think He is?" someone muttered.

"Yeah," another one said, "He's not *that* special. Why, Jesus is just one of a poor carpenter's family. He can't be important."

"We know Jesus' brothers and His sisters," someone else spoke up. "Why, Jesus' brothers, James and Joseph and Simon and Judas, are just plain people, like us. Who does Jesus think He is anyway?"

Jesus' friends and neighbors were actually getting angry at Him! Jesus' friends didn't seem to like Him at all!

Have your friends or neighbors ever been angry at you without a good reason? Tell about a time when your friends decided they didn't like you. How did you feel when your friends did that? Why do you think they were angry or didn't like you?

Jesus hadn't done anything wrong. But Jesus' neighbors were angry at Jesus, and decided they didn't like Him at all. Jesus knew His old friends were rejecting Him. His old friends didn't want anything to do with Him. Being rejected like that always makes people hurt inside. Jesus must have felt hurt too.

Jesus must have felt particularly sad when all His friends and neighbors got up and tried to chase Him out of town! "Go away!" they yelled. Some of them were even ready to throw stones at Jesus, or throw Jesus down to hurt Him. But God took care of Jesus, as He takes care of us.

Do your friends ever chase you away and not want to play with you? How do you feel when that happens? What do you suppose Jesus will do now? How will he feel?

Jesus must have been deeply hurt by the rejection. Everyone is hurt when he or she is rejected. Sometimes we feel angry at our friends when that happens. But Jesus knew that He couldn't be with His friends when they didn't want Him. So Jesus went on to another town, and He began to teach there.

Jesus knew that He was special; even His friends didn't like Him then. Jesus would keep on loving others, and someday many of His old friends would believe in Him, and like Him again.

How long do your friends usually seem not to like you when you are rejected? Can you think of times when your friends didn't want to play one day, but wanted to play with you the next day? If you and I keep on being friendly, our friends will usually want to be with us again soon.

Action Idea

It's likely that simply talking through the Bible story with your child will help him or her feel better about momentary rejection. It may help especially if you encourage your boy or girl to express rejection feelings to Jesus, knowing that Jesus understands, because the Lord had the same experience.

A possible activity is to make a "rejection wheel." Use a paper plate divided into equal pie-shaped segments. Each segment can be labeled in sequence with the words illustrated. Friends may do things that hurt each other, or even not want to be with others for a time. When we are rejected we hurt inside. But by keeping on being friendly, we will usually be friends again after awhile.

The plate can be colored by the child to show how he or she feels at each stage, and thumbtacked to a wall or bulletin board. If you wish, also tack a pointer in the upper right quadrant, and let your child rotate the plate through the cycle as he or she experiences times of rejection. Your goal in making the Rejection Wheel is to help your child have a sense of hope when he or she hurts, knowing that the one who rejected will be a friend again soon.

If you find that the rejection experienced by your child is a common or dominant aspect of his relationships with others, you'll want to follow suggestions given in paragraphs 13 and 14.

Jesus, the Good Shepherd
John 10:1–18

Background

Nighttime fears are so common with boys and girls of six to eight and even older that several stories in this *Handbook* are designed to provide a sense of nighttime security.

One of the most comforting images in Scripture, found in both Testaments, is that of God as our Shepherd. The image was especially meaningful to children of Bible days, who were very familiar with the way a shepherd cared for his sheep. Yet somehow even modern boys and girls quickly sense the caring and commitment which mark the shepherd/sheep relationship.

This very simple story builds on Jesus' presentation of Himself in John 10 as the Good Shepherd. It is designed to help children understand what Bible-time boys and girls knew, and will help our children feel the wonderful peace which comes when we know that Jesus shepherds us. See paragraphs 28 and 33.

The Story Retold

Everyone knew about sheep and shepherds.

Yes, everyone listening to Jesus talk knew just how shepherds took care of their sheep. When people heard Jesus tell them that He is the Good Shepherd, everyone would have known that Jesus was promising to take care of them.

What do you know about sheep and their shepherds? What do shepherds do that makes sheep feel safe? What do you suppose shepherds do at night that makes sheep feel safe in the dark? When

Jesus told us he is the Good Shepherd, he did it so we could always feel safe, too.

At night in Bible times, shepherds kept their sheep in a safe pen. Some pens were made of thorn bushes, with sharp spikes to keep wild animals and robbers out. Inside the sheep would be safe.

The pen for the sheep had only one gate. At night, when the sheep were safe inside, the shepherd didn't leave them alone. He closed the gate with more thorn bushes. And then the shepherd lay down to sleep right by the door. No one could come in to hurt the sheep. The shepherd guarded the sheep at night. The shepherd was there to keep them safe.

Jesus said, "I am the gate." Jesus is our Shepherd, and He protects us. Jesus takes care of us at night and in the daytime. Jesus is always with us to keep us safe.

Let me tell you about a time when I was glad Jesus was with me as my Shepherd [share]. When do you most want Jesus to shepherd you?

Good shepherds loved their sheep. They would do anything to protect them. A good shepherd would fight wild animals to save one of his sheep. Even when the shepherd might be hurt or killed, the good shepherd would fight a lion or a bear or a wolf.

Jesus wanted people to know how much He loves us. So Jesus said, "I am the Good Shepherd. The Good Shepherd lays down His life for his sheep." Jesus loved you and me so much He died on the cross to pay for our sins. Jesus proved then how much He loves us. Because we are Jesus' sheep, we can know that He loves us always.

God wants you and me to know always that Jesus loves us. Jesus is our Good Shepherd. Jesus keeps us safe at night. He knows everything about us, and is with us always. Jesus loves us very, very much.

Action Idea

A number of reassuring activities can grow out of this simple survey of what it means to have Jesus as our Good Shepherd.

For instance, you might learn the familiar chorus, "His Sheep Am I," and sing it with the children at bedtime. You might find a picture of Jesus as the Good Shepherd at a Christian bookstore for your child's room. Another simple but very helpful project is to memorize the Shepherd's Psalm, Psalm 23, as a family project. The Revised Standard Version of this psalm is especially suitable for use with children, and is reproduced here.

> "The Lord is my shepherd,
>   I shall not want;
>   he makes me lie down in green pastures,
> He leads me beside still waters;
>   he restores my soul.
> He leads me in paths of righteousness
>   for his name's sake.
> Even though I walk through the valley
>   of the shadow of death,
> I fear no evil;
>   for thou art with me;
>   thy rod and thy staff,
>   they comfort me.
> Thou preparest a table before me
>   in the presence of my enemies;
> thou anointest my head with oil,
>   my cup overflows.
> Surely goodness and mercy shall follow me
>   all the days of my life;
> and I shall dwell in the house of the Lord
>   forever."

The Good Samaritan
Luke 10:25–37

Background

The story of the Good Samaritan is one of the most familiar in the Bible. It is penetrating, because it cuts through all the differences which divide human beings. The Good Samaritan shows clearly God's concern that we love and have compassion for others. Although the story was told to point up the failure of those religious people who looked for ways to release themselves from the obligation to care, the Good Samaritan has been especially precious to

Jesus' followers. How clearly we sense God's call to us to identify with others in their need, and to reach out with help.

Boys and girls can begin to develop this sensitivity. Although many are not yet able to put themselves in a friend's place, during the childhood years that capacity does develop. We can help our children develop that concern for others, and sensitivity to other's needs, which they will need for healthy Christian relationships with others throughout their lives. We cannot push children to understand how others feel inside before they are able. But we can help children use that ability as soon as it does develop, through Bible stories like this one.

The Story Retold

It was dangerous to travel in Bible times. A traveler might meet wild animals out in the country. Robbers might be hiding alongside the road, looking for a chance to steal from someone who was alone. So perhaps one man whom Jesus told about had a special reason to hurry along the road between Jerusalem and Jericho. He was hurrying. And he was alone.

And then it happened!

Robbers jumped out from behind some rocks. The robbers grabbed the traveler and beat him. They took all his money. They took the packages he was carrying. They even took all his clothes. Then the robbers hit the man some more and left him lying along the side of the road.

The man moaned and tried to move.

But he couldn't move. He was hurt too badly. All the man could do was lie there on the rocky road, while the hot sun burned his bruised skin.

What words can you think of that might tell how the hurt man feels? Have you ever known anyone who might feel hurt (use the words your children might have suggested)? Have you ever felt anything like that man? Tell us about the time.

The traveler lay there in the hot sun. He couldn't help himself. And how he hurt! Then he heard someone coming. Maybe the person would help him. The hurt traveler couldn't even lift his head to look. But he did see feet walking along the road.

The man who was walking by was a priest. When the priest saw the hurt man lying there, with no clothes at all and great bruises on his body, the priest didn't stop. Instead the priest looked around fearfully. Maybe the robbers were still near! Besides, the hurt man looked almost dead. And the priest did have important things to do. Instead of stopping, the priest crossed all the way to the other side of the road, and walked around the hurt traveler. When the priest was past him, he hurried away down the road.

How do you suppose the hurt man felt when the priest went by? Do you think you would like that priest for a friend? Why, or why not? What kind of person would you like as a friend?

The hurt traveler lay there in the hot sun. He seemed to hurt even more. And then the hurt man heard more footsteps. He tried to look up. But all he could see as he lay on the ground was another pair of feet on the road.

When this man saw the hurt traveler, he went to the other side of the road, too. He hurried by the hurt man, trying hard to look in another direction.

What do you think the men who passed by should have done? Was it a good thing to look away and hurry by the hurt man? Why, or why not? How do you and I act when we notice someone who is crying, or looking sad, or maybe is being laughed at by others? How do you suppose we might help?

The hurt man was still lying there in the hot sun. After a while he heard more footsteps. This time the hurt traveler probably thought no one at all cared what happened to him.

But the third man was a Samaritan, a man from the country right next to Israel. The people of Israel and the Samaritans didn't like each other. But this Samaritan didn't ask what country the hurt man came from. Instead the Samaritan felt a great pity for the hurt man.

The Samaritan went right up to the hurt man. He bandaged the hurt man's wounds, put oil on his sunburn, and gave him a drink. Then he helped the hurt man up, and supported him as the hurt man sat on the Samaritan's own donkey. Down the trail the two went. And when they came to an inn, the Samaritan got a room for the hurt Israelite. The Samaritan sat up with him that night and took care of him. When the Samaritan had to leave the next day, he gave money to the innkeeper. "Take good care of the hurt man," the Samaritan said. "If you have to spend more money than this to help him, I will pay you when I come back to your inn."

Of all the travelers, only the Samaritan thought of how badly the man must hurt, instead of thinking of himself. Of all the travelers, only the Samaritan cared.

Would you like your friends to be like the Samaritan? How can friends be like him? Can you think of any time when you've been a good Samaritan, and thought about how others might feel? What did you do then to help? It's good when we can think about how others feel, and care about their feelings as well as our own.

Jesus looked around at the people to whom He was telling this story. "Who was a good friend and neighbor to the man who was robbed?" Jesus asked. One of Jesus' listeners said, "The one who had mercy on him."

Jesus nodded his head. And then Jesus told the man the same thing the Bible tells us.

"Go," Jesus said, "and be just like the good Samaritan."

Action Idea

You'll find suggestions for ways to build on this Bible story in paragraph 13.

Jesus Visits Mary and Martha
Luke 10:38–42

Background

Jesus' visit to Mary and Martha at their home in Bethany led to a conflict between these two adult sisters. Martha was excited about the visit, but felt worried and harried because of her sense of responsibility for necessary preparations. Everything must be just right for Jesus! Mary, a more relaxed personality, simply was delighted that Jesus was coming. She wanted to spend as much time as possible with him, and didn't feel the slightest concern over a fancy, special meal. Mary's reaction infuriated Martha. Here Martha was, working so hard, and Mary was just sitting down listening to Jesus! Finally Martha exploded, expressing all the frustration and self-pity that she felt. Jesus' surprising answer to the complaint of the worried and upset Martha can help our nine- to eleven-year-olds with their own sibling conflicts. And, perhaps more important, the story provides guidance for you and me as parents as we struggle to deal fairly with conflicts between our children.

Perhaps the most important thing we learn is that our children are individuals, as were Mary and Martha. They have different personalities and values. These differences will give rise to conflicts, and we need God's own gift of wisdom not to take sides with one child against the other. Rather we need to help each boy or girl understand himself and his siblings. In the process we will help each grow as a unique individual, whose uniqueness gives him or her significant personal strengths. See paragraphs 70–74.

The Story Retold

"Jesus is coming!"

Mary rushed into the kitchen to tell her sister, Martha. "I just heard, Martha," Mary said. "Jesus is coming to visit us tomorrow."

This wasn't the first time Jesus had stopped in Bethany to visit the home of Mary and Martha and their brother, Lazarus. Jesus was a close friend of the family and liked to visit when He traveled nearby. But it was always a thrill for the two sisters when the Lord came to their house.

When Mary had told Martha, Mary hurried out to give the news to other friends. Mary was that kind of person. She liked to be with people. She liked to talk with them, and listen, and sometimes Mary just liked to sit and look at the sky and think how wonderful God's sunsets are.

When Mary had gone, though, Martha started planning. *Now*, Martha thought, *what will I feed Jesus for supper? It's got to be very special. Maybe I should try that new recipe.* . . . Before you knew it, Martha had a list of all the things she needed to do before Jesus came. Martha was thinking where to go to borrow the extra dishes to feed Jesus' disciples, what to buy to cook for them, what time she'd need to get up to do everything, and many, many other things. Martha was already beginning to feel a little worried and anxious. How could she ever get everything done!

Which of the two sisters are you most like? Mary, who just lets things happen and spends lots of time talking or thinking? Or are you like Martha, who plans work and is very responsible? What do you think mom is most like? Dad? Why? What are some other ways people in our family are different from each other?

Mary and Martha were sisters. But they were very different from each other. That's really all right. Each person is special. God doesn't mind if we're different.

But sometimes the differences between Mary and Martha got the two sisters into trouble. They loved each other, of course. But because they were different, Mary and Martha didn't always understand each other.

For instance, Mary probably helped Martha get the house ready for Jesus' visit. She probably dusted and cleaned, and helped prepare the food to be cooked. But when Jesus came, Mary was so excited. She just wanted to be near Jesus and listen to everything Jesus taught. So Mary slipped out of the kitchen and sat down on the floor near Jesus to listen.

When Martha realized Mary wasn't helping, Martha began to get upset. At first Martha felt sorry for herself. *Here I am, working so hard,* Martha thought, *and nobody even bothers to help me.*

It was hot in the kitchen. And Martha had planned a very special dinner. She had four or five things she was trying to cook, and all Martha could think about was how to get it all done. Finally Martha became so upset she couldn't stand it any longer.

Martha burst into the living room where Jesus and Mary and the others were sitting, and she complained to Jesus. "Lord," Martha said, "don't you care that my sister has left me to do all the work by myself? Tell her to help me!"

What do you think Jesus will tell Martha? Why? Can you think of the last time you complained to mom or dad about your brother (sister)? What was it about? How did you feel when you complained about your brother (sister)? Why do you suppose you felt that way?

Martha knew how she felt. Martha felt upset. Martha was worried about the dinner, and frustrated because there were so many things to do. Martha felt sorry for herself, and angry at Mary—all at the same time! It was so important to Martha to have a fancy dinner for Jesus, she couldn't think of anything else.

But the dinner with all the special foods wasn't that important to Mary. What was important to Mary was to spend as much time as she could with Jesus. Mary wanted to be with Jesus, not be in some hot kitchen. How terrible it would be if Jesus visited, and Mary didn't have any time to be with Him because she was cooking.

What do you think about that? Which was most important? To cook a fancy dinner, or to spend time with Jesus? Why? It isn't wrong to think cooking fancy dinners is important. But it isn't wrong to want to spend the time with Jesus either, is it? Usually when sisters or brothers like Mary and Martha get upset with each other, it's because they have different ideas about what is important.

Jesus heard Martha complain. And Jesus listened when Martha said, "Lord, make my sister come help me."

But Jesus shook His head. Jesus wouldn't make Mary do what Martha thought was important. Mary had a right to choose for herself what she thought was important to her. And Mary was sure that sitting there, to listen to Jesus, was very important indeed.

How would you like it if mom or dad said you had to do what your brother (sister) thinks is important, instead of what you think is important? Do you suppose it would be fair if mom or dad made your brother (sister) do what you think is important? Brothers and sisters can help each other, and can care when each other is upset. But we can't expect others to think the same way we do about what is important to us. We have to let them choose what is important to them.

Jesus tried to explain more to Martha. This time, what Martha had thought was important—making that fancy dinner for Jesus—really wasn't the most important thing.

"Martha," Jesus said, "you're all upset about so many things. Really, only one thing is important. I didn't come here because of what you cook for Me, but to be with you. You could just give me a plate of beans—just that one thing—and I'd be happy. This time Mary made the better choice, and I won't take away her chance to spend time with Me just because cooking is so important to you."

How do you suppose Martha felt when Jesus explained? Do you think Martha learned? What can you and I learn about how to get along better with our brothers (sisters)?

It's not wrong to be different, and have different things

be important to us. But we shouldn't complain if our brothers (sisters) don't think the same things are important. Sometimes when we feel angry and upset, as Martha did, we need to talk about things with our family. Maybe we can find ways to help each other, and we surely can think about what things in our life are most important to God.

Action Idea

When values conflict and stimulate sibling arguments in your home, it's important to help each child talk about what is important to him or her in the situation, and to help each understand the other. Out of understanding three things can emerge:

* When we become sensitive to differences, we see ways to help other family members achieve what is important to them.

* When we talk about differences, we have a chance to discover our own motives and values.

* When we listen to others, we have a chance to measure our values and see if what we have felt is important really should be all that important to us after all.

To help develop this skill, role play Mary and Martha getting ready for Jesus' visit. In the spontaneous conversation, have each character say what is important to her, and try to explain why. After the two sisters have talked, then think together how they might have helped each other, so each gets her important things done. For instance, Mary might have agreed to do certain things *until* Jesus arrived. And Martha might have agreed that she would cook fewer foods, and plan things so Mary could spend time with Jesus—and perhaps so Martha herself could too!

Use this same role play approach to act out ways to handle conflicts between your children. When the next conflict comes, actually do talk it through in this way.

Jesus Teaches on Prayer
Luke 11:1–13

Background

Many of Jesus' teachings on prayer focus on the utter simplicity of relationship with God. We approach the Lord secure in the confidence that God loves us: we are his children, and God is our heavenly Father. See paragraph 90.

All boys and girls who have loving, approachable fathers will quickly transfer the feeling of closeness and confidence to relationship with the Lord. Boys and girls with inconsistent dads, or those in single-parent homes, may hear mixed messages in Jesus' affirmation that God is a good Father. This Bible story is retold with Jesus' own stress: a stress that helps each of us realize that God is our Father, and that God is the best Father anyone could possibly be.

You'll want to introduce this simple retelling to your youngest boys and girls. Awareness of the intimate and open relationship to which we are invited in Jesus Christ is a heritage for them to appropriate as soon as possible.

The Story Retold

Jesus' disciples were confused.

Many religious people in Israel prayed in special ways. Some stood on street corners and prayed out loud. Others came to the temple-church and raised their arms toward the heavens. Some stood and prayed by quoting verses from the Bible. But Jesus didn't seem to do any of these things.

Sometimes Jesus got up early and went outside to pray alone. Sometimes Jesus prayed and thanked God for helping Him heal people. Jesus' prayers were very simple—just like talking with God. Why didn't Jesus pray as other people did?

The disciples watched Jesus for a long time.

Finally the disciples went to Jesus after He finished praying in a quiet place in the country. "Jesus," the disciples said, "will You teach us how to pray?"

Jesus nodded His head yes.

Jesus must have been pleased. Jesus knew that God likes us to pray and talk with Him. And Jesus knew that His disciples needed to learn to talk with God.

So Jesus nodded His head. Yes, Jesus was glad to teach people how to pray.

Do you ever wonder about praying, as the disciples did? Why do you suppose people pray? What do you think people ought to talk with God about? When do you best like to pray?

The most important thing Jesus wanted His disciples to know was this: God loves us very much. When we pray, we do not talk to a God who is a stranger. Oh, no. So Jesus said, when you pray, begin by saying "Father."

Now, not every human father is a good father. Jesus wanted us to know that God is a very good Father. So Jesus told a story.

"Suppose," Jesus said, "you have visitors come, and you need extra food. It's late, but you go next door and knock on your neighbor's door."

"Go away!" the neighbor says. "Stop knocking! I've gone to bed."

Jesus explained. "If it's just a neighbor, you may have to keep on knocking and knocking until finally the neighbor gets up just to keep you from bothering him.

"Well, God isn't like that. God is a good Father. A good father listens to you the very first time, because he loves you."

So when you and I pray, and we say "Father" to God, it's because we know that He loves us. We know that God hears us the very first time we pray.

Jesus even made us a promise. Because God is a good Father, God will give us good things when we ask Him. God loves us and will help us when we pray.

What are some things a bad father might do, or might not do? What are some things a good father will do, or will not do? (Make lists of good/poor father qualities.) What do you think is the most important thing about a good father? (Be sure to include your own thoughts on the list, and share your ideas of important father qualities.)

Jesus wants everyone to know when he or she prays that God is the very best Father there could be. When we pray, and call God our Father, we know that He hears what we say to Him. God loves us very much. Our heavenly Father will listen to our prayers and give us what is best.

Action Idea

At another time look with your children at the special things Jesus taught his disciples to pray about. The following is Luke's version of the Lord's Prayer, with two simple observations on key phrases which you can talk over with your children.

The Prayer:	Insights
Father	*We know when we pray that God loves us and will listen to us.*
hallowed be your name	*God is special. When we pray we can praise him, and tell him how glad we are for who he is.*
Your kingdom come	*Someday everyone will do what God says is good and right. When we pray we can ask God to help us obey, as good citizens of God's kingdom.*
Give us each day our daily bread	*Whatever we need each day, God wants us to tell him about. God loves us and will give us what we need.*
Forgive us our sins	*God wants us to confess our sins when we do wrong. God will forgive us. And God wants us to forgive others who sin against us.*
Lead us not into temptation	*We can ask God to help us be stronger than any temptation, and help us do what is right. We do not need to give in and do wrong.*

Jesus Tells of a Rich Fool
Luke 12:13–21

Background

We live in a materialistic culture. It isn't surprising if our children show an unhealthy concentration on possessions at times—or if we are pulled in that direction ourselves. It's difficult to convince children that possessions are not all that important. It's hard to show that stealing, when it happens, is not only wrong but is also foolish. See paragraphs 37 and 81.

One story which Jesus told his listeners focuses on the foolishness of materialism. In bold, graphic words Jesus described a rich man who thought the meaning of his life was summed up in his abundant possessions. He was wrong. Relationship with God is the basic issue in life, and the rich fool had ignored this relationship.

The impact of this story is clear to adults, but difficult for young children to grasp. It probably should be told to more mature nine- to eleven-year-olds. The *talkables* in the story will help them think through the meaning of this teaching for their lives. The story can be used as a supplement when you are working with your child on allowances or stealing. The basic story related to stealing is found on page 226. The basic story related to allowances is found on page 302.

The Story Retold

"Well, sir," the farm manager said, "I just don't know where we're going to put it all."

The rich man didn't say anything. He just frowned, pretending to be angry with the manager.

Shaking a little bit, because the rich man was very, very rich, the manager said, "You see, sir, you've got so many flocks and so many tons and tons of grain from the last harvest, your barns just won't hold it all. You must be the richest farmer in all of Israel."

Inside the rich man smiled. But outside, he kept on frowning. "Well then," the rich man said harshly, "go tear down the barns that are too small. Build bigger ones. Build the biggest barns in all Israel! Build them big enough to store all the many things I own." The rich man shook his fist at the manager. "Go on, now, and do it in a hurry!"

When the farm manager had gone, the smile the rich man had been hiding came out. The rich man leaned back in his chair. He smiled and smiled. Now and then he laughed too.

Do you suppose you would have liked to be the rich man? Why, or why not? What might be some good things about being rich? What do you think might be bad things about being rich? Do you think the farm manager liked the rich man? Why or why not? Would you want the rich man for a friend?

It's not wrong to be rich, or to own many things. But when a person cares too much about his possessions, there are important things he can forget.

That was the problem with the rich man. He sat there when the manager had gone, and smiled. And he talked to himself. "I'm a lucky person. I have plenty of good things, all laid up for many years. I can take it easy now. I can eat, and drink, and have parties for years and years and years."

The rich man was thinking only about himself, and he thought that his riches would make him happy.

Have you ever felt that there was something you needed that, if you got it, would make you happy for a long time? Tell us about it. Did you get it, and how long did it make you feel happy? (If you didn't get it, how long did not having it make you feel unhappy?) That's one trouble with the things we want to own. Even having a lot of things, or a lot of money, can't really make us happy. What do you think helps a person be really happy?

The Bible tells us how to be really happy. We can try to please God, rather than just think about what we will get. Being rich in God's way means caring about other people, helping them because we love God.

The rich man in Jesus' story had forgotten all about God and what was important to God. All the rich man ever thought about was his money and the things he owned.

The rich man felt very happy that afternoon. He smiled, and now and then he laughed when he thought about the years and years of parties and the riches he would have.

The rich man was very happy all evening. He smiled even more, and began to plan what he would do first to enjoy his riches.

But that night, the rich man died.

And God said to him, "You are a fool. What good do you think all the things you own will do you now?"

Why do you suppose Jesus ended his story this way? The rich man stored up all he owned to use for himself. What do you think he could have done with some of the things he owned that would have been wiser?

God doesn't want any of us to make the mistake of thinking that the things we have or want are most important. Nothing is important enough to do something wrong so we can get it. Things are never more important than helping people who are in need. Things are never more important than wanting to please God.

Action Idea

Hold a family evaluation. How do each of us show that pleasing God is important to us? How do we use our money or other possessions to show that we care about other people? Areas like use of allowances, sharing of some toys, and so on, can all be discussed.

After the evaluation, family members might each try to express one way in which each will seek to better use possessions to please the Lord.

Jesus Teaches about God's Love
Luke 12:22–34

Background

This Bible story is a companion to the preceding story of the rich fool. Through the former story, Jesus wanted his listeners to understand that the meaning of life is not found in luxuries. Through this story, Jesus wants his followers to learn the stunning truth that we need not even focus on the necessities. The point, of course, is that it's not only the rich who are materialistic. The poor may be materialistic too. At heart, materialism is nothing less than acting as if the material universe were the totality of reality, and failing to grasp spiritual realities.

This striking lesson is understood by adults who read this passage thoughtfully. There is also a meaning which comes through just as clearly to children. Boys and girls are dependent on us moms and dads. Few have to worry about having their daily needs met, for that is our responsibility. But even the youngest children can realize that this is a story about God's love. Even the youngest can feel added significance and security as he or she thinks about how important he or she is to our loving Lord.

The Story Retold

Jesus was sitting with His disciples.

The disciples were people who trusted Jesus, and who followed Him. The disciples were Jesus' friends, just as you and I are friends who love Jesus and want to please Him.

Sitting there, close to Jesus, the disciples heard Jesus say, "You don't have to worry." Jesus told them, "You don't have to be afraid."

Why do you suppose Jesus told his disciples that? What do you suppose some of these friends of Jesus worried about? What do you suppose they might be afraid of? What do we sometimes worry about or fear today? (Share some of the things that have caused you worry or fears, as well as encouraging your children to share.)

Jesus loves His disciples very much. Jesus loves you and me. So He told two stories to help us know just how much God loves us, and why we don't have to worry or be afraid.

"I tell you," Jesus began, "don't worry about what you will have to eat or what clothes you'll have to wear. You are very important, and very special, and that's why you don't need to worry.

"Just look at those birds flying over there," Jesus said, pointing to some larger birds in a nearby field. "You know, those birds don't work in any field. Those birds don't have barns to store grain. The birds find what they need to eat each day, for God feeds them.

"You know, you are much more special to God than birds. Surely God, who takes care of the birds, will take care of you. God loves you, for you are very special to Him."

How do you suppose Jesus' disciples felt when they thought about being special to God? How does it make you feel to know that you are special, and that God loves you very much?

Jesus wanted to make sure that His disciples really felt special. So Jesus told them another story.

"Look," Jesus said, pointing out some flowers that were growing in the fields. "See how beautiful these flowers are. You know, those flowers don't worry about what they wear. But God has given them beautiful petals to clothe them. Those petals are more beautiful than the wonderful robes of King Solomon. Now," Jesus went on, "flowers only live for a few days. If God clothes them so beautifully, how much more will God take care of you? You are far more special and important to God than the flowers. So you can trust God, and not be afraid."

Do you suppose Jesus' disciples realized how special they were to God? Just for fun, let's make up some "more special" sayings. For instance, "Jimmy (substitute child's name), you're more special to us and to God than the newest new car." (Let your children make up as many "more special" sayings as they can.)

Jesus told His disciples these stories so they wouldn't worry or be afraid. Jesus wants each disciple to know how special he or she is, and how important we are to God.

And Jesus knew something else, too.

When we know we're special, and that God is taking care of us, we can also choose to do what pleases God. We know that God will take care of us, so pleasing God is the most important thing in our whole life.

Action Idea

Younger boys and girls will appreciate a simple picture panel for their room (see illustrations). On the left panel attach a picture of your child's favorite bird. On the right panel attach a picture of a favorite beautiful flower. In the center panel, attach a picture of the child. You may want to print a phrase from Luke 12 on the picture panel. For instance, "How much more valuable you are" (12:24) or "Your Father knows that you need them . . . . Do not be afraid" (12:30, 32).

It's possible that you may want to explore further the application Jesus made of this story with your older children. His final thrust was to emphasize that, because we have no need to be anxious or focus our life on things, we are free to live generously with others. As we learn to care about other people, and seek to help them, we lay up real treasures for ourselves in heaven.

The Lost Sheep
Matthew 18:10–14

Background

There are few Bible stories which more clearly illustrate the nature of God's grace than the story of the lost sheep. The wandering sheep is not ignored or rejected by the good shepherd. Instead, the loss of the sheep causes the shepherd great anxiety. He goes and searches for the wandering one. When the shepherd finds the lost, grace is most stunningly exhibited. Rather than showing anger and recriminations, the shepherd lifts up the sheep, carries it home, and feels only joy.

This is hard to imitate. When our younger children wander away, or "forget" to come home, we do worry. We find them— and express our worry with anger. When our older children stray from godliness, we all too often become bitter and demanding.

"Your Father knows that you need them... Do not be afraid"

Luke 12: 30,32

Yet God always maintains his attitude of amazing grace toward us, who are also so prone to stray.

In this retelling of Jesus' familiar tale of the lost sheep, we want to help our children who run away sense the anguish they cause, and yet be assured of our joy at their return. Because love is a much more powerful motivator than fear, this story can help you encourage your wandering child to think of you the next time he's tempted to go off on an adventure—and to choose not to run away. See paragraph 40.

The Story Retold

One day Jesus told a story that helps us understand how much God loves us. It was a story about a lost sheep. Let's pretend we're watching the flock of sheep that Jesus is telling about. Let's see what we can imagine . . .

The shepherd we're watching has a hundred sheep. That's a lot of sheep to take care of. But the shepherd knows every one of the sheep. In fact, each of the sheep has his own name, and the shepherd knows each one by name (cf. John 10:14). Every single sheep is important to the shepherd, who loves them all.

But sheep are a lot like people. They are different from each other. Some sheep are very obedient. They love the shepherd, and always do just what the shepherd says.

Some sheep are obedient, but they forget sometimes. They get curious about things and wander off. When the shepherd calls they're too busy to come. They don't mean to be disobedient. It's just that sometimes they don't remember that the shepherd loves them and worries about them when they wander away.

Some sheep are very independent. They know the shepherd loves them. But they have a mind of their own. They want to do what they want to do, when they want to do it. They wander off many times. What they want to do seems more important to them than how the shepherd might feel.

What are the three kinds of sheep in the shepherd's flock? Which kind of sheep do you think you'd like best? Why? If you were a sheep, which of the three would you be most like? Why did you choose that kind of sheep?

Which sheep do you think the shepherd loves most? Why do you think so?

The shepherd loves all his sheep. Every sheep is important to him, even the ones who don't obey, and the ones who don't listen well, and the ones who sometimes run away. In fact, look—(pretend to point to a wandering sheep)—there goes Herbie the runaway now. He's sneaking away while the shepherd is helping another sheep get a stone out of her hoof. The shepherd doesn't see Herbie. There! Now Herbie is hidden beyond those bushes. The shepherd can't see Herbie now. Look at Herbie run!

What do you suppose Herbie the runaway is thinking about as he runs away? Why do you suppose Herbie likes to run away so much? Is Herbie unhappy with the shepherd? Does he think the shepherd loves another sheep more than the shepherd loves Herbie? What do you think? (Accept whatever reason for running away your child suggests as most likely—and be aware of the insight his opinion gives into his own motivations!)

I'll bet you're right. Herbie is running away again because (fill in your child's reason).

Look. I think the shepherd knows that something is wrong. The shepherd is counting his sheep. One. Two. Three. Four . . . it must take a long time to get all the way to a hundred. (Pause.) Ah. Now the shepherd knows. There are only ninety-nine sheep in his flock. One of them has run away.

The shepherd looks around carefully. Yes, you can see the shepherd knows now what sheep is gone. It's Herbie! Herbie has run away again!

How do you suppose the shepherd feels now? Why do you think the shepherd feels that way? How does the shepherd feel toward Herbie? Why?

You can tell how the shepherd feels by what he's doing. Look. He seems to be very worried. He's hurrying to look at that dangerous cliff. He's afraid something bad has happened to Herbie. Now the shepherd looks very sad. See, there's a tear in his eye. I don't think the shepherd is angry. But the shepherd is very, very worried. It really is terrible when someone you love is lost. You think of the bad things that might happen to him (or her) and feel very upset.

See. The shepherd has decided to go look for Herbie.

He's getting all the other sheep together, to make sure they are all right. Now the shepherd is going off to look for Herbie.

What do you think will happen when the shepherd finds Herbie? What do you think the shepherd should do? What would you do if Herbie were your sheep?

Well, the shepherd looked and looked for Herbie. He walked up and down hills. He tore his robe on some bushes. And the shepherd scraped his arm on some sharp rocks, too.

Finally, the shepherd called out gladly. "I've found you. And you're all right!"

The shepherd picked Herbie up in his arms, and headed back to where he had left his flock. All the way the shepherd was very happy. He had found Herbie before Herbie could be hurt or killed by wild animals. Herbie was safe now— until the next time he ran away.

Why do you think the shepherd was happy instead of angry? Do you think the shepherd really loves Herbie? How do you know? Do you suppose Herbie realized how worried the shepherd is when Herbie runs away? What do you think Herbie would do if he realized how upset and unhappy it makes the shepherd when he runs away?

Jesus told this story so people could know how much God loves them. But the story also helps us understand how we can love each other too.

Let's see if we can think how we can love each other, and list some of the ways.

Action Idea

In the shepherd's joy Jesus shows the great sensitivity that God has to us, his straying children. We may deserve punishment. But God gives us warmth and love, and expresses his joy in us rather than loading us with added guilt. This graciousness of God provides a model for us to follow. We are more effective in winning our children to goodness through grace than punishments, although using natural consequences (see paragraph 63) should be one of the ways in which we show love.

One wise thing to do with running away is to delay discussion. Simply bring your child home rejoicing, tuck him or her into bed, tell your child how much you care, and let it go for the moment.

The next day or so, however, you will want to use this Bible study and its follow-up activity. The goal of the story is to help your child gain insight into how you feel when he or she runs away, and to establish expectations, so that fear will not keep him from returning if he should stray again.

Complete the story by listing ways that children and parents can show love to each other. Make two columns on a sheet of paper and have your name(s) at the top of one, and the child's name at the top of the other. Then talk about running away and how each party can show love at key stages. . . .

(1) How can we show love to help a person not run away? (For instance, the child might think of the parent's feelings and decide not to, the parent might be sensitive to a child's upset and listen, and so on.)

(2) How can we show love after a person has run away? (For instance, think of feelings, and come back, go look, and so on.)

(3) How can we show love after the runaway has been found?

Working out such a list can develop a child's sensitivity, and can also help moms and dads be aware of how their reactions affect children's behavior.

The Prodigal Son
Luke 15:11–24

Background

The warm, wonderful story of the Prodigal Son has been told and retold to every generation. How clearly we see in it the loving attitude of God our Father, and his eagerness to forgive. How powerfully we sense the welcome awaiting us when we stray from the Lord. Probably no story tells us more beautifully that God is truly ready to forgive.

Yet the story was first told to set in contrast the character of God with the self-centered character of the religious people of Jesus' day. When the Prodigal Son was welcomed back by the Father, the older son (representing the Pharisees of Jesus' day) was angry. The Pharisees resented the goodness of God.

One of the things we learn as our children grow up is that boys and girls, particularly nine- to eleven-year-olds, are ferociously concerned with fairness. It's hard for them to understand grace. One of the things we ourselves learn as we grow older is that God is most of all concerned with gracious love. God can forgive, fully and freely, without demanding repayment. In fact, in Jesus,

God himself offered full payment to the demands that justice required. See paragraph 69 and 125.

As we tell the Prodigal Son story to our older children, we want to help them understand how sure the promise of forgiveness is—and help them learn to forgive others.

The Story Retold

"Dad, I want to leave home."

Jesus told about the surprising thing the youngest son said to his father.

It was surprising because the youngest son had a very good family. His father loved him. There was work for him to do in the family business. The youngest son had all the food and clothing he needed. And people liked him.

But the youngest son had decided. The youngest son wanted to leave home. So he went to his father. He said, "Father, give me my share of the family business in cash, so I can leave."

How do you suppose the father felt when the youngest son wanted to leave? Where and why do you think the son might have wanted to go? What do you think the youngest son will do with all his money?

The father loved both his sons. But the father realized he couldn't keep the youngest son at home if the boy really wanted to leave. So the father divided up his business, and gave the youngest son the money that would be his share.

Excited about his chance to adventure, the youngest son left home and went to see distant countries.

But the youngest son made some very tragic mistakes. At home the youngest son had been taught not to do bad things. Now the son began to do all sorts of bad things. He spent his money on sinful things. And before the young man realized it, all his money was gone!

Well, the youngest son thought, *I'll just have to get work and take care of myself.* But things were hard in the far country. The youngest son couldn't get a job. Before long he was actually starving!

The youngest son looked and looked, and finally he was

able to get a job, taking care of a farmer's pigs. But all that the youngest son got for his work was a chance to eat the food the pigs were eating. No one was kind to the youngest son, or cared about him at all.

How do you think the youngest son felt then? Do you think he was treated fairly—should he have suffered that way for wasting his father's money, and using it wickedly? What do you suppose the father would think if he knew what the youngest son did?

Sitting there in the pig pen, the youngest son thought about what he had done. He thought about his home. At home, people who worked for his father were given enough to eat. His father's workers were treated kindly. If only he hadn't left home. . . .

And then the youngest son had an idea.

I'll get up, the youngest son thought, *and I'll go back to my father. I'll tell my father I've sinned, and don't deserve to be treated like a son anymore. I'll ask my father if he will let me work for him as a hired man.*

So the youngest son got up and hurried back to his home. It was a long trip. He was very tired and sad when he got home. He thought about his father. He must have wondered what the father would do. *What I really deserve,* the young man must have thought, *is. . . .*

What do you think the young man really deserves? Why? How do you suppose the father will greet him? Will the father feel glad to see the son, or be angry with him, or what? What do you think the father should do?

The father saw the son coming a long way off. How happy and excited the father felt. The father didn't wait for the son to come to him. He jumped up and ran to meet his boy.

The youngest son tried to apologize. "Father," the son said, "I have sinned, and I'm not worthy of being called your son. . . ."

But the father didn't listen to any more than that. The father didn't listen to the youngest son's request to work for him. Instead, the happy father called to his workers. "Quick! Get my son fine clothes. And kill that special calf we're feeding. We're going to have a party. This is my son!

He was lost, but now is found. He was dead, and now is alive again!"

Then the whole household, with all the workers, began to celebrate. The youngest son was home, and he had been forgiven. Now everyone could be happy again.

How do you think we are like the youngest son? How do you think God is like the good Father? Jesus told us this story so we would know, when we sin and do something wrong, that we don't have to run away from God. We can come to God and confess our sin—and know that God will forgive us. When we come to the Lord, or when we come to mom or dad to confess our sin, then we can all be happy together again.

Alternate Ending

There was one person who wasn't happy when the father forgave his youngest son. That was the older brother. The brother was angry. The brother went to the father and complained.

"It's not fair," the older son said. "All these years I've been slaving away for you. I never ran off. I always did what you told me. And you have a party for this wicked son of yours, who ran off and wasted your money so sinfully. It's just not fair."

Can you understand why the older brother felt this way? Do you think he was right? What do you think the older brother would have wanted the father to do? How do you suppose the father will answer the older son?

What the older brother didn't understand was that being fair isn't always the most important thing. The youngest son had done wrong. But he had suffered for it. Now he just needed to be loved and helped. When the youngest son asked his father to forgive him, the father had to celebrate. Being forgiven is the way that people who hurt each other come close, and love each other again.

We can be glad when we hear this story, because we know that God will forgive us when we confess our sins to Him. We can be glad, too, because we know that you and I can forgive others. We don't have to be "fair." People who say "I'm sorry" can be forgiven, even if they have done us wrong.

Let's ask God to help us be like the good father and not like the older son. We can always be glad to forgive.

Action Idea

See if you and the family can locate one or more flat stones, with surfaces as smooth as possible. You can have fun making "prodigal stones" for each person. On one side simply paint the words, "I confess," and on the other, "You're forgiven." Or pick phrases closer to the words of the story, such as, "Father, I have sinned" for one side, and on the other side, "Welcome home."

These stones can be carried as reminders of the fact that when we do sin, we can confess and know that God will forgive us. The stones can also remind us that we are to be as kind and forgiving with others as God is with us. We don't need to hold grudges, or be angry when another person is forgiven for doing wrong.

Jesus Stops to Help
Luke 18:35–43

Background

Illness in the family can bring a number of problems. There may be financial difficulties. There is sure to be anxiety if the illness is serious. There are readjustments each family member must make (see paragraphs 45 and 46). Probably one of the most common stresses originates in the sense of helplessness that often comes. Adults and children may feel extremely insecure and yet may not recognize this source of inner tensions. If the family life has been tightly structured, with an established and familiar routine which is now necessarily broken, the adjustments will be particularly difficult.

Ultimately all of us are vulnerable. We have little control over many aspects of our lives, although we only recognize our helplessness when familiar patterns are broken or tragedy intrudes. But there is one reality which can undergird us. That reality is our personal relationship with a God who is in control—and who cares deeply for us.

This familiar Bible story is told for children of all ages, and designed to provide a basis for inner peace, even when the circumstances of our life are drastically altered by illness.

The Story Retold

"What's happening! What's happening!"

The blind beggar sitting by the road could hear people moving all around him. He could hear excited voices. An even larger crowd was coming. But of course the blind beggar couldn't see what it was.

"What's happening? What's happening?" the blind man asked again. No one answered him. No one paid any attention to the blind beggar at all.

What do you think it would be like to be blind? What would be the worst thing about being blind? It's always hard when people are seriously ill. What has been the hardest thing for us since (name) has been sick?

Probably the hardest thing for the blind beggar was that he felt so helpless. There wasn't much the blind man could do for himself.

Sometimes he felt as if no one cared about him.

Like now.

What *was* happening?

The beggar asked again, reaching out to grab at the people he could hear all around him. "What's happening?"

Finally someone told him. "Jesus. Jesus of Nazareth is walking down our road!"

No wonder everyone was so excited. Everyone in Israel knew about Jesus. Why, Jesus taught about God. And Jesus could make people well!

As soon as the blind man heard that it was Jesus coming by, he started shouting, as loudly as he could.

"Jesus!" the blind man shouted.

"Jesus, Son of David, have mercy on me! Help!"

Well, when the blind man started shouting like that, the people around shushed him.

"Be quiet!" someone said.

"Don't be so noisy," a woman said angrily.

"Yes," the whole crowd around him said. "Be quiet."

But the blind man wouldn't be quiet. He just shouted out as loud as he could. "Jesus! Help me!"

At that the crowd around the man became even angrier.

"Will you quit that noise!" the people said. "Listen," one man explained, "Jesus is much too busy and important to bother about you. You're just a blind man. You're not important at all."

Do you suppose the blind man wasn't important enough for Jesus to bother with? Sometimes we think that God is too busy to care about our problems, or to help us. Have you ever felt that way? Can you tell us about it? How does it make you feel inside when you aren't sure that God really cares?

Jesus heard the blind man calling out, way at the back of the crowd. To Jesus, the blind man wasn't unimportant at all. To Jesus everyone is important.

So Jesus stopped there on the road. Jesus told some of the people to lead the blind man to Him. When the blind man came near, Jesus asked, "What do you want Me to do for you?"

We know what the blind man wanted.

He wanted to see again.

Anytime someone is ill, he wants to get well. So the blind man said to Jesus, "Lord, I want to see."

Jesus nodded His head. "Receive your sight. Your trust in Me has healed you."

And the blind man could see!

How happy the blind man was. How the blind man praised God! The crowd saw it, and they praised God too. Jesus had showed that God cares after all, and that God can help us when we trust Him.

Do you suppose that Jesus cares about everyone who is sick or hurting? No one is unimportant to Jesus. We can't know for sure when we pray that God will make us well—God may have an important reason for us to be sick. But we can know that Jesus listens and cares. God is never too busy to stop and listen to us—and care about us. Let's talk to Jesus now. We can tell Jesus what we want, and how we feel. We can know that Jesus will listen to us and do what is best.

Action Idea

Other stories dealing with different aspects of family illness are found on pages 231, 261 and 346. This story focuses on the comfort

available in knowing that Jesus hears our prayers for our loved
ones.

To reinforce this sense of God's powerful presence, list with
your children other illnesses about which you've prayed. Take
time to praise God together for each time someone has become
well.

The Widow's Gift
Mark 12:41–44

Background

It takes only a few words in Mark's Gospel to describe the
incident. So the incident may seem unimportant. Yet it illustrates
how committed God is to a reality which Paul expresses in 2
Corinthians. It's not the size of the gift. It is the motivation of
the giver which God values.

Some might argue that the significance of the widow's gift is
found solely in the fact that she gave all she had. But her gift is
an expression of the widow's inner motivation, just as the ostenta-
tious public presentation of large amounts of money by the rich
was an expression of their inner motivation. They gave because
they wanted to be seen. They gave because they wanted to be
known as pious men. The widow gave all, despite the contempt
her paltry offering probably generated, because she loved the Lord
and was giving to him, not to be seen by men (cf. Matt. 5:1–4).

This story has direct application when we try to teach our children about giving, and about the use of their allowances (see paragraph 81). Six- and seven-year-olds can sense the importance of
motivation, and be glad that Jesus is happy for whatever they
want to give to God.

The Story Retold

Jesus and His disciples were sitting outside the great temple-church in Jerusalem. As they sat, they watched people
bring offerings to God. In those days, the people brought
their gifts and put them in a big wooden chest outside the
temple.

The gifts they brought were used in many ways. Some
money was used to provide food and clothing for the minis-

ters and their families. Some was used to keep the temple, where they worshiped, beautiful.

What are some of the ways that the money we give at church is used? (If your children are unsure, suggest a family research project. Check the church budget, find pictures and locations of missionaries, mention study materials children use to learn about God, and so on.) We give our money as a gift to the Lord, and it's used in many ways to help people know that God loves them.

Some of the people who came to give money to the Lord walked in proudly. They had a lot of money to give, and they wanted everyone at the temple to see how generous they were. I imagine some of them threw in their gold and silver coins so they clinked loudly. Probably most of the people watching them were impressed.

But not everyone gave a lot of money. Some slipped up quietly to the wooden chest and put just a little money in.

What do you suppose the people watching thought of those who put only a little money in? Why? What do you suppose God thought about them? What is most important when we give money to the Lord?

Jesus and His disciples watched.

And Jesus said something to His disciples.

"Do you see that woman?" Jesus said. Jesus pointed to a woman in old clothes, who looked very tired and thin. "That woman is a widow."

"Yes," the disciples said. "We see her. She didn't put much in the offering, did she?"

Jesus agreed. "No, she put in only two pennies. But those two pennies were more special to God than the thousands of dollars the rich people have just put in."

The disciples were surprised. How could two pennies be more important to God than thousands of dollars?

What do you suppose Jesus will say? How can two pennies be more important than thousands of dollars? What do you suppose God cares most about when we give our offerings to him?

Jesus explained. "The rich people who gave a lot have a lot left over.

"The poor widow didn't have much. She only had two pennies. But she loved God so much she gave all she had to the Lord."

God wants us to give because we love Him. It's not how much we have to give that is important to God. It's how much our gifts come from our love for Him.

Action Idea

Don't press your children to give more, or even to set a specific amount. God's desire is for "cheerful givers," who are motivated by love to share what they have.

But do follow up on the research project of how the Lord's money is used in your church. One basic principle which underlies New Testament giving is that we are moved to give by an understanding of needs. Our giving is purposive, not a ritual obligation. We freely choose what we give, motivated by love for God and for his people.

If your children respond to the story of the widow in some overt way, thank the Lord that he is at work in their hearts, developing the grace of giving, a rich expression of love for God.

Being Faithful in Little Things
Matthew 25:14–26

Background

Boys and girls these days have few opportunities to take significant responsibility. Probably some of us parents are frustrated, trying to find some task around the house our children can do to help them build good work habits. If you've felt that frustration, the parable of the talents, told in this passage, is reassuring. In the parable we see that faithfulness in small things—the kinds of things that children can do—is a vital element in developing responsible adults. Paragraphs 48 and 79 suggest ways to help children develop responsibility and sense personal achievement. This Bible story will help you affirm their successes—and confirm their feelings that they are growing well.

This story should be told after (not before) your child has been faithful in carrying out some regular chore or responsibility. It need not be something big. It can simply be responsible follow-through on homework assignments, or remembering to pick up his toys regularly, or carrying out some other family task. What is important is that the child has been faithful in the responsibility.

For this Bible story communicates God's, and your own, warm approval.

The Story Retold

Once Jesus told a story to help us realize how important little things are. It's a story I'm telling you now, because I think you are like the faithful servants in Jesus' story. Here is what Jesus said:

Once a man planned to go on a long journey. So he called all his servants and gave them special responsibilities.

To one servant, he gave $5,000 to invest for him.

To the second servant, he gave $2,000 to invest for him.

To the third, he gave $1,000 to invest for him. Then the man went on his journey, and left the servants to take care of his money.

While the man was gone, the servants planned how to invest the money their master had left in their care. The servant with $5,000 started a business, and he earned $5,000 more. The servant with $2,000 started a business, and he earned $2,000 more. The servant with $1,000 was different. He hid the money and didn't use it at all!

Some time later the master of the servants came back home from his trip. Then he called his servants to him and asked what had happened to the money each had been given. How had each servant carried out his responsibilities?

The first servant came and brought his master the $5,000 he'd been given—and the $5,000 more he had earned. The master was very pleased. "Well done, good and faithful servant!" the master said. "You have been faithful with a few things; I will put you in charge of many things. Come share your master's happiness."

Now, $5,000 sounds like a lot. But the master was very rich. It was only a little to him. What the master had wanted most of all was for his servant to be faithful and carry out his responsibility. Because the servant had been responsible, the master could trust him with more responsibilities.

Faithfulness in little things makes us all able to grow and be responsible for bigger things.

When the second servant came and brought his master the $2,000 he'd been given, and the $2,000 more he had earned, the master was just as pleased. The master said exactly the same thing to the servant with the $2,000 that he had said to the servant with the $5,000: "You have been faithful with a few things; I will put you in charge of many things. Come share your master's happiness."

What the master was glad about was that the servant had been faithful. The servant carried out his responsibility. The servant had grown up. He could be trusted for bigger things.

But when the third servant came, he brought only the $1,000 he had been given. He hadn't been faithful, or used what the master gave him. The master was very upset with this servant. It wasn't so much the money. It was that the servant had been wicked and lazy. The servant hadn't carried out his responsibility. So the master took the $1,000 away from him and gave it to the first servant, who was responsible.

Now, why do you suppose I told you this Bible story? Can you think of any responsibilities you have had that you've faithfully carried out? It doesn't have to be big or important things . . . our responsibilities can seem small. What counts with God and with me is that you are faithful in doing them.

(Explain the responsibilities you had in mind, and tell your child how happy it makes you to see him or her be faithful. You are happiest because being faithful in little things means he or she is growing up. You are happy and proud that your child is growing up and is becoming more responsible.)

Let's pray, because I want to thank God that you are like Jesus' faithful servants, growing up to be responsible.

Action Idea

As paragraphs 48 and 79 suggest, you need to do all you can to help your child *be* responsible. A boy or girl who is responsible usually has a mom or dad who helped that success come, by providing guidance, support and encouragement, carefully graduated tasks, and so on.

As one level of responsibility is reached and recognized by telling this story, it might be wise to have a family conference on shared responsibility for your family life. Talk together to get everyone's ideas on what needs to be done around your home. Also help each person express preferences for ways he or she can contribute. When children have helped to define and to choose their own tasks, carrying them through will be easier. And the importance of the job to general family well-being will be established.

Don't hesitate to use this story several times. It can become a significant way of affirming your children's growth, of providing them with that sense of accomplishment which is so important in healthy development.

Jesus Prays at Gethsemane
Matthew 26:36–46

Background

Prayer is essentially simple: it is an expression of our relationship with God as heavenly Father. We come to God in trust and dependence to share, praise, and make our requests. Sometimes people try to make prayer complicated, and worry if they are "doing it right." At other times, we even hesitate to encourage our children to pray about serious needs, for fear that if God does not answer the prayer their young faith may be disturbed. When we draw back from prayer, however, we misjudge the nature of our relationship with God—or misjudge the capacity of our children to handle reality. Relationship with God in Christ provides access to a God who truly cares. He is not concerned with forms or with conditions to be met. He is concerned with us (see paragraph 46). Our children can come to terms with a world in which God answers prayers according to God's understanding of what is best for us, not just our desires.

The story of Jesus praying at Gethsemane will help boys and girls from ages six to eleven realize that not all prayers are answered "Yes" by God. Jesus' expression, "Not as I will, but as you will," can help them explore the great truth that God both cares and knows what is best.

The Story Retold

Jesus had just shared supper with His disciples. It was the last supper they would have together, and Jesus was sorrowful. He knew He would soon have to die. They ate, and talked, and they sang a hymn. Then they went outside together.

Jesus led His disciples to a place on a hillside where there was a grove of olive trees. The grove was called Gethsemane. There He told most of His disciples to rest and said, "Wait here while I pray."

When a person feels worried and upset and troubled, and is hurting inside as Jesus was, the best thing to do is to talk to God. We can ask God to help.

That's just what Jesus did. He took three disciples, Peter and James and John, and went on into the grove of trees. Jesus told His disciples how He felt. "I'm overwhelmed with sorrow, so much I feel almost ready to die," Jesus said. Then Jesus went on further and fell on the ground to pray to God the Father.

Have you ever hurt very much inside? Have you felt worried and upset and sorrowful, as Jesus felt that night? Tell us about the time. What did you pray then, when you felt so badly? What do you think Jesus asked God the Father? How do you think God will answer Jesus?

Jesus knew that soon His friends would desert Him. He knew that soon His enemies would capture and beat Him. Jesus knew that very soon He would have to die on the cross. He knew how terribly He would have to suffer. So when Jesus lay there on the ground, feeling so sorrowful, He prayed and said, "My Father, if it is possible, may this cup be taken from Me. Yet not as I will, but as You will" (Matt. 26:39).

Three times Jesus, feeling so sorrowful and upset inside, prayed this prayer to God.

In making his prayer, Jesus said three important things. Why do you think each is important? First, Jesus said "My Father." Why is that important? (Suggest, if the children do not, that it tells us Jesus knew God loved him, and is a loving Father. Because we know God does love us we know he listens to our prayers and wants to help.) Second, Jesus told God the Father what he wanted. Why is that important? (We can always be honest with God. We can tell God what we really feel, and what we want. Jesus didn't want to have to suffer.) Third, Jesus told God, "Not as I will, but as you will." Why is that important? (Jesus knew that God the

Father knows best. God, who loves us, will do what is best. So prayer isn't telling God what he should do. Prayer is telling God how we feel and what we want, but knowing that God will do what is best for everyone.)

Jesus prayed His prayer three times, because He was so sorrowful and upset. God listened to Jesus' prayer, as a loving Father does. God did answer that prayer. He did what was best.

Jesus died on the cross and suffered for us.

But then Jesus was raised to life again.

Because Jesus died for us, and came to life, our sins can be forgiven. One day you and I will be with the Lord forever because Jesus suffered so for us. The Bible says in another place about Jesus, "After the suffering, he will see the light of life, and be satisfied" (Isa. 53:11). After the suffering was over, Jesus was glad that He had asked God to do what the Father knew was best.

Do you suppose we can pray as Jesus did? How? (Help your children see the three elements: come to God as Father, express feelings and requests, ask God to do what is best.) Many, many times God gives us just what we ask for. But sometimes God says no, and we don't get what we asked for. But because we know God loves us, we know that what God does give us may hurt for a time, but will really bring us something that is good.

Action Idea

Talk about prayers that have been answered. If you keep an "I prayed, God answered" book (see page 233), look over the list and see how many times God has said yes to your prayers. Talk too about the "No" answers. Can you see now the good that God intended for you by saying no? We can't always see the good. But because we trust God, we know that he will only give us what is best.

Jesus Is Arrested
Matthew 26:47–56

Background

This is one of a sequence of three Easter stories, found here and on pages 316 and 320. The Easter season is one of the two great highlights of the Christian year. Like Christmas, it marks an event which makes our Christian faith unique. Christmas commemorates the incarnation of Jesus—the great miracle by which God the Son became a true human being.

Easter commemorates the death of Jesus and the miracle of his resurrection: the culminating work of Christ by which he won redemption for us, and promises us resurrection to endless life. Because of the centrality of Christmas and Easter to our faith, it is important for us to emphasize these special days in our homes as well as at church. See paragraph 94.

These three stories do not feature *talkables* within the story. Instead the *Action Ideas* suggest ways to create a context in the home which will help our children appreciate Easter events and enter into both the sufferings and the exaltation of our Lord.

The stories are retold for the whole family. They can be read or told as a family tradition, repeated each year. Used this way they will take on deeper meaning each year, as our children grow older and are better able to understand.

The Story Retold

"This is the last supper we will have together," Jesus told His disciples.

A few minutes before the disciples had been happy. They were eating the Passover supper with Jesus. That supper was a reminder of how God had saved Israel from captivity in Egypt hundreds of years ago. Passover was a happy time for the Jewish people. But tonight Jesus was sad.

Jesus went on to talk to the disciples about many things. He told His disciples He would soon leave them, to go to God the Father. Jesus told them to love each other while He was away.

Jesus didn't tell His disciples the terrible things that were about to happen to Him.

But Jesus knew.

One of the things that Jesus knew was this: one of His own disciples was going to betray Him. So Jesus said it. "I tell you the truth, one of you will betray Me."

Most of Jesus' disciples were shocked. "Is it I, Lord?" they asked. "Surely I won't be the one to betray You."

When the disciple named Judas asked the question, Jesus dipped some bread in wine and gave it to him. "You are the one," Jesus told Judas.

Judas thought he had been hiding his plans from the Lord. But Jesus knew.

Right away Judas got up and went out of the room. Judas went to the chief priests, who were Jesus' enemies. The chief priests had already decided to kill Jesus. They didn't like Jesus to teach about God. And they didn't want Jesus to do miracles.

Judas and the chief priests talked and then made an agreement. "All right," Judas said. "You pay me thirty pieces of silver money, and I'll show you where you can take Jesus prisoner."

The chief priests were very glad. The chief priests knew they could never take Jesus prisoner during the day. Then the people wouldn't have let them seize Jesus. Now Judas would lead a mob of the chief priests' servants and guards to take Jesus when the people of the city were asleep!

Back in the room where the disciples and Jesus were, supper was over. Jesus had told His friends many things after Judas left. Finally they sang a hymn and left.

Jesus and His disciples walked down in the valley and up the side of a hill on the other side—a hill called the Mount of Olives.

There Jesus found a grove of olive trees, called Gethsemane. Jesus stopped to pray. Jesus prayed alone, because His disciples were tired and had gone to sleep.

Jesus knew what was going to happen. He knew how much He would suffer soon. And Jesus wept as He talked with His heavenly Father.

Now Judas led the mob of Jesus' enemies up the side of the Mount of Olives. Judas knew where Jesus would go. Jesus usually stopped and rested there when He left Jerusalem.

Jesus knew that Judas was coming.

He woke up His sleeping disciples.

He was ready to be arrested, and to suffer, and to die.

When Judas came up to Jesus and the others, he went right up to the Lord. Judas gave Jesus a kiss and said, "Greetings!"

That kiss was a signal.

Judas had agreed to betray Jesus, and to point Jesus out to the high priest's guards. "The one I kiss will be the one you want," Judas had told them.

Now, when Judas kissed and greeted Jesus, some of the mob rushed forward and grabbed Jesus. Jesus was their prisoner!

Only one of Jesus' friends tried to help. Peter grabbed a sword and swung it wildly at one of the high priest's servants.

"Put your sword away," Jesus said. "Don't you know that I can call on God the Father, and God will send armies of angels to help Me? But what the Bible says must happen has to happen."

Jesus must die for our sins.

He must rise to life again.

This must happen, even though death for Jesus meant terrible suffering.

As the mob roughly dragged Jesus down the hill, all Jesus' followers ran away in fright.

Jesus was alone.

In the next hours Jesus would experience much suffering— and then He would die.

(Pray together, thanking Jesus for being willing to suffer for us.)

Action Idea

Symbols can help to make this time special for children and for adults. See if you and your family can work out a symbol to help you remember Jesus' suffering this Easter time. It might be something as simple as a teardrop, drawn on a 3x5 card. It might be something more complicated, such as a large circle divided into sections, each of which has a picture representing some Easter event (such as a crown of thorns, a cross, and so on).

Begin your Easter remembrance on Good Friday eve. Read this first story in the Easter sequence. Then together work out your family Easter symbol for this year.

Peter Denies Jesus
Matthew 26:69–79

Background

Two common childhood themes are picked up and amplified in this familiar Bible story. Boys and girls, particularly as they move through early childhood into ages nine and eleven, feel great pressure to conform to their peers (see paragraph 17). In addition, children of all ages find it as easy, as do adults, to shade the truth, or to tell outright lies to avoid unpleasantness (see paragraph 38). Certainly the apostle Peter must have been able to understand those pressures. The night of Jesus' arrest and trial, Peter surrendered to peer pressure and lied about his relationship with the Lord.

In another story, which you may wish to associate with this one, the Bible tells us how Peter was forgiven, restored, and given an important ministry. Our failures do not condemn us to be set aside. In this Bible story, you will lead your children through the *talkables* more suitable for older children, though you may wish to share them with mature seven- and eight-year-olds if relevant problems emerge.

The Story Retold

"You're one of His followers!"

It was just a servant girl who said it, but Peter looked around, frightened.

"Yes, you are," the girl said. "You were with Jesus in Galilee."

Peter didn't know what to do.

That night Jesus had been arrested. Jesus was inside the house of the high priest, being tried by His enemies. Peter had followed the gang of guards who captured Jesus. Now Peter was sitting in the courtyard outside the house of the high priest, worrying about what was going to happen to Jesus.

Peter thought he was safe.

Peter thought no one knew him.

But then the servant girl said, out loud, right in front

of all the others outside the house that night, "You are one of Jesus' followers."

How do you suppose Peter felt when she said that to him? Why? Everyone was looking at Peter, waiting to see what Peter would do. How do you think that made Peter feel? Have you ever felt that everyone was looking at you, wanting you to do something you didn't think you should? Can you tell us about it?

Peter looked around. Everyone was looking at him. Peter knew that none of those people liked Jesus. He was afraid if he told them he really was one of Jesus' followers, the people in the courtyard might hurt him. So Peter did a terrible thing. He lied and said in front of everyone, "I don't know what you're talking about."

Then Peter hunched down inside his cloak, trying to pull back into the shadows.

Have you ever been afraid of what others would think or do if you did something you knew was right? How did you feel inside then? Can you understand why Peter was so afraid? What do you think about what Peter did? When you were afraid of what others might think of you, what did you do?

Peter must have been very ashamed of himself for lying about his friendship with Jesus. But Peter had been afraid of the other people. Now he hunched back in the shadows. When it seemed people were still looking at him, Peter got up and went outside the gate.

There another servant girl saw him. She pointed at Peter and told the people who were waiting outside the gate, "This fellow was with Jesus of Nazareth."

Now Peter had a chance to do the right thing! People were still looking at Peter. People who didn't like Jesus were watching. And the girl said it again. "This fellow was with Jesus."

What do you suppose Peter feels now? What do you think Peter will do? Will it be hard or easy for Peter to admit he is one of Jesus' friends?

Peter looked around at the people who were watching him. He was still afraid. Before he knew it, Peter spoke up and said roughly, "I don't know the man. I swear it, I don't even know this Jesus."

Peter lied again!

Peter had been afraid of what others would think and do to him, and Peter had lied.

Sometimes when we worry about what other people will think of us, we do things that are wrong too. Do you suppose it's more important to do what our friends want, or what's right? Why? What do you think could help people in situations like Peter's to do right?

Peter must have felt really ashamed now. But before Peter could slip away, several men in the group came up to Peter. "We think you are one of the followers of Jesus. You talk with a Galilean accent, and Jesus is from there. The way you talk gives you away."

This was the third time now that people were staring at Peter. Peter looked around. He was still afraid. Peter worried more about what other people would think of him than about what Jesus would think of him. For the third time, Peter lied about his friendship for Jesus.

In fact, Peter tried so hard to convince the men that he was on their side and not on Jesus' side that Peter swore oaths and made all sorts of promises that he was telling the truth. Peter said, "I tell you, I don't know the man!"

As soon as the words came out of Peter's mouth, a rooster crowed nearby. Then Peter remembered something Jesus had said. Just that night, before Jesus was taken prisoner, Jesus told Peter, "You will deny Me three times before the cock crows to announce the morning."

Now it had happened.

Now Peter realized what a terrible thing he had done. Peter had lied about being a friend of Jesus. Peter had cared more about what people might think than about pleasing God.

Now Peter felt sorry and was very ashamed. As Peter left the yard of the high priest's house, he wept bitterly.

Have you ever felt like Peter did, guilty and ashamed and sorry after you'd done something wrong? Can you tell us about that time? How much better it would be if Peter—and you and I—could remember to do what pleases God. We don't need to let fear of what other people might think lead us to do wrong.

Let's ask God to help us make choices that please the Lord.

Action Idea

To remind the children to make right choices, make a small "rooster" symbol. It can be attached to school books or playthings as a reminder to please Jesus instead of friends, when friends want us to do something that is wrong.

Jesus Is Condemned and Crucified
Matthew 26,27; Luke 23; John 19

Background

This is the second in a series of three stories retold especially for family Easter observance. The first story is found on page 309 and the third is on page 320.

Easter affirms a central teaching of the Christian faith. Jesus, the Son of God, did die on a cross for our sins. Jesus did rise again to endless life, as our Lord. Because Jesus died for us and rose again we have forgiveness, and the promise of our own resurrection to endless life with Jesus. Easter's great truths need to be reaffirmed in our family each year. Building family Easter time around retellings of these three great Easter stories is one way to annually affirm our own commitment to our crucified and risen Lord. See paragraph 94.

In our family, we found that it helped make Easter and Christmas special to hold private family services later at night, after our children's usual bedtimes. Getting to stay up late was exciting to the children—and one way to underline the specialness of the occasion. Nightime candlelight services, with the family gathered close together to share the wonder and glory of Jesus' self-giving, can enrich the faith of each individual in your home.

The Story Retold

"Hit Him!" one of the leaders shouted.

"Yes, hit Him!" And the men began to hit Jesus and spit on Him.

For hours the enemies of Jesus had tried to get witnesses to lie about Jesus, so their court could condemn Him. Finally the high priest asked Jesus: "Tell us the truth. Are You the Christ, the Son of God?"

Jesus answered them honestly.

After all, Jesus had told everyone so many times. "Yes," Jesus said, "it is as you say. And in the future you will see Me, the Son of Man, sitting at the right hand of God the Father, coming on the clouds of heaven."

It was then the leaders shouted, "Hit Him."

Jesus had claimed He was the Son of God.

Because the leaders didn't believe Jesus, they thought what Jesus said was a great crime. "He deserves to die," the leaders said. In their anger, they slapped Jesus and hit Him with their fists.

But the high priest and the leaders of the Jewish court had a problem. Israel was governed by Rome. It was part of the Roman Empire. The Jewish court didn't have power to put anyone to death.

So after they had beaten Jesus, the leaders took Jesus to Pilate, the Roman governor. They told the Roman governor that Jesus was a criminal and ought to be killed. "Why," the leaders said, "this Jesus says He is our King."

When the Roman governor heard their charges he wanted to talk with Jesus. "Are you really King of the Jews?" Pilate asked.

Jesus answered Pilate. "Yes. But My kingdom is a heavenly kingdom, and My followers don't fight."

After Pilate talked with Jesus, he knew that Jesus was innocent. The Roman governor realized that the chief priests and religious leaders were just jealous of Jesus. So Pilate wanted to let Jesus go.

Pilate called all Jesus' enemies back into the courtroom. "I know this Man is innocent," Pilate said.

But the enemies of Jesus shouted and screamed. "Crucify Him! Crucify Him!"

Pilate didn't want to have Jesus put to death. So he tried something else. Every year at the time of the Passover Feast, the Roman governor released a Jewish prisoner as a special favor. The governor let the people of Israel choose who should be released.

So Pilate had an idea. "Should I release Jesus for you, or should I release Barabbas?"

Barabbas was a brutal criminal, who had robbed and killed. Jesus was a good man. He taught about God and healed the sick. Pilate thought for sure that the crowd would want Jesus released rather than the evil Barabbas.

But Jesus' enemies had stirred up the crowd against Jesus. When the Roman governor asked the crowd to choose, Jesus' enemies began to shout. "We want Barabbas!" "Turn Barabbas loose!"

Pilate was surprised.

"What about Jesus?" Pilate asked.

"Kill Him!" the crowd shouted. "Crucify Jesus! Yes, crucify Jesus!"

Pilate didn't want to crucify Jesus. He knew Jesus was innocent. But Pilate was afraid. Pilate, the Roman governor of Jerusalem, was afraid that the Jewish leaders who hated Jesus would go to Rome, and say that Pilate let someone go who claimed to be a king. So Pilate gave in.

"It is your responsibility," Pilate said to the crowd. And then Pilate gave the order.

Jesus was to be crucified.

The first thing that happened, the Roman soldiers took Jesus to a nearby guardroom. There the soldiers beat Jesus with whips. This was to make Jesus bleed, to make Him weak from loss of blood. Jesus would die quicker if He was weak.

The soldiers also put a crown made out of sharp thorns on Jesus' head. Then the soldiers beat Jesus some more. They spit on Him and made fun of Him.

Jesus just stood there, quietly accepting the suffering.

Finally it was time for the execution.

The soldiers took Jesus outside and tried to make Him carry the long wooden pole used to make the cross. Jesus staggered under the heavy weight. He stumbled along the stone streets. Finally Jesus fell under the weight of the cross.

The soldiers grabbed an onlooker and made him carry the cross. Jesus, weak from loss of blood, staggered on through the city streets after them.

Finally they all came to the city gates.

Just outside the gates was a hill, a hill that looked like

a skull. In Hebrew its name was Golgotha. We usually call the hill Calvary.

The soldiers took Jesus' clothes and then threw Him down on the ground. They nailed Jesus' hands and feet to the wooden cross. Then they lifted the cross up and stood it upright in a hole that had been dug.

Jesus was hanging on the cross.

He was about to die—for our sins.

While Jesus hung on the cross, wonderful things happened. Even though it was about noon, the sky suddenly became very dark. The whole land was covered with darkness, as if it were night. The watching soldiers were amazed. They began to realize that Jesus was special after all.

Jesus wasn't crucified alone.

Two thieves were crucified at the same time. At first the two ridiculed Jesus. They said, "If You're really God's Son, come down from the cross." All the crowd watching the crucifixion jeered and said the same things.

They didn't know that Jesus was dying for our sins.

Later one of the two thieves changed his mind. "Don't you know," that thief said to the other, "that we are dying for our crimes? Jesus hasn't done anything wrong." And the dying thief said to Jesus, "Remember me when You come into Your kingdom." Jesus promised, "Today you will be with Me in Paradise [heaven]."

The thief who believed in Jesus was forgiven.

Jesus was dying to pay for the thief's sins, and for our sins, too.

Jesus suffered on the cross for a long time.

It wasn't just the pain, even though crucifixion hurts terribly. What made Jesus suffer most was the weight of sins that He carried there—the sins of the whole world. For the very first time, God the Father had to turn away from God the Son. Jesus took on Himself all our sins. He died for the wickedness that human beings have done.

Then it was time.

Jesus looked up to heaven and dismissed His spirit. His suffering was over, and Jesus died.

Jesus didn't have to die.

Jesus was God, and He could have come down from the cross. Jesus could have destroyed all His enemies. But Jesus chose to die, because Jesus knew that your sins and mine must be paid for. Jesus wanted to forgive us, so we could become members of God's family.

Jesus suffered.

But Jesus was glad to suffer.

Jesus suffered for you and for me.

Action Idea

Conclude the reading of this solemn account of the Crucifixion with a family communion. You can read the service from 1 Corinthians 11:23–26, or write your own communion service. As your children grow, your communion service can be expanded, modified, or rewritten yearly in preparation for the special family time when you remember together Jesus' death.

Jesus Is Risen!
Matthew 28, John 21

Background

The Russian church greets Easter morning with a symbolic search, followed by glad cries of "He is risen! He is risen indeed!"

In the deepest sense, Easter is the highlight of the Christian year. On Easter we mark the triumph of our Savior over mankind's grim enemies. Christ is risen. He is Victor over death. Jesus had broken the bonds of sin which held us. See paragraph 94.

Jesus' resurrection stands in history as glowing, final proof of all our Lord's claims about himself. Easter reveals Jesus as the triumphant Son of God. Easter reveals all the divine power and the glory that were masked during our Savior's years on earth.

Because Easter is so special, we will want to share its joy in our family. This Bible story is suggested for use early Easter morning, to set the tone for the day's joyful celebration at worship. This is the third in a series of three stories for use during the Easter season. The first two stories are found on pages 309 and 316.

This Bible story, like the other two, does not feature *talkables*. Instead, it is a simple affirmation of that great event which brings the fullness of hope to believers. The accompanying *Action Idea* suggests ways to shape the family context for a special annual Easter celebration.

The Story Retold

"He's alive!"

The women were almost out of breath when they ran into the home where Jesus' disciples were mourning.

Mary took a deep breath and choked out the exciting news: "It's really true. Jesus is alive!"

The disciples of Jesus looked at the excited women—and they couldn't believe what they heard!

The disciples had been heartbroken ever since Jesus had been crucified. They had seen Jesus die. Some had helped take Jesus' dead body down from the cross. Others had wrapped Jesus' body in linen cloths. They had carried the body to a nearby garden. There the disciples had watched tearfully as Jesus' body was put in a tomb carved in the rock. The disciples had said good-by to Jesus. They had loved Jesus so much. But the soldiers rolled up a great, heavy stone and closed the tomb door. So the disciples knew that Jesus was dead. They just couldn't believe what the woman told them.

Besides, the disciples must have thought, the chief priests put soldiers at the tomb to guard the door.

Jesus *must* be dead.

The disciples had wept and sorrowed after Jesus died. Each one of the disciples knew he would weep and feel awful sorrow for the rest of his life because Jesus was dead.

But the women knew better. Loudly, the women shouted out their story to the sorrowful disciples.

"Listen," one of them probably said. She told the disciples how they went to the tomb early in the morning, with flowers and with spices for Jesus' dead body. But when the women got to the tomb, the guards were gone and the stone was rolled away. Jesus' tomb was open. An angel, as bright as the brightest lightning, sat on the stone that had locked Jesus' body in.

The woman told the disciples how the angel had talked

with them. "Don't be afraid," the angel said. "Jesus, who was crucified, isn't here. Jesus has come to life again, just as He said He would. Jesus is risen from the dead."

The angel then told the women to go look inside the tomb. The women looked. The angel was right! Jesus wasn't there at all. Jesus had come back from the dead!

Then the angel sent the women to the disciples. "Go quickly," the angel said, "and tell His disciples that Jesus has risen from the dead and is going to Galilee." The angel promised that the disciples would see Jesus there.

The women started to run.

They ran as fast as they could.

Suddenly, there in front of the hurrying women, was Jesus Himself! The women actually saw Jesus! Full of joy they fell at Jesus' feet and worshiped Him. Now the women knew for sure. Their friend Jesus, the one whom they loved so much, really was the Son of God.

When the women reached the disciples, all out of breath, they shouted out the good news.

"Jesus is alive!"

"He lives. We saw Him ourselves."

When Jesus' disciples heard the story, they began to wonder. Could it be true?

Two other disciples were beginning to believe too. Peter and John had not been with the rest. Even earlier that morning, Mary Magdalene had visited the garden tomb. Mary Magdalene thought someone had stolen the body, so Mary came, crying, to tell Peter and John.

Peter began to run toward the tomb. John followed. Because John was younger he outran Peter. When John and Peter reached the tomb, each looked inside. There were the strips of linen cloth Jesus had been wrapped in. But Jesus wasn't there! How could the linen be there, and Jesus be gone?

Peter and John looked. And they began to believe. Jesus really had risen from the dead!

That night all the disciples met together in a private room. The door was locked, and the disciples were talking. What had happened? Was Jesus really alive again?

And suddenly, there was Jesus.

Alive.

Right there in the room with the disciples!

"Peace," Jesus said to His amazed disciples. Then Jesus showed them His hands, where the spikes were driven when He was nailed to the cross. Jesus showed them His side, and they saw the wound made by a Roman soldier's spear.

It really was Jesus!

There could be no mistake.

Jesus was alive again.

And the disciples were filled with joy.

Jesus *is* alive. Today. Because Jesus lives, we will live too, forever and forever with God.

Action Idea

Early Easter morning, why not imitate the Russian Church's practice? Get up at dawn. Search through your whole house, and outside too. Jesus' body is not there. He is risen.

Greet each other with the words of joy:

"Jesus is risen. Jesus is risen indeed."

Then fill your home with joyful Easter music until you go together to church, to celebrate, with other believers, the resurrection of our Lord.

Jesus Trusts Peter
John 21:15–19

Background

It's discouraging for you and me when our children show little progress, and the same faults show up over and over again. It's discouraging for the children too. Should our boys and girls sense that we've given up on them, it's all too easy for them to give up on themselves. They feel that they simply cannot do better than they have. The hope of growth and change, and expectation of a better future, are lost.

One of God's greatest gifts to us, and one we can give our children, is the gift of confidence that they will grow and change. When we believe in our boys and girls, it's much easier for them to believe in themselves. How exciting that, as Christians, we *can* believe in our children, no matter how slow their progress may seem to be (see paragraph 52).

One beautiful Bible story helps our children and us understand the transforming power of forgiveness. When God forgives us, he breaks the bonds forged by our past failures. God tells us to look ahead. Looking ahead, we realize that God intends to help us grow to spiritual maturity. God intends to use us and to make us spiritually significant persons.

Children (of any age) who feel discouraged about their failures will sense God's love and his belief in them as you share this Bible story of Jesus' conversation with Peter after Peter had denied Jesus three times (see page 313).

The Story Retold

Jesus stood up.

Jesus had been crouched over a fire, cooking some bread and fish for His disciples. The disciples had gone fishing. But when a Man on shore called them and then brought them food, the disciples knew it was Jesus.

When the food was passed around, Peter held back. Peter stood behind some of the other disciples, keeping them between him and Jesus. Peter did this because he was ashamed. He was afraid of what Jesus might say to him.

You see, just before Jesus was crucified and raised again from the dead, Peter had done a terrible thing. Peter had been so afraid of what people might think that Peter lied three times about his friendship for Jesus.

Three times on the night Jesus was on trial, Peter had told others that he didn't know Jesus.

Now Peter remembered how terribly he had failed. So Peter didn't want Jesus to see him. Peter just wanted to hide.

What words do you suppose might describe how Peter felt then? Have you ever failed and just didn't want others to see you? Can you tell us about one time? How did you feel about yourself then? How do you suppose Peter felt about himself?

Peter felt very ashamed. Peter felt as if he was no good at all. He had failed Jesus and had failed himself too. Now Peter was afraid that Jesus would never trust him again.

But Jesus didn't let Peter hide.

When they finished eating, Jesus looked right at Peter. "Peter," Jesus asked, "do you truly love Me more than these?"

Peter nodded. "Yes, Lord. You know that I love You."

Then Jesus said, "Peter, take care of My sheep."

Jesus asked Peter again, "Do you love Me?"

Peter gave the same answer. "Yes, Lord, You know that I love You." Then Jesus said, "Peter, take care of My sheep."

Peter had denied Jesus three times. So Jesus asked Peter His question a third time. "Peter, do you love Me?"

Peter felt hurt that Jesus questioned him a third time. "Yes, Lord," Peter said, "You know all things. You know that I love You."

Then Jesus said to Peter, "Feed My sheep."

We know that Jesus' "sheep" are people who love God and believe in Him. What Jesus did was to give Peter a special job. Peter was going to be a leader and a teacher, to love and care for the people whom Jesus loves.

Do you think Peter was a good choice for this important job? Why—or why not? When Peter denied Jesus, Peter failed terribly. Why do you suppose that Jesus would trust someone who had failed him so badly?

Jesus knew how badly Peter had failed. But Jesus knew that Peter really did love Him. Jesus knew that Peter, even though he had failed, would become a good leader for God's people. He trusted Peter enough to give Peter an important job. Jesus knew that Peter would grow and change. Jesus knew that God would help Peter become a good leader in spite of his failures.

How do you suppose it feels to keep on failing, until you don't think you'll ever be any good? Have you ever felt that way? What about?

Everyone has times when they fail and fail. When that happens to you, I don't give up on you. I know that you will keep on growing. I know that God will help you grow, as he helped Peter. God will help you be able to succeed.

(Pray together, thanking God that, as we love him, the Lord does help us grow. God will help us become able to succeed instead of to fail.)

Action Idea

Make a poster for your child's room on an "I'm Growing" theme. You can use any of a number of possible motifs to represent growth. Trace a caterpillar from cocoon to a butterfly. Trace a seed from sprout to plant to flower. You can also include a helpful saying, such as, "I don't give up. God isn't finished with me yet."

Work together to design and make each child's own unique "growing" poster. How good to know that you truly can believe in your child, whatever his failures, because God *isn't* finished with him yet. God is at work. Jesus in our lives brings solid hope for the future.

Jesus Returns to Heaven
John 14:1–4; Acts 1:1–11

Background

Death and dying are facts of life, even for children. Few experiences are likely to cause more grief than the loss of a beloved family member. Few experiences are likely to create more doubts and concerns about a child's personal future. While six- to eight-year-olds and nine- to eleven-year-olds typically have different questions about death (see paragraph 88), each does need a basis for hope, and some knowledge of what lies beyond this life.

Several Bible stories in this *Handbook* are related to death. Each focuses on some specific childhood concern. The story of the death of Moses is designed to help a child deal with the death of a grandparent or other older person. The story of Stephen deals with sudden, unexpected death. This Bible story explains what happens when a believer dies, and it recalls Jesus' own words about what he is now doing in heaven to prepare a place for us. Another Bible story (pages 349–352) suggests answers to the unanswerable question which children have, "What is heaven like?"

You may want to use this as part of your Easter sequence (see pages 309, 316, and 320) and retell it each year during the Easter season. This way the story will be preparation for tragedies which must someday come. Or you can tell the story after a death, when children ask, "What happens when we die?"

The Story Retold

It was time to leave.
Jesus took one last walk with His disciples.

How excited the disciples had been when they learned that Jesus was alive. When Jesus was crucified, and died, all that the disciples felt were sorrow and grief. How lonely the disciples had felt then. It seemed to them that they were empty inside. Jesus was dead, and the disciples thought they would never see Jesus again.

How do you suppose the disciples who loved Jesus felt when he died? What do you suppose the disciples thought about? Why is it so hard for us when someone we love dies?

It was hard for the disciples when their friend Jesus died. But how excited and joyful they felt on Easter morning, when they discovered that Jesus was alive again! Death hadn't been the end for Jesus. Jesus came back from the dead, to be with His friends.

But Jesus wasn't going to stay with the disciples. That's why the walk Jesus and His friends took one morning was their last walk. Jesus was going to leave them. The disciples knew that Jesus was alive. But Jesus would soon be gone, as if He'd taken a long trip.

(If you've gone on a long trip, or your family members live at a distance, talk about this as analogous to dying. We are not with our distant loved ones every day. But we know they are all right. We may miss them. But we don't feel sad, as though we would never see them again.)

Jesus told His disciples that He would soon leave them. The last supper that the disciples had with Jesus, just before Jesus was crucified, Jesus told them where He would go, and why.

"Don't let your hearts be troubled," Jesus had said. "Trust in God; trust also in Me. There are many rooms in My Father's house. I am going there—to be with God the Father. When I go I will prepare a place for you."

Jesus was going to heaven to be with God the Father. Jesus would have heaven ready for you and me. Jesus wanted the disciples to know that when they died, there was a special place all ready for them with God. Dying is like taking a long trip for us too. We go to be with Jesus, in a wonderful place Jesus is preparing for us.

How do you suppose the disciples felt when Jesus told them about heaven? What made them most happy—to know that when their bodies died they would go on living? To know that when they died they would be in a beautiful place prepared just for them? Or to know that when they died they would be with Jesus always? Or perhaps to know that the people they loved who had died were still alive in heaven, so some day they would be together again? Which of these seems most important to you when you think about dying?

Jesus made another wonderful promise to His disciples. Jesus told them that He would prepare a place for them. And Jesus told them, "I will come back, and take you to be with Me, that you also may be where I am."

Jesus would leave.

But He will come back again.

Then all of us—people who are alive then, and people who have died—will be together again. Then we will all be together, with Jesus, forever.

Maybe the disciples remembered what Jesus had said when they walked with Him on that last walk. Maybe the disciples had forgotten. But on that walk Jesus talked with them for a while, and then, right in front of their eyes, Jesus began to float up, higher and higher, into the air! The disciples watched, amazed as Jesus went higher and higher. Finally Jesus was hidden by a cloud.

When Jesus was gone, and the amazed disciples were still looking up, two angels stood beside them.

"Men of Galilee," the angels said. "Why do you stand here, looking into the sky? This same Jesus, who has been taken from you into heaven, will come back in the same way you have seen Him go into heaven."

Then the disciples knew for sure. Jesus was gone, and they wouldn't see Him again here on earth. But when the disciples died, they would go to heaven, and Jesus would be there. Someday, perhaps soon, Jesus will come back again. Then we will all be together in heaven, forever and ever.

Action Idea

The sense that people who die are not just gone and forgotten is important to children. You can help them by talking about loved ones who have died, whom you are looking forward to being with when Jesus comes again. Tell stories about your own parents (if they have died) or about grandparents or friends you knew as a child. Speak of them with warmth and humor and gladness, as though they were still living (for they are), but simply are far away. Your own expression of confidence in the promise Jesus made will go far to build your child's faith and hope.

The New Church Lives in Love
Acts 2:44–47

Background

It was astonishing. The people of Jerusalem looked with amazement at the new community that formed after Jesus' resurrection and said of the Christians, "See how they love each other!" That new community, marked by sharing and love, is described in many New Testament passages. We read of its life style in nearly every epistle, and gradually grasp the importance of the acceptance, forgiveness, mutual support and encouragement which made the early Body of Christ such a dynamic witness. These people truly cared about each other. That caring, in a world in which people are hungry for love, is a warm call to come to Jesus and so become one of Jesus' people.

The first New Testament passage which gives insight into the life style of the new community is Acts 2:44–47. This imaginary Bible story is designed to pick up and highlight the ways of living reflected in the Acts 2 passage, and to help children both select close friends, and evaluate their own treatment of other people. The story as told reflects issues discussed in paragraphs 10 and 13 of this *Handbook*. It may also be used to give insight in brother/sister relationships (see paragraph 75).

The Story Retold

It was so exciting. To have real friends at last! That's what Jedediah was thinking as he hurried to the home of his neighbor, Jeremy.

Jedediah was a Christian in the very first church, a church started in Jerusalem after Jesus' resurrection. Jedediah and Jeremy are made-up names. But the Bible tells us the kind of things that happened to them as they learned how to live together in love.

One of the things that made Jedediah so happy about

his new Christian friends was that people were so unselfish. When Jeremy's family ran out of money, because Jeremy was hurt and couldn't work, other Christians brought food and money to help them. Jedediah didn't have much, but he brought some food for the family too. Jedediah had to skip his own lunch. But it made him very happy to be able to help others. *Yes,* Jedediah thought, *being one of Jesus' people made one feel very happy. Joyful even.*

It was also fun to be together. The new friends got together almost every day. They ate at each other's homes and liked to be with each other. These were friends a person could talk to. You could talk to these new friends about your problems, or tell them if you felt upset. These friends really cared. Why, they even prayed for each other. They talked to God about what was important to each other.

For Jedediah, real friends were special. These friends of his had many things in common. They believed in Jesus as their Savior. They all tried to please the Lord. Oh, Jedediah had friends who weren't Christians, of course. But his closest friends were people like him, who tried to please the Lord because they loved Jesus. Worshiping God together, and knowing that your friends would want to do what is right, was good. These friends wouldn't try to get you to do something wrong. That was one of the things that made the new church so warm and wonderful.

When Jedediah was with his Christian friends, Jedediah knew he belonged. He was with people whom he was learning to love. Jedediah knew that these friends would love him, too, always.

Oh look! There is Jeremy now.

"Hi Jeremy!" Jedediah shouted. He hurried toward Jeremy. Jedediah was with his friends.

Talkables

Rather than weaving the talkables in, here are a number of ideas for following up on themes introduced in the story. You may want to talk about all or just some of these areas.

1. *How did people like Jedediah, in the first church, show they loved each other? (List from the story, or read it through again to make a complete list.) Which way of showing love do you think was most important? Can you think of other ways good friends act, that show they care about each other? What don't friends do? What do friends do?*

2. *Who are your closest friends? Why do you enjoy being with them? How are they like you? How are they different from you? What is the most important way that they are like you? Jedediah's closest friends were Christians who wanted to please God, as he did. Why might it be important to have close friends who want to do what's right?*

3. *What are some ways that you can let your friends know that you care about them? Jedediah said he knew people cared because they weren't selfish, and shared. Also he could talk his problems over with his friends, and they would listen. Can you think of other ways that you know your friends like you, or that your friends know you care?*

4. *How can our family be like the first church, and love each other better? Are there things that any of us do that make you feel unloved? Can you tell us about them? How can we show more love to each other?*

Action Idea

If you apply this story to your family, work together on a mural or collage which will express ways to live with each other in love. You can use drawings, cut out the pictures and words, and so on. The finished product will remind you of how to better love each other at home, and experience the joy that comes when we really care.

The Believers Pray
Acts 4

Background

When the disciples proclaimed the resurrected Jesus, and their message was authenticated by miracles, the religious leaders who had plotted to have the Lord crucified were stunned. The death of Jesus hadn't stamped out the movement after all!

Immediately the leaders attempted to put pressure on the disciples. The leaders threatened them and warned them to stop preaching in the name of Jesus. Under this threat, the disciples gathered together. The early church went to God in prayer.

The prayer of these tested believers is fascinating. The church brings the problem before the Lord. The believers express confidence that God truly is Sovereign Lord. Then, instead of asking God to remove the opposition, these believers simply ask for boldness and courage to continue proclaiming Jesus.

In their prayers they did not beg God to change the difficult situation. Instead the apostles accepted responsibility for facing the difficulties and asked only for God's help and empowering, that they might do what is right.

In our attempt to help our children grow up as responsible persons, we need to teach them the joy of this kind of prayer. God often will not change the circumstances of our lives. What God will do is to give us strength to overcome. As we overcome, we grow in confidence in ourselves, and confidence in the Lord. See paragraph 79.

The Story Retold

"Bring them in here," the officer said harshly.

The guards dragged Peter and John into the courtroom. Now Peter and John stood in front of the very men who had condemned Jesus to die just a few weeks before.

The judges in that courtroom were very angry. The judges had killed Jesus because they didn't like what Jesus taught, and they didn't believe that Jesus is the Son of God. Now Jesus' followers were preaching all over the city. Jesus' disciples were saying that Jesus really was God's Son. Even worse, some of the disciples of Jesus had healed people. Then they claimed that Jesus' power was what performed the miracles. The judges were sure they had to hush up people like Peter and John. If they didn't, pretty soon everyone in the city would blame the judges for killing the Lord.

That day in court, the judges angrily asked Peter and John how they had healed a crippled man.

Boldly, Peter spoke up. "We healed the crippled man

by the power of Jesus Christ of Nazareth, whom you crucified, but God raised from the dead. You rejected Jesus,
but I tell you that Jesus is the only way a person can be
saved."

The judges were shocked and amazed.

These were followers of Jesus, all right. And the cripple
Jesus' followers had healed was standing right there beside
them. So the judges couldn't say that the healing didn't
happen. What could they do?

The judges sent Peter and John out of the room, and
talked it over. "What are we going to do with these men?"
they asked each other.

Finally they decided.

Everyone in the city of Jerusalem knew the man had been
healed. So the judges were afraid to punish Peter and John.
Instead, the judges called Peter and John back, and threatened them.

"Don't you dare speak or teach in the name of Jesus,"
the judges said. "We have the power to punish you. If you
do talk about Jesus, we'll make you suffer!"

After the judges threatened Peter and John, they let them
go.

Right away Peter and John went to join other Christians.
Peter and John told about the judges' threats and warnings.
The Christians began to pray.

*What do you suppose the disciples and the Christians prayed?
If you had been there, what do you think you would have wanted
God to do? Do you suppose they will pray that Jesus' enemies go
away and stop threatening them? Why, or why not?*

*Have you ever had a time when you were afraid or worried, about
what might happen if you did the right thing? How did you feel
then? If you had prayed then, what do you think you would have
asked God for? (Tell of such an incident in your own life if one
comes to mind).*

Peter and John had been threatened by the very men
who ordered Jesus killed. These men had power to hurt
Peter and John, too. But when Peter and John prayed, the
two disciples didn't ask God to destroy their enemies. Instead, the disciples prayed this way.

First, Peter and John told God they knew that only He

is truly powerful. "Sovereign Lord," they said, "You made the earth and the seas and heaven, and everything in them." Peter and John knew the court that threatened them really didn't have any power at all. God is in charge of our lives. God can protect us. Only when God lets it happen for a good reason can anything bad happen to us.

Second, Peter and John asked God for help.

Peter and John didn't ask for their enemies to be destroyed. Instead the disciples prayed, "Lord, consider their threats, and enable Your servants to speak Your Word with great boldness." Peter and John only wanted God to help them be strong inside, so they would do the right thing in spite of the threats.

Praying doesn't always change things outside.

Sometimes praying is to change us inside, to make us strong so that we can do something that is hard for us.

Why do you suppose Peter and John prayed that kind of prayer? Do you think they wanted their difficulties to go away? Or did they think it was better to have difficulties? Why?

God did answer Peter and John's prayer. The Bible says that God the Holy Spirit gave Peter and John the strength they needed inside, so Peter and John did speak boldly about Jesus. God answered their prayer for strength inside. That was even better than if God had made the enemies go away.

God wants us to grow so we can be strong inside and do hard things. If you were to pray today for strength inside to do something that is difficult for you, what would you probably pray about? (Share your own need for strength inside, as well as listen to the children.)

Let's pray together that God will give us strength inside us, as God gave strength to Peter and John. God will help us do what we believe is right, too.

Action Idea

Make it a practice for the next few weeks when you pray together to pray for strength inside. If you are careful to continue this pattern, you can build into your children's lives a wonderful prayer experience. You can help them develop a confidence which comes only when we know God is with us, to help us do what is right.

The Believers Share
Acts 4:32–37

Background

Old and New Testaments both affirm the rights of the individual to have personal possessions. But both Testaments also enjoin generosity. What we have is ours. But when we love others, and are sensitive to their needs, we will be quick to respond by sharing.

It is striking that the term used in the New Testament to express giving is "fellowship"—a word which renders the Greek word *koinonia,* and which means "sharing." God gives us the privilege of so sharing the joys and sorrows of others that we become sensitive to their needs, and motivated by love to reach out and help.

One key to helping our children learn to relate to others effectively is development of sensitivity (see paragraph 13). This story is designed to help your boys and girls think with you about the importance of understanding how others feel. It will encourage their natural generosity and lead them to reach out to help. This story is suitable for children of all ages. But probably only children eight and older will have the role-taking skills it encourages (see paragraph 74).

The Story Retold

"Zachari looks pretty upset these days," Jedediah said to some of his Christian friends.

Zachari and Jedediah aren't mentioned in the Bible. But what happened to them is the kind of thing that the Bible book of Acts tells us about. When Jesus had died and come to life again, the people who believed in Him got together often. Jesus' followers talked about the teachings of the leaders who wrote our New Testament. And Jesus' followers learned to love each other very much. They were the closest of friends.

That's why Jedediah was concerned when he noticed that Zachari seemed upset. Friends care about each other. If one friend is worried or upset, other friends want to help.

Who are the friends whom you care about the most? Do they care about you, too? How do you suppose we know when our friends really care about us? What are some things about (name of a friend identified by your child) that helps you feel he is a real friend?

Jedediah showed he was a friend by noticing that Zachari was upset. Jedediah noticed Zachari didn't smile as much as he used to. Zachari looked sad. Or Zachari stood off alone to one side when others were talking. When we see a person do those things, we can be pretty sure that something is wrong.

When times really got hard in Jerusalem, and many people had no way to earn money for food, some of the Christians sold land or houses. The Christians brought the money from the sale to the disciples. The disciples, like Peter and John, gave away the money and saw that no one would go hungry. Because Jesus' people really did love each other, they were ready to share.

God doesn't ask us to sell everything and give it away. But God does want us to be sensitive. When our friends are feeling badly, God wants us to help. Sometimes we may need to give others money to help them out. But sometimes we can help just by listening to them. Or we can help by working with a friend on a hard schoolwork assignment. We can help by having others over to play with us when they're lonely. One wonderful way to show our love to God is to love others, and help them when they need us to care.

Action Idea

Make a list with your children of times when their friends or they might feel upset or unhappy or lonely. When the list is as long as you and your children can make it, write each problem area on a separate 8½ x 11 sheet of paper.

Draw a vertical line dividing the paper into two sections. On one side of the paper, try to list with your child as many clues as possible that might indicate a friend is having problems. Listing things that your children can observe from the behavior of others will help them become sensitive to other's feelings.

On the other side of each paper, list possible ways you and your children might be able to help a person with a particular problem. A lonely child might be invited to a party, invited to stay overnight, and so on. You might tell a worried boy or girl you will pray for him or her, tell your parents about the problem and see if they can help, and so on.

As you work through this process together you can help your children grow significantly in their ability to relate well to others. You can also help them develop the Christian grace of caring love.

Learning to Be Fair
Acts 6:1–7

Background

The early New Testament church was vital and loving. But it was not without problems. In a way, that church was much like a good home. The members of a family do love each other. But things happen which lead to disputes, to hurt, and even to anger.

Paragraphs 36 and 39 explore how to deal with anger and jealousy in your family. This Bible story, about the settlement of a dispute in the Jerusalem church, can be very useful in working out family ground rules for handling disputes in your own home.

One of the most important things for us to realize as parents is that problems are opportunities. It is through conflicts and their resolutions, through problems and their solutions, that people grow. This is especially true with children. Our boys and girls don't need to be told that particular patterns of behavior are wrong as much as they need to be helped to find better ways to deal with the experiences which may stimulate wrong actions. The dispute over fairness that caused bitterness in the early church is like many disputes over fairness that take place in every home. What our children need, and receive in this Bible story, is a way to work through disputes: a way that shows love and is fair to all.

The Story Retold

"It isn't fair!"
"They're cheating us."
"How come they get more than we do?"
All these things were being said in the first church in Jerusalem. People were upset and angry. Some of the people were very jealous too.
"It isn't fair for them to get more than we do!"
Have you ever felt the way those people felt? When are you most likely to feel upset and angry because you feel someone isn't fair? (Be sure to share times when you may feel this way, too.) What do you suppose we can do when we feel we're not treated fairly? Just staying angry doesn't help, does it?

The people who were part of that first Jerusalem church had one special difference between them. Some of those Christians had grown up speaking the Greek language, and some had grown up speaking the language of Palestine, called Aramaic. When these people became Christians, they became part of God's one family. But they still had their differences.

What happened was that the widows and orphans, who had no one to help them earn money for food, were given food by their Christian friends. But the Christians who spoke Aramaic thought their Aramaic-speaking widows weren't getting their fair share. They were sure the Greek-speaking widows were getting more. That's why they were upset and angry.

"It isn't fair," the Aramaic-speaking Christians said to each other. The more they thought about it, the more angry they became. And they began to feel bitter toward those who spoke Greek.

Do you think the Aramaic-speaking Christians were right to feel upset? I think it's all right to be upset when we believe something isn't fair. But getting angry and bitter doesn't help. What do people who are angry at not being treated fairly usually do? What do you suppose a person could do that would really help?

The people in the Jerusalem church were part of God's family. They loved Jesus, and they loved each other. Being upset wasn't something the Jerusalem Christians liked. But they were hurt when they felt others didn't treat them fairly.

So the Aramaic-speaking Christians did something. They complained. Instead of keeping their feelings bottled up inside, or trying to hurt their Greek-speaking brothers, they told how they were feeling. Then Jesus' disciples, who were the leaders, called everyone together to talk about the problem.

The disciples listened to the people who felt upset and hurt. Jesus' disciples didn't blame anyone. Instead, the disciples cared about the feelings of the people who thought the way the food was given out wasn't fair. Then they did something very important.

The disciples told everyone, Aramaic and Greek-speaking alike, "You choose seven good men, who love God and who are wise, and we will make them responsible for giving out the food. They will take responsibility, and see that everyone is treated fairly."

My, what a good idea, everyone thought. And all the Christians worked together to choose men who would be fair, and who would see that all the widows had whatever they needed.

The early Christians did several things to solve the problem of people being hurt and angry when they weren't treated fairly. Which of these things do you suppose was most important, and why?

1. *The Aramaic-speaking Christians told the leaders how they felt.*

2. *The leaders listened and called everyone together to hear how the Aramaic people felt.*

3. *The leaders didn't get angry or blame people for how they felt, or blame the others for what they had done. Instead the leaders tried to solve the problem.*

4. *The leaders and the people figured out a way to be sure everyone was treated fairly.*

Do you think we could use a plan like this in our family, to help solve problems that come when someone feels he or she isn't treated fairly?

In Jerusalem a wonderful thing happened. The seven men that everyone chose to take care of the widows all had Greek names! The Aramaic-speaking Christians really did know that everyone was part of God's family. They knew that family members do love each other. The Aramaic-speaking Christians knew that since everyone understood how they felt, the Greek-speaking Christians would be fair.

Action Idea

Discuss the idea of setting up a family council. You can set up family council rules, based on what happened in the Acts church. Possible rules are:

1. Everyone can tell parents how they feel, and ask for a family council.

2. At the council, everyone can tell how they feel about what is happening.

3. No one can blame other people. Instead the council will try to understand why there is a problem.

4. The family council will try to figure out a way for everyone to feel he or she is treated fairly.

Stephen Is Killed
Acts 6, 7

Background

A death in the family is always difficult for children. It is most difficult if the person who dies is a parent, or a brother or sister. Somehow even children expect older people to die. But sudden, unexpected deaths are disruptive and traumatic.

As paragraph 88 discusses, children typically have different kinds of questions and concerns about death at different ages. Yet perhaps the most difficult question when death strikes unexpectedly and too soon is "Why?"

There is no satisfactory answer to the "Why?" question. But it is important for children and for us to know that death need not come as punishment, or as a result of wrongdoing. And it's important for us to remember that death is not the end. Death is a door, opening to an even richer experience of life. Each of these themes is expressed in the Bible story of the martyrdom of Stephen. Stephen was a godly young man, much loved by believers in the early church. Stephen's violent death came at the hands of a mob. His murder was unjust as well as unexpected. But while dying, Stephen saw a vision of Jesus and commended his spirit to the Lord.

This story, retold especially to be used after the sudden death of a loved one, does not include talkables. It is intended simply to be told, without discussion. Later your child may ask for the story again. Or later he may want to talk about the story. The *Action Idea* suggestion gives several themes from the story that you may pick up and talk about, when your child is ready.

The Story Retold

"It's Stephen," the old lady said happily.

Stephen was one of the men in the Jerusalem church who helped take care of widows and orphans. Stephen was a good man, and the Christians in Jerusalem loved Stephen very much.

No wonder the old lady was happy to see Stephen come to visit. Stephen not only saw to it she had food to eat; Stephen took time to talk with her, too.

Stephen was a good man. And no one expected that anything bad would happen to Stephen.

One of the things that Stephen liked to do was to tell the people of Jerusalem about the Lord Jesus. God even helped Stephen heal the sick and do other wonderful things to show how much God loved Stephen.

That was why it was so hard to believe when Stephen was killed. Stephen was a good man, and people loved him. Jesus loved Stephen too.

There were some men in Jerusalem who didn't like Stephen. These were men who had hated Jesus and didn't want Stephen to speak about the Lord. These men argued with Stephen. But every time they argued, Stephen was so wise, and so right, that they could never win.

Finally the enemies stirred up a mob against Stephen. The angry mob dragged Stephen to the very court that had condemned Jesus to death.

But Stephen was a good man.

Stephen was a man whom other Christians loved.

Stephen was a man whom God loved, too.

Certainly nothing bad could happen to Stephen.

When the judges let Stephen speak, his face shone like that of an angel. He boldly told the judges how, all through history, God's Old Testament people hadn't listened to God or obeyed the Lord. Stephen told the judges that they had done the most terrible thing of all. God had sent His Son, Jesus. Instead of loving God's Son, those judges betrayed and murdered Jesus.

Everything Stephen said was true.

Because it was true, the judges on the court were furious.
They howled in anger and glared at Stephen.

Then Stephen looked toward the heavens and saw Jesus!
"Look," Stephen said. "I see heaven open, and the Son of
Man, Jesus, standing at the right hand of God the Father."

The judges of the court and Stephen's other enemies were
so angry! They yelled at the top of their voices and dragged
Stephen outside the city.

Stephen was a good man.

Stephen was a man whom all the Christians in Jerusalem
loved.

Stephen was a man whom God loved.

Stephen hadn't lied, or done anything wrong. Stephen
had only told the judges of the court the truth.

Even though Stephen was a good man, the crowd dragged
Stephen outside the city and began to throw great rocks
at him. The stones knocked Stephen to his knees. Stephen
knew that he was going to be killed.

Then Stephen looked up to heaven and prayed.

"Lord Jesus," Stephen said, "receive my spirit." Then
Stephen asked Jesus to forgive the people who killed him.
And Stephen died.

How sorrowful the Christians in Jerusalem must have
been. Stephen was just a young man; he wasn't old enough
to die. Stephen was a good man, whom everyone loved.
God hadn't been punishing Stephen. God loved Stephen
too.

No one in Jerusalem knew just why Stephen had to die
so young. But everyone was glad for one thing. Stephen
was with Jesus in heaven. Stephen was gone, and everyone
would miss Stephen very much. But Stephen was with Jesus.
Someday the Christians of Jerusalem would see Stephen
again.

Action Idea

When telling this story the first time, it's probably best to make
no comments unless your child raises questions. It's probable that,
if the story meets a need, your boy or girl will ask for the story
again. After the second or third retelling, you may want to talk,

as comfortingly as possible, about the person who has died in your family.

Talk quickly about ways that person was like Stephen. He or she was a good person. He or she was loved by the family. He or she was loved by God too. We don't know why he or she died. But we do know that God loved him or her, and that he or she is now with Jesus.

It's likely that weeks or months may pass before other questions about death and what happens after death will surface. When questions do emerge, you can answer them by telling the Bible stories on pages 179 and 316 of this *Handbook*.

Paul and Barnabas Break Up
Acts 15:36–41

Background

Divorce by mom and dad can be a shattering experience for children. Research has shown that divorce is always harmful, though not necessarily as harmful as staying together may be. Our challenge when a divorce does take place is to minimize any damage to the children. Paragraph 89 discussed some of the most common emotional problems which occur and explores ways to solve them. This Bible story is designed to help you do one of the most important things: encourage the children to express and talk about their feelings, frustrations, or fears.

There is no Bible story that deals directly with divorce. But the report of the argument which led to the breaking up of the missionary team of Paul and Barnabas contains many parallels. These two missionary leaders had shared many experiences. They were bonded together by a deep affection, by a common commitment to share Christ, and by a common commitment to obey God's Word. They were as close as friends could be. And yet there came a time when a dispute erupted which the two could not resolve. The disagreement became so sharp that the missionary team broke up, and Paul and Barnabas parted company.

There is little indication here that one was "right" while the other was "wrong." Both were probably to blame for the painful separation that took place. It is doubly significant that each of the men was a godly leader, and each continued in leadership in the early church. It's tempting for us to think that if they had only followed principles of reconciliation that each taught, some compromise could have been worked out.

But it didn't happen that way.

As in so many families these days, a time came when the two, who had bonded their lives together, came to that painful point at which they felt they must separate—rightly or wrongly.

Without condoning or condemning, this story is to help your children discover the parallels between Paul and Barnabas' breakup and your divorce. It is to help your children begin that essential process of talking about their thoughts and feelings, which will help them cope with the reality of what has happened in your family.

The Story Retold

"You can't be together as long as Paul and Barnabas have, and then just break up."

At least, that's what people at the church in Antioch thought when Paul and Barnabas began to have terrible arguments.

Why, Paul and Barnabas had been together for years, traveling as Christian missionaries. Paul and Barnabas had worked together, and eaten together, and preached together, and prayed together for years. People who have been together for years just don't break up. At least, that's what the people at Antioch thought. Besides, Paul and Barnabas did love each other. They had been the best of friends. When you've been so close, how can you ever break up?

Do you suppose people who have been as close as Paul and Barnabas—very, very good friends—can break up? What do you think makes people who care for each other break up? How do you feel about breaking up? (Share some of the things that were hard for you about breaking up with your spouse.)

What happened with Paul and Barnabas was that they had a disagreement. You see, Barnabas and Paul were planning to go back as missionaries, to visit churches they had started before. Barnabas wanted to take along a helper named Mark. But Mark had gone with Paul and Barnabas once before, and Mark had quit when he was needed. Paul didn't want Mark to come. Mark had quit, and Paul didn't think he could trust Mark to be a good helper.

It may not seem like much to argue about. But it was very important to Barnabas that Mark be given a second chance. And it was very important to Paul that any helper be trustworthy.

What are some of the things you think people might break up over? What do you think the most important reason people have for breaking up is? How do you feel about breaking up when people have reasons like that? Are there things you feel badly about? Are there things you feel are better after breaking up?

We don't know how good the reasons Paul and Barnabas had for breaking up were. We do know that neither one was happy about arguing. When people care about each other and have been together a long time, it's very hard to decide to break up. But finally the arguments became so bad, and Paul and Barnabas hurt each other so much, that they parted company.

Barnabas took Mark and went to Cyprus to be a missionary. Paul took a helper named Silas, and Paul went to a different country to be a missionary.

Both Paul and Barnabas felt badly about their argument. They felt badly about breaking up. But Paul and Barnabas must have felt that breaking up was the best thing to do.

When do you think people ought to think about breaking up? Breaking up always hurts people in some ways. Divorce is breaking up, and often people feel hurt. (Talk about some of the ways you feel hurt, and your ex-spouse felt hurt.) What are some of the ways that breaking up made you feel hurt?

While it always hurts when people break up after being together for a long time, we have to believe when it happens that it will be for the best. God was with Paul and Silas, and God was with Barnabas and Mark too. Paul and Silas often had many wonderful adventures. Paul broke up with Barnabas. Barnabas did help Mark become a trustworthy and faithful Christian. In fact, that Mark is the same Mark who wrote the Gospel of Mark that we have in our Bible. So God was with each person after they broke up. God loved Paul and Barnabas after they broke up, just as God loved them while they were together.

We don't know what will happen now that mom and dad have broken up. But we know that God loves daddy.

God loves mommy. And God loves each of you children too.

Somehow God will help everything come out for the best for each of us.

God never deserts us, even when families break up.

Action Idea

This story will indicate your readiness to talk about feelings children may have about the divorce. Even though it is likely to be painful for you, do encourage children to share their feelings. Listen sensitively and share in return. Your boys and girls can cope with divorce. A new base of security is most likely to be developed when you communicate freely about this painful experience, which has affected you all.

Paul Stays Sick
2 Corinthians 12:7–10

Background

Unanswered prayers usually trouble parents more than they do children. Very seldom is the faith of our boys and girls disturbed when God says "No" to one of their requests. But there are times, when a great need exists, and a prayer isn't answered the way we yearn, that disappointment may stimulate doubt or even anger. One of the serious issues which may stimulate this response is sickness. Another is the death of a loved one. Another may be a family breakup. Essentially those things which threaten the family system, and thus the child's base of security, are the kinds of things that may stimulate serious prayer. If an undesirable outcome still occurs, it may lead to bitterness or even apparent abandonment of trust in God. See paragraphs 45 and 46.

Most times such reactions do not happen. But unless we help our boys and girls work through their disappointment and hurt, express their feelings, and discover that what has happened does not mean God has abandoned them, doubts may come.

This *talkable Bible story* relates a "No" answer to prayer given the apostle Paul. Paul had healed so many sick persons. But Paul himself was not healed from a debilitating disease which many biblical scholars believe was an eye disease. Paul's experience, and Paul's response to it, can help our children realize that "No" is a possible answer to the most heartfelt prayer. Even "No" can be an expression of love. God will never abandon us in our hurts.

The Story Retold

Paul's eyes hurt.

Paul wanted to rub his eyes so badly. But the apostle Paul didn't rub his eyes. He knew it would only make them hurt worse.

Paul peered out of his swollen, watering eyes, trying hard to see the people he was talking with. The people looked all blurry to Paul. What was worse, Paul knew how ugly his swollen, red and watery eyes made him look to others. He wanted to tell people about Jesus. Would anyone listen when his sickness made Paul look so ugly?

There was another terrible thing about Paul's sickness. He couldn't read the Scriptures. He could hardly even see to write the letters he sent to churches to help them understand more about Jesus. The last letter Paul wanted to write he had to dictate. Paul had someone else write it down while he talked. At the end of the letter Paul added some words in his own writing. But he had to write the words in big scrawling letters. Paul could hardly see what he was writing, so Paul filled a whole page with just a few words (cf. Gal. 6:11).

Paul just hated being so sick. He wanted desperately to be well again.

What are some of the feelings Paul must have had when he was sick? Are they like the feelings you have because you (or dad, mom and so on) are sick? How does your sickness make you feel? (Share your own feelings and worries too.)

In this Bible story Paul is the apostle Paul, who wrote many of our New Testament letters. It must have seemed strange to people that this Paul was so sick.

Many times Paul had prayed, and God healed other people who were sick. Once a young man fell out of a window in a building where Paul was preaching. The young man was killed. But Paul prayed, and God brought the young man's life back into his body. You would have thought that Paul, who healed so many other people, would have been able to make himself well without any trouble.

But Paul hadn't really healed anyone. It was Jesus who healed when Paul prayed.

So now Paul did a very wise thing.

He prayed and asked the Lord to make his eyes well.

What do you suppose will happen when Paul prays? How many reasons can you think of why the Lord would answer Paul's prayer, and make Paul well again? Can you think of any reasons why the Lord wouldn't make Paul well?

The apostle Paul knew that God loved him. Paul loved Jesus, too. He had spent his whole life teaching others about Jesus. God had answered many, many of Paul's prayers. So when Paul prayed that God would make his eyes well, he really expected God to do it. And soon.

But Paul didn't begin to get well.

Paul prayed, but his eyes remained red and swollen. Paul prayed, but he still looked ugly. Paul prayed, but he still couldn't read or write well. Paul still had trouble seeing the people he talked with about Jesus.

So Paul prayed again.

Paul prayed very hard a third time. He pleaded with the Lord to make him well. He wanted so very, very badly to get well again. But still Paul didn't begin to get well.

How do you suppose Paul felt, after praying so hard, and not beginning to get well? (Together list a number of feelings.) Which of those feelings do you suppose would be hardest for Paul? What feelings have you had when God hasn't answered some of your prayers? It's all right when we feel (fill in child's strongest feelings), and even when we begin to doubt that God really loves us. It's very hard when God says "No" to something we want very badly.

The apostle Paul wanted to be healed so very badly. But God said "No" to Paul's prayer.

Then God told the apostle something very special. And Paul wrote it down in the Bible, for you and me. God told Paul the Lord would give Paul enough grace to be able to live with his sickness. God promised that when Paul felt the weakest, God would be there to give him strength.

Paul's being sick didn't mean that God did not love Paul. Not at all. Bad things that happen to us don't mean that God has stopped loving us, either.

In fact, God can be even more real to us when we are

weak. Then we know how much we need God's help.

What kind of strength do you think we need from God to help us with your (or dad's, and so on) sickness? Sometimes we need strength to keep from being afraid. Or we need strength to keep on trying when we feel like giving up. Can you think of other kinds of strength we can ask for?

It's all right to keep on asking God to make us well. Usually God will, even if we're sick for a long time. But we can also ask God to give us strength inside. We can ask God to help us. God can give us the strength we need when we feel worst.

The apostle Paul probably kept on feeling unhappy about his sickness at times.

But it helped Paul to know that God still loved him, even though he didn't get better. After a time Paul even began to feel glad about his sickness. "When I am weak," Paul wrote in the Bible, "then I am strong." Paul knew that because he was weak, it must be God who helped Paul be strong and cheerful and loving in spite of the sickness. God still loved Paul. And Paul knew God loved him. Even when Paul was sick.

Action Idea

If you tell this Bible story during a serious family illness after you and the children have prayed together often for healing, you'll not need any particular follow-up process. The Scripture will have its own ministry and help your boys and girls realize that God hasn't abandoned them. None of you may understand the "why" of the sickness. But the Bible's affirmation of God's love, and of his commitment to strengthen you in your trial, will be healing and reassuring.

What Is Heaven Like?
Various Bible Passages

Background

We don't know much about heaven. The Bible does give us word pictures of a coming time when Jesus will rule on earth.

There are glimpses of a time beyond even that, when God will make a new heaven and earth. We're given insights in Revelation into the close relationship with God which a redeemed and holy humanity will have. Still, the details of what life will be like in eternity simply are not provided.

Even so, heaven remains a dominant image in Christian faith. The promise of eternal life is ours, and even our children have questions about what eternity will bring. Their questions usually occur some time after the death of a friend or family member. Several stories in this *Handbook* are specifically designed to help your children deal with their feelings about the death of a loved one (see paragraph 88, and pages 179–181, 316–320, 340–343). This story is different. It is designed to deal with children's curiosity about the future life after the traumatic emotions have subsided and new, normal patterns of life have been reestablished.

The approach is suitable for children of all ages, though it is more likely to fit the ways of thinking and understanding of your nine- through eleven-year-olds.

The Story Retold

Everybody has some idea of what heaven is like. But it's hard for us to know for sure just what it will be like when we are there. We do know that we'll be with our friends and family who love Jesus. And we do know that God will be there with us. Most people have some other ideas too about what heaven will be like.

What do you suppose heaven is like? How would you like to draw a picture of your idea of heaven? (Distribute paper and crayons to all family members, including yourself.) Let's draw a picture of what we think heaven may be like, and how we'll feel there. (When the pictures are completed, have each person tell about what he or she has drawn, and explain his or her picture.)

The Bible gives us some word pictures to tell us about heaven.

Let me read you some of the words in the Bible that tell us about heaven.

In the Old Testament book of Isaiah (65:17–25) God tells us about a wonderful new world He will make. Here is what God tells us:

"Behold, I will create new heavens and a new earth,
the former things will not be remembered, nor will they
come to mind,
But be glad and rejoice forever in what I will create. . . .
The sound of weeping and of crying will be heard in
it no more.
Never again will there be in it an infant that lives but a
few days, or an old man who does not live out his years!
They will build houses and dwell in them; they will plant
vineyards and eat their fruit, . . .
They will not toil in vain
or bear children doomed to misfortune;
for they will be a people blessed by the Lord. . . .
The wolf and the lamb will feed together,
and the lion will eat straw like an ox. . . .
They will neither harm nor destroy in all
my holy mountain."

The New Testament book of Revelation talks about heaven
too. Here are some of the things the Bible says about heaven
in Revelation 21 and 22.

"I saw a new heaven and a new earth, for the first
heaven and earth had passed away, and there was no
longer any sea. I saw the Holy City, the new Jerusalem,
coming down out of heaven from God. . . . I heard a
loud voice from [God's] throne saying, Now the dwelling
of God is with men, and he will live with them. They
will be his people, and God himself will be with them
and be their God. God will wipe away every tear from
their eyes. There will be no more death or mourning or
crying or pain, for the old order of things has passed
away. . . .
"The city does not need the sun or moon to shine on
it, for the glory of God gives it light, . . . On no day
will its gates ever be shut, for there will be no night
there. . . . Nothing impure will ever enter it, nor will
anyone who does what is shameful or deceitful. . . .

Then the angel showed me the river of the water of life, as clear as crystal, flowing from the throne of God and of the Lamb, down the middle of the great street of the city. On each side of the river stood the tree of life, bearing twelve crops of fruit, yielding its fruit every month. And the leaves of the tree are for the healing of the nations. No longer will there be any curse. The throne of God and the Lamb will be in the city, and his servants will serve him. They will see his face, and his name will be on their foreheads. There will be no more night. They will not need the light of a lamp or the light of the sun, for the Lord God will give them light. And they will rule for ever and ever" (21:1–4, 23, 25, 27; 22:1–4).

What are some of the things you learned about heaven? How is what the Bible says like the picture you drew? How is what the Bible said not like your picture? If we were to make a family mural— a very big picture that we all drew and painted together—what would we want to show on that picture-mural?

Let's read through the Bible passages again. Whenever you hear something you think ought to go on a picture-mural, stop me and we'll write it down.

(Reread the passages, letting your children take notes).
Which of the things about heaven do you suppose you'll like best?
Let's thank God that He loves us so much that He's prepared a wonderful place for us to be, forever and forever.

Action Idea

Make a "heaven" mural together. Let each family member represent things about heaven that seem special to him or her on a single mural sheet. Use crayons or water-based paints to create your mural.

We will not be able to accurately represent the wonderful eternity God has planned for us. But a sense of assurance and comfort will be ours as we focus on the endless love of God for Jesus' people.

SUBJECT INDEX